Building Your Church Through Counsel and Care

Library of Leadership Development

9707

LIBRARY OF Leadership DEVELOPMENT

Building Your Church Through Counsel and Care

30 Strategies to Transform Your Ministry

Marshall Shelley, General Editor

BETHANY HOUSE PUBLISHERS
MINNEAPOLIS, MINNESOTA 55438

Published by Bethany House Publishers
A Ministry of Bethany Fellowship, Inc.
11300 Hampshire Avenue South
Minneapolis, Minnesota 55438

Printed in the United States of America.

Library of Congress Cataloging-in-Publication Data

Building your church through counsel and care: 30 strategies to
transform your ministry / by Marshall Shelley, General Editor.
    p.   cm. — (Library of leadership development)
    ISBN 1-55661-966-9
    1. Pastoral theology. 2. Pastoral psychology. I. Shelley, Marshall.
II. Series.
BV4017.B85   1997
253—dc21   97–21029
                                                       CIP

Contents

Part 4
Crisis Situations

Part 5
Specific Care

Introduction

The purpose of sound counsel and effective care is cultivating mature Christian character.

—Marshall Shelley

O ne of the best definitions of a leader is "someone who is willing to take responsibility for someone else." Lots of people want to absolve themselves of responsibility for anyone but themselves (and some try to dodge even that).

But Christians who've heard the call of God know that ministry is about caring for others. "Care" isn't just an emotion, a warm feeling toward people in general, or an affection for a few individuals. No, care implies making sure that basic needs are met.

Pastoral care means taking responsibility for the spiritual well-being of a group. The "pastoral epistles" are filled with the apostle Paul's instructions about caring for the flock—details of organization and administration are part of it, but the emphasis is on sound counsel (through personal conversation and through teaching and preaching) and effective care. The purpose: cultivating mature Christian character.

In recent years, psychology and counseling have dominated the field and shaped people's expectations. Many pastors feel ambivalent about that form of pastoral care.

"I love it, and I hate it," said Pastor Rob Morgan, in a recent LEADERSHIP article. "It's exhilarating, and it's exhausting. Pastoral counseling is part of who I am and what I do, yet it often feels as if it's an invasion into my life."

Despite the helpful contributions of psychiatrists, psychologists, and psychotherapists, they can never replace the work of *pastoral* care. After all, says Morgan, "the prefix 'psych' means 'soul'—and pastors are tenders of the soul."

In putting together this book, we built on some assumptions. These provide the power for effective pastoral counsel and care.

1. *We represent Christ.* When people come with their problems to a Christian minister (clergy or lay), they come not only to a professional but to an embodiment of the love of Christ, a channel of his grace.

2. *We're there in all of life.* The Hebrew word for "shepherding" is closely aligned to the Jewish word for "friend." That's often what people need. In its essence, Christianity is nothing more than personal relationships—with God and one another.

A therapist recently told Rob Morgan, "You pastors have a real advantage because you're part of a person's life more than I can ever be. Counselors get intimate with people quickly; then we're gone. You are in a person's life consistently. My role is short-term; yours is long-term, and it's the long-term role that usually proves most valuable."

3. *Our care can be reinforced every Sunday.* In a church context, person-to-person ministry doesn't stand alone. It's reinforced each week by the preaching of God's Word, which helps correct, refocus, and encourage. It's also given in the context of sacraments, small group relationships, service opportunities, and a recurring focus on redemption.

As Pastor Morgan concludes, "There is no better tool than Scripture for penetrating soul and spirit, joints and marrow, thoughts and intents. It is the Bible in all its authority—specifically the promises in all their sufficiency—that revives the soul, makes wise the simple, gives joy to the heart, and light to the eyes."

This is the challenge of pastoral care—to help individuals see how God is involved in their specific circumstances. And helping you provide that care is why *Building Your Church Through Counsel and Care* was put together.

God bless you as you counsel and care and make a difference for eternity.

—Marshall Shelley
Senior Editor,
LEADERSHIP

Contributors

Randy Alcorn is founder and director of Eternal Perspective Ministries. Before that he co-founded and pastored Good Shepherd Community Church outside Gresham, Oregon. He is author of *Money, Possessions, and Eternity; Christians in the Wake of the Sexual Revolution*; and *Dominion.*

Danny Armstrong is a chaplain on Fairchild Air Force Base in Washington.

Greg Asimakoupoulos is pastor of the Evangelical Covenant Church of Naperville, Illinois. Before that he pastored Crossroads Covenant Church in Concord, California. He is coauthor of *The Time Crunch.*

James D. Berkley is senior associate pastor of First Presbyterian Church in Bellevue, Washington. He is a contributing editor to LEADERSHIP. He is the author of *Making the Most of Mistakes* and the editor of *Leadership Handbooks of Practical Theology.*

Andre Bustanoby is a marriage and family therapist in Bowie, Maryland. He is a member of the American Association for Marriage and Family Therapy and past president of the mid-Atlantic division. He is the author of numerous books, including *But I Didn't Want a Divorce* and *Just Talk to Me.*

Randy Christian is pastor of adult education and family ministries at Beaverton Christian Church in Beaverton, Oregon. He is a member of the National Council on Family Relations and is a licensed professional counselor.

James Dobson is founder and president of Focus on the Family, a nonprofit organization that produces his internationally syndicated radio programs. His numerous books include *The New*

Dare to Discipline, Love Must Be Tough, and *Parenting Isn't for Cowards*.

Richard Exley is a freelance author and speaker. Before that he served as pastor for twenty-six years. His books include *The Rhythm of Life* and *The Making of a Man*.

Gary L. Gulbranson is pastor of Westminster Chapel in Bellevue, Washington. Before that he was pastor of Glen Ellyn Bible Church in Glen Ellyn, Illinois.

Richard C. Halverson (1916–1995) was former Senate chaplain and long-time pastor of Fourth Presbyterian Church near Washington, D. C. He was a member of LEADERSHIP's inaugural advisory board.

Archibald D. Hart is a professor and dean of the Graduate School of Psychology at Fuller Theological Seminary. He is a member of the editorial advisory board for LEADERSHIP. His numerous books include *Healing Adult Children of Divorce* and *The Hidden Link Between Adrenaline and Stress*.

Bruce Larson is academic dean of International School of Communications at Crystal Cathedral in Garden Grove, California. Before that he was co-pastor of Crystal Cathedral and pastor of University Presbyterian Church in Seattle, Washington. He is author of numerous books including *What God Wants to Know, Living Beyond Our Fears*, and *Faith for the Journey*.

Kathryn Lindskoog is author of numerous books including *Light Showers, Fakes, Frauds and Other Malarkey*, and *C. S. Lewis: Mere Christianity*.

Victoria Martin is a psychiatrist practicing in the Dallas-Fort Worth, Texas, area.

S. Bowen Matthews is pastor of Brandywine Valley Baptist Church in Wilmington, Delaware.

Louis McBurney is founder and medical director of Marble Retreat, a counseling center for clergy in Marble, Colorado. He serves on the advisory boards of LEADERSHIP, *Marriage Partnership*, and Called Together Ministries. He has written *Every Pastor Needs a Pastor, Counseling Christian Workers*, and *Families Under Stress*.

Aldean (Al) Miles is a chaplain and coordinator of hospital ministry of The Queen's Medical Center in Honolulu, Hawaii. He is a writer and lecturer on grief and spiritual care in the health-care environment.

Robert J. Morgan is pastor of Donelson Fellowship in Nashville, Tennessee. He is the author of *Empowered Parenting, On This Day: 365 Days with Preachers, etc.* and editor of *The Children's Daily Devotional Bible.*

Eugene H. Peterson is the James M. Houston Professor of Spiritual Theology at Regent College in Vancouver, B.C. He is contributing editor to LEADERSHIP. His many books include *The Message: The New Testament in Contemporary English* and *The Psalms: The Message.*

Michael E. Phillips is pastor of Riverside Alliance Church in Kalispell, Montana. He is the author of *To Be a Father Like the Father.*

Gary D. Preston is pastor of Bethany Baptist Church in Boulder, Colorado. Before that he served as associate pastor at Foothills Bible Church. He also served as senior pastor of Mountain Christian Fellowship in Golden, Colorado.

Kevin E. Ruffcorn is pastor of Trinity Evangelical Lutheran Church in Appleton, Wisconsin. He is author of *Rural Evangelism: Catching the Vision; God's Word of Encouragement,* and *Share the Word.*

Dale S. Ryan is CEO of Christian Recovery International, the parent organization to the National Association for Christian Recovery and Confident Kids Support Groups. He is coauthor, with his wife, Juanita, of the *Life Recovery Guide* series of Bible studies.

Hal B. Schell is co-founder and chairman of the board of Equipping Ministries International. He has developed numerous courses including *Biblical Sexuality* and *Unhook Me, Lord: A Christian Walk through the Twelve Steps of Wholeness.*

Marshall Shelley is editorial vice-president at Christianity Today, Inc. and senior editor of LEADERSHIP. He is author of *Well-Intentioned Dragons* and *Helping Those who Don't Want Help* and coauthor of *The Consumer Church.*

Gary R. Sweeten is co-founder and chairman of the board of Lifeway Counseling Centers. He consults and trains pastors and therapists to set up holistic communities of care and counsel, and has a daily radio program in Cincinnati, Ohio.

Matthew Woodley is pastor of Cambridge United Methodist Church in Cambridge, Minnesota. Before that he was pastor of Barnum United Methodist Church in Barnum, Minnesota.

PART 1

Ministry Philosophy

1

Reforming Spiritual-Health Care

The vocational reformation of our own time is a
rediscovery of the pastoral work of the cure of souls.

—Eugene H. Peterson

A reformation may be in process in the way pastors do their work. It may turn out to be as significant as the theological reformation of the sixteenth century. I hope so. The signs are accumulating.

The Reformers recovered the biblical doctrine of justification by faith. The gospel proclamation, fresh and personal and direct, through the centuries had become an immense, lumbering Rube Goldberg mechanism: elaborately contrived ecclesiastical gears, pulleys, and levers rumbled and creaked importantly, but ended up doing something completely trivial. The Reformers recovered the personal passion and clarity so evident in Scripture. This rediscovery of firsthand involvement resulted in freshness and vigor.

The vocational reformation of our own time (if it turns out to be that) is a rediscovery of the pastoral work of the cure of souls. The phrase sounds antique. It *is* antique. But it is not obsolete. It catches up and coordinates, better than any other expression I am aware of, the unending warfare against sin and sorrow and the diligent cultivation of grace and faith to which the best pastors have consecrated themselves in every generation. The odd sound of the phrase may even work to advantage by calling attention to how remote present-day pastoral routines have become.

I am not the only pastor who has discovered this old identity. More and more pastors are embracing this way of pastoral work and are finding themselves authenticated by it. There are not a lot of us. We are by no means a majority, not even a high-profile minority. But one by one, pastors are rejecting the job description that has been handed to them and are taking on this new one or, as it turns out, the old one that has been in use for most of the Christian centuries.

It is not sheer fantasy to think there may come a time when the number reaches critical mass and thus effects a genuine vocational reformation among pastors. Even if it doesn't, it seems to me the single most significant and creative thing happening in pastoral ministry today.

What Do We Do?

There's a distinction between what pastors do on Sundays and what we do between Sundays. What we do on Sundays has not really changed through the centuries: proclaiming the gospel, teaching Scripture, celebrating the sacraments, offering prayers. But the work between Sundays has changed radically, and it has not been a development but a defection.

Until about a century ago, what pastors did between Sundays was a piece of what they did on Sundays. The context changed: instead of being with an assembled congregation, the pastor was with one other person or with small gatherings of persons, or alone in study and prayer. The manner changed: instead of proclamation, there was conversation. But the work was the same: discovering the meaning of Scripture, developing a life of prayer, guiding growth into maturity.

This is the pastoral work that is historically termed the cure of souls. The primary sense of *cura* in Latin is "care," with undertone of "cure." The soul is the essence of the human personality. The cure of souls, then, is the Scripture-directed, prayer-shaped care that is devoted to persons singly or in groups, in settings both sacred and profane. It is a determination to work at the center, to concentrate on the essential.

The between-Sundays work of American pastors in this century, though, is running a church. I first heard the phrase "run a church" only a few days before my ordination. After thirty years, I can still remember the unpleasant impression it made.

I was traveling with a pastor I respected very much. I was full of zest and vision, anticipating pastoral life. My inner conviction of call to the pastorate was about to be confirmed by others. What God wanted me to do, what I wanted to do, and what others wanted me to do were about to converge. From fairly extensive reading about pastor and priest predecessors, I was impressed that everyday pastoral life was primarily concerned with developing a life of prayer among the people. Leading worship, preaching the gospel, and teaching Scripture on Sundays would develop in the next six days into representing the life of Christ in the human traffic of the everyday.

With my mind full of these thoughts, my pastor friend and I stopped at a service station for gasoline. My friend, a gregarious person, bantered with the attendant. Something in the exchange provoked a question.

"What do you do?"

"I run a church."

No answer could have surprised me more. I knew, of course, that pastoral life included institutional responsibilities, but it never occurred to me that I would be defined by those responsibilities. But the moment I became ordained, I found that indeed I was defined both by the pastors and executives over me and by the parishioners around me. The first job description given me omitted prayer entirely.

Behind my back, while my pastoral identity was being formed by Gregory and Bernard, Luther and Calvin, Richard Baxter of Kidder-Minster and Nicholas Ferrar of Little Gidding, George Herbert and Jonathan Edwards, John Henry Newman and Alexander Whyte, Phillips Brooks and George MacDonald, the work of the pastor had been almost completely secularized (except for Sundays). I didn't like it and decided, after an interval of confused disorientation, that being a physician of souls took priority over running a church, and that I would be guided in my pastoral vocation by wise predecessors rather than contemporaries. Luckily, I have found allies along the way and a readiness.

among my parishioners to work with me in changing my pastoral job description.

Curing Souls vs. Running a Church

It should be clear that the cure of souls is not a specialized form of ministry (analogous, for instance, to hospital chaplain or pastoral counselor) but is the essential pastoral work. It is not a narrowing of pastoral work to its devotional aspects, but it is a way of life that uses weekday tasks, encounters, and situations as the raw material for teaching prayer, developing faith, and preparing for a good death.

Curing souls is a term that filters out what is introduced by a secularizing culture. It is also a term that identifies us with our ancestors and colleagues in ministry, lay and clerical, who were and are convinced that a life of prayer is the connective tissue between holy day proclamation and weekday discipleship.

A caveat: I contrast the cure of souls with the task of running a church, but I do not want to be misunderstood. I am not contemptuous of running a church, nor do I dismiss its importance. I run a church myself; I have for over twenty years. I try to do it well.

But I do it in the same spirit that I, along with my wife, run our house. There are many essential things that we routinely do, often (though not always) with joy. But running a house is not what we *do*. What we *do* is build a home, develop in marriage, raise children, practice hospitality, pursue lives of work and play. It is reducing pastoral work to institutional duties that I object to, not the duties themselves, which I gladly share with others in the church.

It will hardly do, of course, to stubbornly defy the expectations of people and eccentrically go about pastoral work like a seventeenth-century curate, even if the eccentric curate is far more sane than the current clergy. The recovery of this essential between-Sundays work of the pastor must be worked out in tension with the secularized expectations of this age: there must be negotiation, discussion, experimentation, confrontation, adaptation. Pastors who devote themselves to the guidance of souls must do it among people who expect them to run a church. In a determined and kindly tension with those who thoughtlessly presume to write job descriptions for us, we can, I am convinced, recover our proper work.

Pastors, though, who decide to reclaim the vast territory of the soul as their preeminent responsibility will not do it by going away for job retraining. We must work it out on the job, for it is not only ourselves but our people whom we are desecularizing. The task of vocational recovery is as endless as theological reformation. Details vary with pastor and parish, but there are three areas of contrast between running a church and the cure of souls that all of us experience: initiative, language, and problems.

Initiative

In running the church, I seize the initiative. I take charge. I assume responsibility for motivation and recruitment, for showing the way, for getting things started. If I don't, things drift. I am aware of the tendency to apathy, the human susceptibility to indolence, and I use my leadership position to counter it.

By contrast, the cure of souls is a cultivated awareness that God has already seized the initiative. The traditional doctrine defining this truth is *prevenience*: God everywhere and always seizing the initiative. He gets things going. He had and continues to have the first word. Prevenience is the conviction that God had been working diligently, redemptively, and strategically before I appeared on the scene, before I was aware there was something here for me to do.

The cure of souls is not indifferent to the realities of human lethargy, naïve about congregational recalcitrance, or inattentive to neurotic cussedness. But there is a disciplined, determined conviction that everything (and I mean, precisely, everything) we do is a response to God's first work, his initiating act. We learn to be attentive to the divine action already in process so that the previously unheard word of God is heard, the previously unattended act of God is noticed.

Running-the-church questions are: What do we do? How can we get things going again?

Cure-of-souls questions are: What has God been doing here?

What traces of grace can I discern in this life? What history of love can I read in this group? What has God set in motion that I can get in on?

We misunderstand and distort reality when we take ourselves as the starting point and our present situation as the basic datum. Instead of confronting the bogged-down human condition and taking charge of changing it with no time wasted, we look at divine prevenience and discern how we can get in on it at the right time, in the right way.

The cure of souls takes time to read the minutes of the previous meeting, a meeting more likely than not at which I wasn't present. When I engage in conversation, meet with a committee, or visit a home, I am coming in on something that has already been in process for a long time. God has been and is the central reality in that process. The biblical conviction is that God is "long beforehand with my soul." God has already taken the initiative. Like one who walks in late to a meeting, I am entering a complex situation in which God has already said decisive words and acted in decisive ways. My work is not necessarily to announce that but to discover what he is doing and live appropriately with it.

Language

In running the church I use language that is descriptive and motivational. I want people to be informed so there are no misunderstandings. And I want people to be motivated so things get done. But in the cure of souls, I am far more interested in who people are and who they are becoming in Christ than I am in what they know or what they are doing. In this, I soon find that neither descriptive nor motivational language helps very much.

Descriptive language is language *about*—it names what is there. It orients us in reality. It makes it possible for us to find our way in and out of intricate labyrinths. Our schools specialize in teaching us this language. Motivational language is language *for*—it uses words to get things done. Commands are issued, promises made, requests proffered. Such words get people to do things they won't do on their own initiative. The advertising industry is our most skillful practitioner of this language art.

Indispensable as these uses of language are, there is another language more essential to our humanity and far more basic to the life of faith. It is personal language. It uses words to express oneself, to converse, to be in relationship. This is language *to* and *with*. Love is offered and received, ideas are developed, feelings are articulated, silences are honored. This is the language we speak spontaneously as children, as lovers, as poets—and when we pray. It is also conspicuously absent when we are running a church—there is so much to *say* and *do* that there is no time left to *be* and no occasion, therefore, for the language of being there.

The cure of souls is a decision to work at the heart of things, where we are most ourselves and where our relationships in faith and intimacy are developed. The primary language must be, therefore, *to* and *with*, the personal language of love and prayer. The pastoral vocation does not take place primarily in a school where subjects are taught, nor in a barracks where assault forces are briefed for attacks on evil, but in a family—the place where love is learned, where birth takes place, where intimacy is deepened. The pastoral task is to use the language appropriate in this most basic aspect of our humanity—not language that describes, not language that motivates, but spontaneous language: cries and exclamation, confessions and appreciations, words the heart speaks.

We have, of course, much to teach and much to get done, but our primary task is to *be*. The primary language of the cure of souls, therefore, is conversation and prayer. Being a pastor means learning to use language in which personal uniqueness is enhanced and individual sanctity is recognized and respected. It is a language that is unhurried, unforced, unexcited—the leisurely language of friends and lovers, which is also the language of prayer.

Problems

In running a church I solve problems. Wherever two or three are gathered together, problems develop. Egos are bruised, procedures get snarled, arrangements become confused, plans go awry. Temperaments clash. There are polity problems, marriage problems, work problems, child problems, committee problems, and emotional problems. Someone has to interpret, explain, work out new plans, develop better procedures, organize, and administer. Most pastors like to do this. I know I do. It is satisfying to help make the rough places smooth.

The difficulty is that problems arrive in such a constant flow that problem solving becomes full-time work. Because it is useful and the pastor ordinarily does it well, we fail to see that the pastoral vocation has been subverted. Gabriel Marcel wrote that life is not so much a problem to be solved as a mystery to be explored. That is certainly the biblical stance: life is not something we manage to hammer together and keep in repair by our wits; it is an unfathomable gift. We are immersed in mysteries: incredible love, confounding evil, the Creation, the Cross, grace, God.

The secularized mind is terrorized by mysteries. Thus it makes lists, labels people, assigns roles, and solves problems. But a solved life is a reduced life. These tightly buttoned-up people never take great faith risks or make convincing love talk. They deny or ignore the mysteries and diminish human existence to what can be managed, controlled, and fixed. We live among a cult of experts who explain and solve. The vast technological apparatus around us gives the impression that there is a tool for everything if we can only afford it. Pastors cast in the role of spiritual technologists are hard put to keep that role from absorbing everything else, since there are so many things that need to be and can, in fact, be fixed.

But "there are things," wrote Mariann Moore, "that are important beyond all this fiddle." The old-time guide of souls asserts the priority of the "beyond" over "this fiddle." Who is available for this work other than pastors? A few poets, perhaps; and children, always. But children are not good guides, and most of our poets have lost interest in God. That leaves pastors as guides through the mysteries. Century after century we live with our conscience, our passions, our neighbors, and our God. Any narrower view of our relationships does not match our real humanity.

If pastors become accomplices in treating every child as a

problem to be figured out, every spouse as a problem to be dealt with, every clash of wills in choir or committee as a problem to be adjudicated, we abdicate our most important work, which is directing worship in the traffic, discovering the presence of the Cross in the paradoxes and chaos between Sundays, calling attention to the "splendor in the ordinary," and, most of all, teaching a life of prayer to our friends and companions in the pilgrimage.

2

Strategically Unstrategic Care

The greatest baggage a pastor carries to a new ministry assignment is ready-made programs.

—Richard C. Halverson

After my first pastorate, 1944–1947, in Coalinga, California, I never intended to pastor again; I didn't think I was good enough material. So I worked with small groups as an associate minister for eight years and then joined International Christian Leadership for three years. After the Lord led me to Fourth Presbyterian Church, I realized I didn't have a ready-made ministry program. In fact, I was so out of touch I didn't even know what programs other churches were using or what programs were available.

Now, after twenty-one years at Fourth, I look back on that "problem" as one of the greatest assets I took to the church.

The greatest baggage a pastor carries to a new ministry assignment is ready-made programs. He is programmed to think he should try out this program as soon as he's finished trying out that program. He's buried in an avalanche of "how-to's." He continually compares program ideas with his colleagues. Consequently, ministries never become indigenous.

To make a ministry indigenous requires a more inductive approach.

Keep Things Simple

In those early days at Fourth, God taught me two things: First, treat the Sunday morning congregation the same way you'd treat a small group of people meeting in your living room. Second, fully implement the commandment Christ gave: "Love one another as I have loved you, and you will demonstrate to the world that you are my disciples."

I was captured by a simple little statement in Mark: Jesus chose twelve and ordained them to be with him. Suddenly the word *with* became a big word, one of the biggest in the New Testament, because implicit within it is *koinonia* prayer and support. That word convinced me to have a ministry of being *with* people. I didn't worry about what I was going to do with them; I didn't need an agenda. Jesus began a movement that would be universal and that would last forever, and yet he spent most of his time with twelve people.

I'm not saying the most effective church structure is one composed of small groups; I'm saying that the right *attitude* about and *approach* to ministry is more effective than a lot of canned expertise.

For example, I have a regular Wednesday breakfast with some lay leaders. I learned long ago that if I came to the breakfast burning with a message I had prepared in my study, it would invariably fall like a lead balloon. Afterward the guys would say, "Halverson, it just wasn't the same this morning." It took me time to understand there is a chemistry about each group that generates its own agenda. I believe it comes from the Holy Spirit in our midst. That doesn't mean I should neglect preparation, but it does mean that I have to prepare with a high degree of awareness and execute with a high degree of sensitivity. Even when a congregation or group is silent, something is still transmitted to the speaker.

Avoid the Canned Approach

We had a Gordon-Conwell student who recently interned at Fourth Presbyterian. I advised him, "John, you have learned many things at Gordon-Conwell, and before that you gained some valuable experience working with the Navigators. As you go to your first pastorate, you'll be tempted to bring to that new situation all of the ideas, plans, and programs that you picked up in your training, and you won't be patient enough to discover what is already there. Take the time to become part of what is there, and then these things you have learned will find proper adaptation and application; they'll become indigenous to that situation. You can grow a dandelion in just a few hours, but it takes seven years to raise an orchid."

I have real problems with the humanistic assumption that we can find the "right way" or the "best way" to do everything, and that if we find it, we'll get the desired results. When I went to Fourth Presbyterian in 1956, I had come out of eleven years of small-group ministry. I thought I was a small-group expert. I wasn't, but that's the way we operate in this culture; when you've done something a few years you become an expert.

The man who led me to Christ was my first pastor, and he taught me how to handle ideas. He taught me to treat ideas like good seeds and showed me how to plant them in the soil of a heart or mind and let them grow. I have a bias against "canned" or ready-made, mass-distributed church programming. My style is to plant a seed, water it, and watch it grow.

We begin every worship service with a little greeting that reminds the people of the importance of their contribution to what is about to happen. The greeting is: "There is something to be captured in this moment that we can never give or receive at any other time or in any other situation. Let's be alive to what Christ wants us to do here and now."

I began to visualize myself standing in the pulpit on Sunday morning and talking to a group of people who have been literally inundated all week long with words. Now I want them to listen to my words. I suppose that's what originally challenged me years ago to treat my congregation like a small group of people in my living room. When you invite a few people to your home for an evening, you don't line them up in rows and lecture them unless you're an absolute bore. Although the task of host or small-group leader may require you to focus the thinking or the discussion of the group, the objective is to get them involved in the process, to get them to participate.

On Sunday mornings, I try different things. One time I'll say, "Here's what Jesus said . . . now do you hear that? Do you hear it?"

If the congregation just sits there, I'll persist, "Do we hear it?"

I'll begin to get a response. "What did he say?" I'll wait until somebody says it out loud from the congregation. I don't see any point
in throwing words out at people if they are not listening and responding to them.

Identify Your Core Philosophy

I see the ideal organizational structure for a church in a model
of concentric circles. I don't like to diagram church organization
on a vertical plane.

The scriptural model might start with John, who was called
"the beloved." At the Last Supper, he laid his head on Jesus' chest;
somehow, the intimate relationship John had with Jesus, the first
circle, so to speak, was not a problem to the others. In the second
circle were Peter, James, and John; Jesus took them to the Mount
of Transfiguration and to the Garden of Gethsemane. Somehow
Peter, James, and John had a relationship with Jesus that was not
enjoyed by the nine but was accepted by them, even though the
disciples were a normal group of human beings and prone to peer-
group jealousy.

The core group around Jesus was the twelve; then there were
the 70 around the twelve, and the 120 around the 70, and out beyond that the 500. The church should be the same.

This is how I approach pastoral care. Paul says in 1 Corinthians
12:25, "That the members should have the same care for one another" (NKJV). A true Christian community is not something you
organize. Now, I'm not saying you should never have a specific
program, but the more spontaneous the caring is, the better it is.
My mind keeps coming back to the Sunday morning service, which
I believe is the pastor's greatest opportunity for real caring.

For years the back page of our bulletin has been called "The
Family Altar" and is devoted to congregational needs: the sick, the
shut-ins, the students, and four or five "Families of the Week."
During our service we have a period of time called the "Praise and
Prayers of the People." This is followed by a period of silence in
which we urge our people to pray for one another. Then we ask
them to touch someone near them. I personally step down from
the pulpit and walk into the congregation and touch various peo-

ple. Other pastors do the same. Then we pray for the people on the back page. These simple gestures encourage an environment of caring.

Model Supportive Relationships

We encourage small groups, but we don't try to organize them. It's common for people to come to me and say, "We'd like to start a small group. Will you meet with us?" I usually do, and in the first session I show them how to study the Bible inductively and encourage them to make the group experience more that just a straight Bible study. Every small group has the potential to become a support church.

Within our church, this dynamic is modeled for our small groups by the steering committee of the small groups. I meet as often as I can with all of our steering committees. The other pastors do the same. We try to model supportive relationships. Sometimes we fail, but that's good for us.

Twenty-one years ago we started with the "flock system," whereby each lay leader was responsible for a certain number of members. That responsibility was clearly defined. For example, they were to meet with each member at least once a year, maintain contact at least twice a year, and so forth. It never worked. One reason was the nature of community life in metropolitan Washington. Some of the members said, "We don't like to be thought of as sheep." That was the final blow that killed the flock idea. More seriously, the sense of regimentation didn't seem to set very well.

So we tried other programs. We have tried fellowship committees and other forms of congregational care. Right now we have a Ministry of Concern office. We were fortunate to secure the services of Pat Brown, a lovely woman from South Carolina with a beautiful southern accent. She obviously likes people and cares for them, and they in turn immediately respond to her. She creatively handles all kinds of situations.

For example, if a family is being evicted, they call her. If somebody can't pay a hospital bill, she acts as a liaison with the deacon board. She's developed what she calls a "Going Forth" ministry. This is a group of people who make themselves available to help others wherever she sends them. She has also organized what she calls "Family Connection," an event-centered ministry of fellowship that encourages entire families to do things together. For example, Family Connection will be going to this month's home game of the Redskins. During the summer they attended an outdoor concert at Wolftrap, and soon they will be chartering a train to spend a day together at Harper's Ferry.

This kind of fellowship brings together young and old, married and single. Pat's office tries to be especially sensitive to the need of singles who want contact with married couples, and to young people who want contact with older persons.

The point is that in all of these things we are less than perfect, but we are going to come back tomorrow and try harder.

Read the Culture

When I first came to Fourth, I did a lot of conventional visitation nearly every afternoon in the week. Little by little I discovered that suburban culture doesn't allow for effective pastoral calls.

In the first place, it's almost impossible to find the family together. Second, the suburban housewife tends to be very busy, and she usually doesn't see any particular value in sitting down with the pastor and visiting for thirty minutes. Third, when children are present, a pastoral call can be looked upon as a family intrusion. I've had the experience of calling on families where they tried to accommodate me with one eye while watching television with the other.

In place of home visitation, we have assigned each of our pastors the responsibility of a certain number of members to contact by phone four times a year. That kind of contact has been very satisfying to me. I'll take a couple of hours on a regular basis, sit at the phone, call a family and say, "Hi, this is Dick Halverson. I'm just calling to find out if you have any special needs I ought to be praying about today."

We recently revived a term used a great deal when I was in seminary: care of souls. I hadn't heard that term for years. Dr. Bonnell, who was in the vanguard of pastoral counseling, taught a course by that name which was required for seniors. His objective was to make us as sensitive as possible to the needs of the believer and to the many different means we could use to meet those needs. However, the emphasis was always on the person's needs, not on the method to meet those needs.

Learn to Listen

When I began my ministry, I had taken a required course in counseling at Princeton and had read the one or two books available on this subject. I really wasn't well prepared to face the problems that came my way. So I had to learn counseling by listening to people. Let's face it, there is no substitute for being with people and trying to understand them and empathize with their needs.

For example, I was counseling a church member who was a closet homosexual. In our sessions I could sense he was getting close to admitting his problem. Instinctively I knew that if there was anything in my facial expression, anything at all that would indicate shock or change in attitude when he admitted his problem, I'd lose him. I so well remember how I prepared myself for the moment he shared who he was.

I made a few major mistakes in counseling, mostly when I failed to spiritually prepare for my task or allowed outside pressure and personal frustrations to desensitize me to the situation.

I'm embarrassed to admit this, but early in my ministry at Fourth, a couple—she was Japanese, he was Jewish—came to me for help. Their marriage was in terrible shape; I spent hours with them. It seemed at some point in every session the young man would rise and start pacing back and forth. Then he would start talking, getting louder and louder until he worked up into a frenzy.

One Sunday morning right after church they asked to see me, and as soon as he was in my office he began his little act, thoroughly embarrassing and intimidating his wife. He ended his performance by saying, "You know, if it weren't for my wife, I'd take my life." By then I was fed up with him, and in anger I said, "Well, you sure aren't much use to her now."

Monday morning I found he had attempted to take his life. I went to the hospital and the first thing he said was, "Mr. Halverson, you told me to do it."

I had failed him—both of them, because I stopped listening and allowed myself to become insensitive to the real problem. Even to this day I rarely give what might be considered direct advice.

Handle Criticism Firmly

The plant-and-watch-it-grow philosophy doesn't preclude conflict. Recently, a family whose fifteen-year-old boy was in trouble with the law made some critical comments about me. His father called me by phone, leveling me about my personal failures and the failure of our church. It wasn't all true, but there was enough truth in it to make it hurt.

Even more devastating was a letter I received from one of our former elders who is now separated from his wife—two pages of very nasty notes about the church's failure.

I had to face conflict head-on. In the case of the former elder, I called him as quickly as I could after receiving the letter. He didn't want to talk, but I persevered. I let him say everything on the telephone he had already said in the letter. Then I apologized: "I'm sorry. I'll accept this criticism for myself personally, and I'll apologize for the church." Since then, I've been talking to him by phone on a regular basis, and we are going to get together in two weeks.

In the case of the father and son, I went first to our director of youth ministry. The night after I talked to the father, the director went to their home and spent a couple of hours talking with them.

I prefer to handle criticism quickly, directly, and sensitively. But the emotional trauma that conflict creates deep in my soul is not as quickly handled. There's a story about a frog that fell into a pothole. Regardless of what his frog friends tried to do, they couldn't help him out of his dilemma. Finally, in desperation they left him to his destiny. The next day they found him bouncing around town as lively as ever. So one frog went up to him and said, "What happened? We thought you couldn't get out of that hole." He replied, "I couldn't, but a truck came along and I had to."

I don't know any other answer to jumping out of the pothole of conflict despair than "you just have to." Many times I would love to run away, ignore the situation, or try to justify it, but Christ has given us very specific instructions in Matthew 5:24. If you know you have offended a brother, you must go to him; if he has offended you, you must go to him. We have to do it!

The ancient image of the pastor being the shepherd with the long crook on one arm and a cuddly little lamb in the other is only one perspective. The other is the shepherd who must look disease right in the eye and come up with a cure or a recommendation for a cure no matter how painful it might be. Cancer can't be treated with a skin salve.

Evaluate the Right Thing

The word *success* troubles me. The implication pervading the Christian church equates bigness with success, and I think that's absolutely wrong. Most criteria for success have their roots in materialism: congregation size, budget size, building size. These aren't bad in themselves, but they are not criteria for success.

I'm very concerned about people who pastor small churches, for there is an unspoken assumption in our culture that if one is really doing a good job he'll eventually become pastor of a large church.

Size is not the criterion for success.

Chuck Colson of Prison Fellowship recently told me he had hired someone to travel the country and evaluate their ministry. I asked Chuck what criteria he used in the evaluation. Not one item on his list was statistical. Every one had to do with values: What was the spiritual climate of a group of Christian brothers in a prison? Were they studying the Bible? Did they have the spirit of reaching out to others? These are some of the criteria for successful ministry.

Be Free to Fail

I'm always amazed by the grace of God. Paul Tournier, the Swiss physician, points out that some parents are extremely authoritarian and others are extremely permissive, but most parents are somewhere in the middle. Then he says that regardless of the parental style, if one's children turn out all right, it's by the grace of God. I like that—a grace that allows me to fail.

I think one of the greatest freedoms any pastor has is the freedom to fail. Again and again, in my private life and in my public ministry, I've had the pressures build until I think I can't stand it any more. When I stop long enough to take a spiritual inventory, I discover that I've failed many times in the past, and it's likely that I will fail again. How liberating!

This past Tuesday morning I awakened about four o'clock after some kind of dream about which I couldn't remember a thing except that I had failed. I tried to go back to sleep, but I couldn't relax. I felt like my skin was crawling right off my body. I finally slipped out of bed onto my knees and began to pray. As I talked to my Father, I again eventually realized that my failure does not constitute God's failure. It was so liberating to say, "Lord, when I fail, I know your grace will be there to cover the bases."

Obviously, we can't presume on God's grace or use his goodness as an excuse for negligence, but likewise, we don't need to fear failure. Failure is a part of the forging process. Failure is God's way of consuming the dross so the gold may remain.

3

Pastor-Teacher or Super-Counselor?

*Counseling is like the proverbial camel that sticks its
nose into the tent and, once allowed that liberty, follows
with its shoulders and forelegs, pushing
till there's room for nothing else.*

—Randy Alcorn

W hat's it like to be a counselor?"
The question often comes my way, usually from young
men and women interested in a counseling ministry. They often
ask with a sort of awe, convinced that counseling is the most fulfilling of all vocations, that counselors are the most fortunate of
mortals.

Though counseling has been a central part of my pastoral ministry for seven years, I never know quite how to answer their question.

From a distance, counseling has a pretty face—it seems mys-
terious, stimulating, and challenging. Up close you see the pock
marks. Because counseling is difficult, draining, and sometimes
frustrating, it's easy to lose the sense of wonder about it.

Pastor, Not Psychologist

I'm not a psychologist. I'm a pastor called to minister God's
Word. Nevertheless, for some years I've borne the title "Pastor of
Counseling and Family Ministries." I've worn two hats, the pastor's
and the counselor's, which is a real juggling act, and I've discovered I'm not always a good juggler.

I had always considered counseling as just one phase of the pastoral ministry. Now I know how easily it can overshadow not only your ministry but your entire life. It's like the proverbial camel that sticks its nose into the tent and, once allowed that liberty, follows with its shoulders and forelegs, pushing till there's room for nothing else.

In my case, the counseling mantle fell to me by accident. There were originally two of us on the church staff, and we split the responsibilities down the middle. Counseling was one of my responsibilities and I welcomed it. I always had a sense of satisfaction in helping another human being (and hearing them tell me what a help I'd been).

People's needs were ever-present, and I seemed reasonably successful in dealing with them. Within a year and a half counseling became my primary, almost exclusive domain. It was another two years before I realized the mistake that was. Along the way, I've learned some lessons.

Counseling can't be taught. Professors can teach you *about* counseling. But they can't teach you counseling *per se.* They can't prepare you for the physical, emotional, and spiritual drain that comes with a counseling ministry. At least, they didn't prepare me.

Counseling is an art. But it is unlike the physical arts that allow the artist to escape from people to maximize creative potential. Often the counselor performs his art under duress, in the crucible of human pain and conflict. A surgeon of the soul, he cannot dismiss himself from the operating room to read up on the latest surgical technique.

Only in actual practice can the counselor develop the skills and perspectives so essential in addressing the specific needs of human beings. Until then, you can't appreciate the fact that counseling's effects, both good and bad, are felt not only in the life of the counselee but in the life of the counselor as well.

The better you do the more you get. In the seven years since we started the church, we have grown from forty families to over 1,000 people.

I'm thankful, of course. To a preacher, such growth is gratifying. For the counseling pastor, however, it can be a nightmare. When one person walks in the door, twenty personal needs come along, needs that someone must help meet. There may be others qualified to counsel, but it never seems like enough. The shepherd's heart of the counselor gets panicky when numerical growth outstrips resources. Soon "super-counselor" tries to do it all, and that means a *lot* of unfinished dinners, changed plans, interrupted days off, and exhausting days on.

I started as a pastor of people but soon became a pastor of problems. The more experienced I became at counseling, the more the difficult counseling situations came my way. Initially, counseling successes gave me satisfaction. But my sense of satisfaction in being used of God quickly diminished. That is partly because the more your reputation spreads, the more demands are placed upon you—"He helped me. I'm sure he can help you too. Besides, he doesn't charge $60 an hour." In my case, the quality of my counseling decreased as its quantity increased. I was doing less and less good for others, and none at all for myself.

Counseling can change your personality. As I became more and more involved in counseling, I underwent what one friend described as a personality change. Once outgoing and always available, I found myself holding back, inviting fewer people over, introducing myself less frequently. It was only later I realized what had happened. It was a matter of self-defense—the survival instinct in its rawest form. Many pastors overburdened by counseling know exactly what I mean.

The problem? Each new person I met was a potential counseling appointment. It might be him, or it might be his suicidal cousin, his lesbian sister, or his neighbors involved in a messy divorce. But one way or another his presence meant more responsibility for me—an already overburdened pastor trying to *avoid* additional responsibilities. My unconscious defense mechanism was to avoid the problems by avoiding the people (though it never seemed to work).

Once my work day was done (pastors will chuckle at that thought), people became intrusions. When the phone rang in the evening at home, my stomach literally ached. (I shared this with another pastor and he was shocked—he thought he was the only one whose phone rang in his stomach.) Like Pavlov's dog, I was conditioned to associate the ring with a negative experience.

The doorbell had a similar effect. Sometimes, when we would have preferred to stay home, we packed up the family and left for the evening, just to ensure we wouldn't be interrupted. (The *fear* of interruption is sometimes as bad as the interruptions themselves.)

When I came into the church office I hoped that for once the junk mail would outnumber the pink slips. (These messages from my secretary had the same symbolic effect as phone calls and ringing doorbells.)

Church retreats and banquets were really tough. I longed to relax and have informal fellowship. What better place than a social gathering? Invariably, however, the people we sat next to grabbed the opportunity to talk to me about their problems. My wife was left out completely. During one retreat I barely saw her—I was doing marriage counseling the whole weekend. Believe me, I resented it.

Living With the Guilt

You may be thinking, *What a terrible attitude for a pastor.* I felt that way for a while and suffered from the guilt. Ironically, though people's problems burdened me and robbed me of strength and sleep, I felt I was becoming callous, insensitive, uncaring. To a counselor, such things are the ultimate shame and cause for alarm—as frightening as a surgeon helplessly watching arthritis creep into his hands.

I felt more than psychological pain, though. I began to experience the physical symptoms of stress. I was *always* tired. I could honestly not remember the last time I *wasn't* tired. And I was constantly fighting colds. Sore throats would often last for months— one year the same cold and sore throat lasted from August to February.

Of course, I didn't let sickness interfere with my work! When I was so sick that even I could justify staying home, I couldn't rest. This was my only chance to get things done around the house, to do some writing, and get caught up on paperwork and phone calls. I refused to listen to the message my body was sending me.

Here I was—less than ten years in the ministry, and contemplating whether I had hit mid-life crisis fifteen years early! I began to wonder if the longevity of pastors was comparable to that of professional football players. If the press had interviewed me, I would have said I was waiting till the end of the season before deciding whether or not to retire. If I made it to thirty-five, they'd be calling me "the old man"—and they'd be right!

The one thing worse than the guilt and fatigue was the price my family was paying. I thought I was a loyal family man. I was even occasionally criticized for leaving meetings at 10:00 P.M. out of courtesy for my wife. I "put in my time" with the family, as any good family man should, but I gave them second best. By the time my energies were poured out at the office, I often arrived home about 6:30 for a late dinner. Typically, I struggled to stay awake at the dinner table. I would have traded anything for a half hour nap on the recliner. But I knew I should spend time with my girls before they went to bed. So I did. It took every ounce of energy I had to wrestle with them on the living room floor. The delight of reading them "Harry the Dirty Dog" and their favorite Bible stories was gone. Even "One fish, two fish, red fish, blue fish" became a chore. I had once been a very good listener (aren't all counselors?). Now my girls had to repeat themselves and raise their voices to get my attention.

For a period of three years or so, I experienced most of the symptoms described in the books on burnout. I felt lonely, depressed, physically and emotionally exhausted. My morale was low, and I was sensitive to criticism (a disastrous condition in the ministry). I was defensive and resented the fact (or was it only my imagination?) that the ministries of other staff members were often publicly applauded, but mine was not.

A barrier slowly grew between me and the others on the church staff. Though we loved each other and had unusual rapport, our busy schedules hindered communication. It bothered me to emerge between counseling appointments only long enough to overhear important staff discussions I wanted to be in on. I felt increasingly "in the dark." Of course, the root of the problem was not theirs, but my own overspecialization and consequent lack of availability of time.

Perhaps the best indicator of how deeply I was hurting is the way I reacted when people complimented and encouraged my teaching and preaching. Sometimes, it actually bothered me. Why? Because those things were such a small part of my ministry (maybe 20 percent), and compared to the counseling, it seemed to me an easy part ("the grass is always greener . . .").

Those were dark days; I was prideful on the one hand, yet felt tremendously inadequate on the other. I had a classic case of job saturation, an inability to leave my work behind me. The problem is common to all the helping professions, especially the ministry, but I didn't know that—I felt terribly alone. And when I tried to share my dilemma with others, between the pain and frustration I never seemed to communicate well. I ended up feeling more alone and misunderstood than ever and determined not to open up again.

I felt trapped—the victim of circumstances. I tried everything I could think of to resolve my overextension problem, but I could not say no to people who were hurting. I still cared deeply for them and was often moved to tears at their emotional and spiritual problems. At the same time, I didn't realize how severe my own problems were becoming. The challenge "Physician, heal thyself" was for me "Counselor, counsel thyself." Finally, I did.

Perspective Rediscovery

For me, the key to physical, emotional, and spiritual healing was getting some extended time off. My church granted me a two-month sabbatical for my six years of service. It was a good investment.

I spent a week alone, meditating and writing. Then I spent nine days at the Oregon coast with my family. It was the time of our lives. We played, bicycled, ate out, picnicked, and consumed a lot of ice cream. It was the first time in years that I was not constantly aware of my ministry responsibilities. I ran on the beach, walked out on a 500-foot jetty, and sang to the Lord as I was drenched by the mist of waves beating against the rocks. I had no idea how much I needed those times, both alone and with my family.

After I'd been away for a few weeks, and knowing I still had plenty of time left, my head began to clear. I was able to see myself and my ministry in perspective, something that had time and time again proven impossible when I was in the thick of things. Often I had identified the problems, but despite my most sincere and diligent efforts, the obstacles to a fulfilling ministry had persisted. At last they seemed to, if not disappear, shrink to a manageable size. I did three further things that began to revitalize my ministry.

1. *I recognized I was a sheep first, a shepherd second.* My biggest mistake was forgetting that my primary calling is to be a sheep in need of guidance, affection, protection, provision, and peaceful rest in the presence of my Creator. I relearned the lesson through prayer and study.

During the time away I read two helpful books: Tim Hansel's *When I Relax I Feel Guilty,* and Don Baker and Emery Nester's *Depression,* in which Pastor Baker recounts his personal struggles and trauma in the midst of a highly successful ministry.

I also studied Mary and Martha in Luke 10:38–42, and mulled over the implications of their different approaches to life and ministry. Martha was first a worker, only secondly a worshiper. This is what I had become—a worker, pure and simple.

As a counselor I had learned a forbidden art—how to keep giving out when my reservoir was dry. Like Martha of Bethany, I excelled at doing rather than being, at labor instead of love. I was a servant but not a saint, a do-er not a pray-er, a giver who had forgotten how to receive. And, ironically, since I had stopped receiving, I had little of quality left to give.

2. *I attempted to delegate more.* You've probably wondered why I didn't delegate in the first place in order to get the job done without killing myself. I did, to a degree. In fact, I taught a nine-month counseling course to sixty committed and capable laymen in our church. I delegated many counseling situations to these people, and it was a terrific investment in every way. But there was one problem I hadn't bargained for. Still seeing myself as super-counselor, I delegated to laymen those that were less serious and less complex. This reserved for myself, of course, the really hard cases.

The problem was that these really challenging cases (extreme depression, deep sexual problems, major marital crises, etc.) were abundant. And many of them couldn't afford to see a Christian psy-

chologist. I was really in a mess. I had managed, by delegating, to
avoid all the mild problems, while I filled every hour with the severe ones! I had become a specialist. I was a pastor in psychologist's clothing, who sometimes wasn't doing a good job as either.
Not only that, but I couldn't find time to follow up on the lay counselors I had sent people to. I seemed further behind than ever.

I began to miss all those "easy" cases—you know, the dear
people who really want to grow in Christ and simply need some
good biblical input, a time of prayer, a practical assignment, and
an encouraging pat on the back now and then. These are the people who praise you for working wonders in their lives, when all
you've done is listened and shared a little Scripture! They were the
kind of folks who convinced me I was gifted in counseling in the
first place. Now I saw them only on Sundays. I was surprised to
find how much I missed their spiritual contribution to my life.

Delegation didn't really pay off until I got hold of my schedule.
I had often tried to change my schedule before, but never with
lasting success. Perhaps what made the difference this time was
my degree of desperation. I forced myself to start saying no not
only sometimes but much of the time. I realized that merely because something would be good to do didn't mean it was the best
thing to do. In fact, if I wasn't careful, I could spend the rest of my
life doing good things without ever doing the best.

I no longer felt I was saying no, but yes, when I delegated
counseling to qualified laypeople and professional Christian counselors. And as the fog cleared, I realized I had no right to resent
people for their "demands" on my time. After all, my schedule was
my responsibility, not theirs.

3. *I diversified my ministry.* I undertook new ministries that
brought me closer to thriving, growing people who not only receive from me, but give to me. I counseled less, and by my request
the church provided financial aid to those who needed professional help. (Back when I was super-counselor, I never put funds
for this in the counseling budget—after all, wasn't I paid for this?).

Moving into some other areas of ministry did wonders. My relationship with the other staff members is better than ever. I feel
part of the team once more. And I love to meet new people again.
The phone can still be a problem, but I'm getting more calls for

spiritual guidance—many are asking advice in working with a friend instead of sending the friend to me. Not every call is a crisis, and that makes the real crises much easier to deal with. For the first time in years, I feel like I'm a pastor first, a counselor second.

Nothing has magically fallen together. I still experience pressure, and occasionally it gets the best of me. Still, the change is significant and noticeable. I am studying and teaching more, and finding time for some of the people with the "little problems." I'm also learning to approach life less like Martha and more like Mary. My family has seen a tremendous difference, and now, life at home is more than leftovers. It's a feast again, and I thank God for it. Now I feel I can look forward to many more rewarding years of ministry.

4

Regeneration, Deliverance, or Therapy?

Ultimately, calling people to respond to God's grace through regeneration has to be our primary focus.

—Archibald D. Hart

Pastor Jones was perplexed. For the fourth time this month Cynthia, a twenty-four-year-old single woman, had come to see him, each visit more puzzling than the last.

Cynthia had grown up in his church, where her parents were long-standing members. Cynthia had professed faith at a youth meeting when she was fourteen and had been a leader in the youth group before going away to college. Now she was home again, looking for a job.

At her first session, Cynthia explained that two years earlier she had started dating a young man. They became serious but fought often and frequently broke up.

"A year ago, I discovered I was pregnant," she finally said. "And against my better judgment, I had an abortion."

Troubled by both the relationship and the abortion, she felt "locked in," unable to extricate herself from either the relationship or her past behavior.

"What can I do?" she wailed. "Where can I go to get away from all of this? What's wrong with me that I can't break off this sick relationship?"

Pastor Jones listened to Cynthia with deep sympathy. He reasoned with her and then prayed for her. She felt better.

But a few days later she was back again. He listened to her reiterate her anxieties and guilt. *She seems worse, maybe even de-*

pressed, Pastor Jones thought. *Why isn't she experiencing forgiveness and freedom? Has she really experienced conversion? Is perhaps some demonic power at work in her?*

Not that he'd had much experience in spiritual warfare, but so many groups were talking about it he couldn't help but consider it.

Still, he repeated his standard counseling format: he helped her confess her sins and pray for forgiveness. Then he hoped God would work a miracle.

Twice more she came back, even more troubled. Pastor Jones was baffled and even a little irritated. He wondered, *Could she have some deep-seated emotional problem? Has something snapped in her mind, or is there something from her childhood coming back to haunt her?*

He felt inadequate. But he hesitated to refer her to someone else for fear Cynthia and others would think him incompetent. This seemed to be a spiritual problem. Why couldn't he just do his job as a pastor? He stewed about what to do.

Pastor Jones is not alone. I have heard this story, with minor variations, over and over from pastors. No pastor can become an expert in every aspect of the human condition.

And yet every pastor has to diagnose, if only at a rudimentary level, a troubled person's problem: Does this person need to be pointed toward making a commitment to Christ and thereby experiencing the new life of regeneration? Does this person need some supernatural intervention? Or is this a case for psychotherapy or counseling?

Before I set out some guidelines for diagnosing people who come to see pastors, first let me discuss two factors that complicate a diagnosis: (1) how psychological factors, especially childhood experiences, can impact or impede spiritual healing; (2) the difference between demon possession and its most popular imitator, schizophrenia.

Psychological Scars

Hardly anyone reaches adulthood without collecting a few psychological scars along the way. Even Christian homes can be severely dysfunctional and anxiety-producing. Abuse can take many forms. The worst is not physical but emotional.

Divorce is increasingly common even in Christian circles, wreaking havoc on the social and emotional lives of children. Or, psychological damage can be caused by bad parenting—neglectful, overly permissive, or overly repressive.

In later life these scars can interfere with a person's spiritual development and prevent a free, unhindered experience with Christ.

For example, our understanding of God is very much shaped by our childhood experiences with people significant to us. When a father, for instance, is abusive, demanding, cold, or unforgiving, we are likely to assume that most authority figures, even God, are that way.

One woman told me, "I can't approach God without confusing him with my father. I can't pray with my eyes closed because if I do, I see images of my father towering over me and making threats. I can't even pray the Lord's Prayer because saying 'Our Father' sends fears flashing through my body. God and my father seem to be the same—emotionally I can't tell the difference. When someone speaks of God's love, I don't have the slightest idea what they are talking about. It's all very confusing to me."

This woman will have great difficulty in developing a healthy and balanced spiritual life. Scores of people in most churches suffer from such distorted images of God. When these people are in emotional pain, these distortions will hinder their ability to appropriate God's help.

A pastor counseling such a person will need much wisdom in correcting these distortions. Merely educating people in the "attributes of God," teaching them about who God really is, is only part of the counseling task.

The psychological damage needs to be healed, and while God does sometimes intervene in wonderful ways to erase these scars, other times such supernatural intervention does not occur. (God does not always short-circuit the healing process, I believe, because in the long run we are better off having "worked through" these problems by God's grace rather than experiencing instantaneous cures.)

False guilt is another example of psychological damage that can hinder spiritual growth. Many children raised in devout Christian homes are traumatized by excessive and unrelenting guilt. Sometimes parents, yearning to raise "God-fearing" children, impose rigid discipline and practice severe punishment.

For instance, one Christian family, who lived in a house next to ours when we first arrived in the United States, had strict rules about whom their three daughters could talk to. The parents were so scared that their girls would become "contaminated by the world" that they told them: "You may not have any conversation with a non-Christian child. If we catch you talking to such a person, we will punish you."

These children developed intense guilt about talking to non-Christians. My daughters (who were allowed to be their friends) would listen for hours to their fears. Our neighbor's daughters grew up to be excessively guilt-ridden; one now suffers from a major emotional disorder.

This sort of guilt is often referred to as "neurotic" or "false" guilt, as opposed to true or healthy guilt. Although many psychologists see all guilt as false, I do not. We need healthy guilt. We need to develop a clear sense of right or wrong. But when we feel condemned by arbitrary rules, or when the guilt we feel is far in excess of what is appropriate, then it becomes neurotic.

Why is it neurotic? For one important reason: such guilt does not respond to forgiveness, whether it is offered by human beings or by God. It only knows punishment. It demands to be punished. It won't let up even when all is fully restored.

This was the problem with Cynthia (the person Pastor Jones was counseling). Her upbringing made her conscience oversensitive and out of control. She could find no way out of the prison of guilt brought on by her wayward behavior. Having strayed, she could not find her way back to the peace of mind that forgiveness from God should have provided.

Is this purely a spiritual problem? Obviously not. Can God not miraculously cure such a problem? Yes, but often he doesn't. God's wisdom is far greater than ours, and his concern is much more for our sanctification than our comfort. Cynthia needed to replace her neurotic guilt with a healthy sense of guilt. She also needed to experience forgiveness—the deep and profound forgiveness that God offers—so that she can come to live with her imperfections.

Schizophrenia and Demon Possession

If psychological trauma, especially in childhood, can impede spiritual growth, what about spiritual powers? How do these impact psychological or spiritual problems?

I encounter scores of emotionally troubled people every year who at one time or another have been told they have an "evil spirit" or a "demon" possessing them. But demon possession is not always the problem.

Not every person who has a sexual addiction is under the control of a "lust demon." Lustful thoughts and behavior can be the consequence of poor self-control, inappropriate exposure to sexual activity as a child, sexual abuse, or ordinary sin. We don't need to jump immediately to exotic explanations.

In addition, it can be harmful to assume demon possession too readily. No doubt Satan appreciates the extra publicity, but even worse, the hopelessness that such a label, especially when untrue, engenders in the victim (especially after exorcisms fail to cure the problem) can often do more harm than the original problem.

Falsely attributing emotional problems to demons has several dangers. It removes the victim from responsibility for recognizing and confessing *human* sinfulness. It enhances Satan's power inappropriately. But most importantly, it delays the introduction of effective treatment. And delaying treatment for a problem like schizophrenia can significantly decrease the likelihood of the sufferer's return to normalcy.

Schizophrenia is a physical disease. Because it exhibits bizarre symptoms, it is frequently labeled as demon possession. Epilepsy is another disease formerly labeled as demon possession, but now we know that both epilepsy and schizophrenia are the result of a defect in brain chemistry. Medication can bring a cure.

Any delay in starting the right medication for treating schizophrenia can impact the sufferer's long-term recovery. Misdiagnosis can have serious consequences. This is especially true for a form of schizophrenia that starts in late adolescence.

Every pastor, therefore, should be able to recognize the basic
symptoms of schizophrenia. Frankly, those who cannot should not
be counseling. Some basic symptoms include

- marked social isolation or withdrawal;
- marked inability to function as wage-earner, student, or homemaker;
- marked peculiar behavior (collecting garbage, talking to oneself in public, hoarding food);
- marked impairment in personal hygiene and grooming;
- digressive, vague, over-elaborate conversation, or lack of conversation, or lack of content in conversation;
- odd beliefs or magical thinking that affect the person's behavior (superstitiousness, belief in clairvoyance, telepathy, "others
  can feel my feelings");
- unusual experiences (recurrent illusions, sensing the presence
  of a force or person not actually present);
- marked lack of initiative or energy.

Naturally, schizophrenia is a complex disease. But if a pastor
suspects it in a client, he or she should make the appropriate referral as quickly as possible.

If schizophrenia is identified, what does demon possession
look like? The characteristics of demon possession are not neat
and simple to discern, but those with extensive experience with
possession look for such things as

- the presentation of a new personality. The person's voice and
  expressions change, and he or she begins acting and speaking
  like a different person. However, this is also seen in "multiple
  personality disorders," a severe psychological problem asso-
  ciated with "splitting" and childhood abuse. It takes someone
  trained in psychopathology to tell the difference.
- a striking lack of human warmth. The possessed seem barren
  and empty, and they lack empathy.
- marked revulsion to Christian symbols. The cross, the Bible,
  and other Christian symbols make those who are possessed extremely uncomfortable. However, I also see many schizo-
  phrenics evidence this reaction. Consequently, this sign, by it-

self, is not evidence of possession.

- physical phenomena. Many describe an inexplicable stench, freezing temperatures, flying objects, and a "smooth, stretched" skin (see Malachi Martin's *Hostage to the Devil*).
- behavioral transformations. The victim has "possessed gravity," in other words, cannot be moved physically or can levitate or float.

Obviously, then, possession is not as common as is supposed, and many so-called possessions have more natural explanations. Diagnosis of demon possession is usually made after first eliminating the obvious causes of the problem.

How should the pastoral counselor set about making a diagnosis of demon possession? By ensuring that other professionals also examine the person to be certain that no obvious cause of the problem is being overlooked. If all natural explanations are exhausted and several of the above symptoms are present, then the pastor may wish to proceed with such a diagnosis.

The Law of Parsimony

In all matters of discernment the principle that should guide us is the "law of parsimony."

In essence, this law requires that we try to understand a problem at its most obvious and fundamental level. Simplicity is the rule. When diagnosing a problem, we must *first* try to find the most obvious and natural explanation *before* moving on to explain it in more complex or less obvious ways.

For instance, if I have a headache, I first try to see it as a result of stress or eyestrain (depending on the circumstances). If rest doesn't cure it, I may then need to consider whether I have a bad case of the flu. If that hypothesis doesn't pan out, I may need to go to a neurologist to check if I have a brain tumor.

But unless the symptoms obviously suggest a brain tumor, I don't immediately jump to the conclusion that every time my head hurts I have a tumor. All diagnostic processes follow this law.

Here's how we can apply that law to the pastoral counselor's task of determining the nature of a person's problem.

Take a careful history. This lesson we can borrow from other disciplines like medicine. Most pastors are not trained to take a thorough history, but it is vitally important to do so if you are not going to miss an obvious cause of a problem. A history should include the following:

- Details of family background;
- History of dysfunctional patterns in the family;
- History of mental illness in the family;
- History of the presenting problem;
- When it first occurred;
- How often it occurs;
- The changes that have taken place in recent history;
- History of spiritual experience and practice;
- Experience of conversion—when, where, and how?
- Patterns of spiritual development since conversion.

A thorough history should provide a clear picture of what troubles the person, how it started, and the context of the problem.

Consider obvious causes first. Following the law of parsimony, you now try to explain the problem in the most obvious or natural terms.

For instance, if there is a history of mental illness in the family and the person you are counseling is experiencing bizarre behavior or emotions, the most obvious cause is likely the familial pattern of illness. Genetic factors strongly influence severe mental disorders. Unless you are trained in psychopathology, however, the most responsible action you can take is to refer the troubled person to a psychologist or psychiatrist for diagnosis.

Intervene at the most obvious level first. It is helpful to think of counseling intervention in hierarchical terms. Not only does diagnosis work upward from the obvious level of explanation, many interventions should also follow this approach. Treat the basic symptoms first, then move on to more complex symptoms.

For instance, a man may be behaving bizarrely, saying he sees things or hears voices that no one else sees or hears. The first intervention should be to refer the man to a competent professional who will treat these unusual behaviors and hallucinations.

While treatment for the bizarre behavior is underway, you may wish to counsel the person in the steps of Christian commitment, encouraging a "surrender" to the claims of Christ. (Your responsibility as pastor doesn't end when you make a referral.) Of course, the one intervention (professional treatment) may need to temporarily take precedence over the other (spiritual guidance) simply because the disease needs to be under control before the person can adequately comprehend spiritual matters.

Consider supernatural causes. At what point should one consider the possibility of supernatural or demonic causes for a problem and invoke deliverance as the remedy? Only when the more obvious causes have been eliminated.

If there is a history of schizophrenia in the immediate family of a troubled person, for instance, the treatment of schizophrenia must be given first consideration. I think it is gross negligence to move beyond this diagnosis without addressing the presenting issue.

But what about less bizarre behaviors? The same principle applies. Find the most obvious cause and treat this first. If you have eliminated the obvious, or if the symptoms are so strange as to rule out any natural cause, then you might want to consider moving directly to supernatural factors.

Some words of caution:

- Never try to diagnose supernatural causes by yourself. Always seek corroboration from others and hold yourself accountable to corporate discernment.
- Remember that many experts believe that possession doesn't usually manifest itself in bizarre behavior. Satan is more creative than that. We may need to look elsewhere for it.
- Even when you think there is a state of possession, remember that psychological or psychosomatic problems accompany and complicate possession. These may *also* need treatment.
- While Jesus instructed his followers to deal with demons (Luke 9:1), we find no injunction to seek them out. In other words, avoid preoccupation with these causes. Focus rather on the victory and protection we have in Christ.

Consider the need for regeneration. One of the great draw-backs of counseling or psychotherapy is that it does not deal directly with the core problem of human existence: our alienation from God.

Whatever the problem that a troubled parishioner presents, the question of regeneration is always a legitimate one. Without the regeneration that God works in the core of our being, all human endeavor to improve the quality of life (mental or physical) is limited. Pastoral diagnosis must always address the question of whether or not regeneration has occurred.

I am not suggesting that we judge people's salvation. But we have a right to call people to accountability for their souls. This is the work of evangelism.

During emotional turmoil people are more open to spiritual interventions. The caring pastor will carefully suggest ways the client can experience renewal by receiving God's grace. *Regeneration* literally means "rebirth," and only when the core (or "heart") is regenerated can counseling or psychotherapy make a significant difference.

As Christian counselors we can prepare a person to be receptive to God's work. We can help remove the obstacles of childhood traumas or distorted God-images so that his grace can be effective. Therapy or counseling does not do the work of grace; it merely aids it. It is nothing more than burden-bearing as instructed by Galatians 6:2, 5, and Romans 15:1. It is helping others to rely upon the greatest burden bearer of all (Matthew 8:17).

Don't delay in referring. Whenever a problem is complicated or when you feel that it is beyond your training or expertise, refer the person to someone capable. Develop a relationship with a group of trusted professionals to whom you can make referrals.

Let me emphasize the word *trust*. Unless you know these professionals personally, you will not have complete trust in them. Cultivate a relationship. Go to lunch and talk with them so that they understand where you are coming from. Find out their orientation. If you are not satisfied, move on to someone else.

And even after you've made your referral, maintain ongoing contact so that you can evaluate progress and decide when and how you will intervene with spiritual direction.

While I suggest a parsimonious model of diagnosis, I cannot stress too strongly the importance of continuing education for pastors, especially in the area of understanding the human condition. Ignorance here is dangerous and can do much harm.

The misapplication of a spiritual solution may delay appropriate treatment of serious mental disorders. By the same token, the exclusive use of psychological treatments for spiritual problems is costly and dangerous to the soul.

Ultimately, calling people to respond to God's grace through regeneration has to be our primary focus. After all, "What good will it be for a man if he gains the whole world, yet forfeits his soul?" (Matthew 16:26).

For many, however, evangelism may mean helping them overcome the psychological obstacles to surrendering to this grace. This is where Christian counseling becomes a means of grace.

5

Old-Fashioned Pastor in a Therapy Age

If applied wisely and in partnership with Scripture,
many psychological principles can lead
people down discipleship's road.

—Louis McBurney

Years ago, a pastor attending Marble Retreat was trying to climb out of the deep gorge of despair. Several years before coming to Marble, she had taken her struggles to a psychotherapist and wound up in bed with him. Her troubles, as you might imagine, compounded exponentially.

In one of our first counseling sessions, I asked her what seemed like an obvious question.

"How have you dealt with your sin of adultery?"

A funny look crossed her face. "No one has ever called it that before," the pastor said. "But it is sin, isn't it?"

"Yes, it is."

Right then and there she repented. It was the catalyst to her recovery.

Later, the irony hit me: this pastor's adultery had happened several years back, but apparently nobody in her church, denomination, or circle of friends had mentioned that what she did was a sin. Neither had the professional counsel she'd received after her affair. I was flabbergasted.

The Therapeutic Invasion

The North American church has been invaded by what some call the "therapeutic culture"—a culture that promotes openness, acceptance, and tolerance, with a value system of listening, empathy, and support.

This phenomenon began in the 1960s, in what psychiatry called the Age of Anxiety. The cultural unrest of that period conceived and gave birth to despair, a despair that has continued for some thirty years. Today's lonely crowd has lost the capacity to cope. Many feel hopeless and aimless. The evening news reports the grim result: suicide, child abuse, spousal abuse, divorce, violence—the rates in recent years have skyrocketed.

Paralleling this despair has been the proliferation of support groups and professional counselors—the secular recovery movement—which provided many hurting people a safe, structured environment for dealing with their problems. By the late 1980s, in fact, seeing a counselor or attending a support group was considered chic; you had a doctor, a lawyer, and a therapist.

What began in the general culture, then, spread (some would say metastasized) to the church. Local churches allowed AA groups to meet in their facilities and sponsored support groups on divorce recovery, grief recovery, and overcoming sexual and drug addictions. Each spring Christian schools now graduate an army of counselors outfitted to help people work through their problems. These soldiers of healing find their way into local church settings or start counseling businesses. The language of recovery saturates the Christian air waves. At Christian bookstores, believers hungrily buy up millions of dollars worth of self-help books that tell how to set boundaries, identify anger, and discover patterns of family sin.

These changes have affected how pastors feel about what they do. As parishioners get help from counselors and fill up support groups, pastors can feel threatened. Their skills may seem obsolete. Leading Bible studies, preaching, visitation—these seem to be anachronisms. *What good am I*, a pastor may think, *if people are getting all their good stuff from their support group? What's my role around here, anyway?*

One pastor came to Marble troubled. He felt like an outsider; everyone was "recovering" except him. "I'm supposed to be leading these people," he said, "but I've never been where they've been. I don't feel good asking them, 'Hey, what do you have that I don't have?' "

What are we to think of this new phenomenon?

Its Benefits

While some pockets of the church have embraced the recovery movement, others have criticized it heavily—and with good reason. Many philosophical elements of popular psychology are clearly at war with Scripture.

No doubt much of popular psychology is laced with narcissism. Self is often exalted above all. The word *sin* is no longer used. Many efforts to help people with their problems completely ignore the spiritual dimension. Everyone is a victim. Parents, spouse, genetics—these all get blamed while individuals in therapy seem to be absolved of responsibility.

But I'm not prepared to wash my hands of psychology. The tendency is either to reject or embrace it. I'd like to suggest a third approach: reject the non-Christian elements and embrace the principles that help individuals exhibit the fruit of the Spirit. In fact, if applied wisely and in partnership with Scripture, many psychological principles can lead people down discipleship's road.

Here's one helpful technique of therapy, for example, that breaks entrenched patterns of sin. Let's say someone who is struggling with pornography comes to me. Using behavioral modification principles, I point out the pattern or steps leading to sin: the stimulus, immediate response, and habitual behavior. A stimulus might be his feeling anxious or tense or depressed. His immediate response is to seek release from that discomfort. And through the years, he's developed an entrenched habit that acts like a tranquilizer: watching porno-movies or flipping through *Playboy* and then masturbating to release his anxiety. As soon as he feels a certain level of anxiety, the dominoes begin to fall: anxiety, pornography, masturbation. The pull seems inexorable.

When asked, men who fight this problem can often list, with great precision, the events leading to their action. By pointing out these patterns, I help a man identify the early stage, say, when he begins to feel anxious or tense. The stimulus will still be there—he still may feel anxiety—but his habitual response can change.

Being aware of the dynamics and creating a new habit can halt the
stimulus' response/behavior chain. As soon as he recognizes what
is happening, he can pray, read Scripture, or talk to a friend. In
short, the therapeutic techniques can help him develop one of the
fruits of the Holy Spirit: self-control.

Not only do insights and practices from recovery have practical
benefits, they also build community. Our culture creates loneliness. In an age of despair, people need more than ever a place of
hope, where it's okay to admit your problems, where people accept you, where "everybody knows your name."

That's the genius of support groups, a tool we have found ben-
eficial at Marble Retreat. The pastors and spouses who sign up for
two weeks of counseling and support have been emotionally beat
up and bruised by adultery, marital struggles, addiction, burnout,
depression, or the vicious sheep in their flock.

For two-week periods, four couples meet together regularly
with ample time for group sharing. We encourage participants to
let down their guards and share frankly without fear of recrimi-
nation. The groups provide a safe place where any feeling is allowed and unconditional acceptance is the only rule.

One pastor came to Marble with his ministry and marriage
hung up on the rocks of self-doubt. He felt extremely ineffective
and threatened as a person and as a minister. Over the days he
spent with us, childhood problems bubbled to the surface, deep-
soul issues of acceptance and identity. As he grew up, the messages he received from his parents were uniformly negative. When
he found Christ as an adult, his life turned around, but through the
years he still agonized over his adequacy.

His time at Marble was a turning point for him. The group
helped him to see himself in a different light, affirming who he was
in Christ and what they appreciated about him. One of the discussion questions the group was asked to answer was simply,
"What's new?" That simple question came to have profound significance for him. It became the symbol of change in his life. In a
recent letter, he wrote:

> Well, what's new? Me! That's what's new. Those first
> three words have had a powerful impact upon my life and

those last four words are just beginning to sink in. I thank the Lord for the freedom that I am beginning to experience. For example, I often found myself calling myself "dumb" or "stupid" when I would forget something or mess up. I still do that, but I find it's merely out of habit. When I do it now, there is no power in those words, and often I find myself chuckling about it.

You know, I'm really starting to like myself, and it sure is neat. I'm beginning to see that I have worth not because of who I am or what I do, but simply because God loves me. Can you imagine that? God loves me! I must tell you that it's great to be loved. . . . And what is so neat is that God rescued me because he delights in me (Psalm 18:19). He delights in ME!

His letter went to all the group members, thanking them for helping him to understand God's love. This is just one example of how the recovery movement within the church can offer a fresh witness of the gospel.

Link Therapy With the Word

However, the "therapeutic world order" places new burdens on church leaders. Today's church culture, for example, puts a premium on pastors who are warm, relational, and vulnerable. What many churches want in a pastor is an empathetic support group leader; a healer who listens first, then makes poignant insights into people's lives, nurturing them on the road to emotional health.

Not every pastor is wired for that. Nor should every pastor be. Though the ground has shifted, pastors must stick to being pastors. Someone must still point to the Word and to Christ—that's always been in the job description of a spiritual shepherd. What's happening in counseling and support groups must be linked with God's Word. Here are several ways to make that happen.

- Encourage people to outgrow their status as victims. Children naturally interpret their world as orbiting around themselves. In a home, say, where the father gets drunk repeatedly, causing chaos and turmoil, a five-year-old child can easily come to believe, on an emotional level, that she is responsible for her daddy's problems. *I must be a bad person,* she thinks, *for allowing this to happen.* She grows up feeling shameful and responsible for not only her daddy's problems, but also for the problems of her husband and others.

Years later, let's say, she finally gets into counseling. An initial step in therapy is helping the patient get in touch with her brokenness. She begins to see she wasn't responsible for her father's rampages. This revelation often causes a geyser of anger and resentment to spew forth—a necessary but painful step in the healing process.

While I may squirm at this anger, I shouldn't squelch it or encourage her to deal with it quickly. Anger itself is not sin. When these feelings are identified, talked about, and accepted as valid, only then should I encourage her to take the next step of releasing them in forgiveness.

Yet, she *must* take this next step. Too often people stay angry and blame their parents and everyone else who has victimized them.

This is where pastors, in their preaching, counseling, and leadership, must play an important role. They must lead their people to where they can say, "What happened to me was awful. I wasn't responsible for it, so I don't have to assume guilt or shame for it. But neither do I have to be stuck there. The people in my life were fallen creatures just as I am. They sinned and as children probably were sinned against."

We should expect anger and resentment, but must gently encourage, in due time, moving toward forgiveness.

- Link the recovered self with the serving Christ. One of the most important but gritty tasks of Christian discipleship is moving people from being takers into givers. In recent years, this has grown only more difficult. Those who have received counseling often feel released from the ought-to's and obligations that before shackled them. As they get in touch with their own needs, which is necessary in the recovery process, they can become selfish, focused merely on their needs.

To move beyond that, they must see their self in relation to Christ. Their identity is not merely in discovering who they are but who they are in Christ. One is inwardly focused; the other Christ-centered.

Simply put, who we are in Christ is this: redeemed sinners. When we absorb this truth, it leads to sacrificial giving. When a person truly sees who he is in Christ, he is freed from the pride of thinking he's better than others and also from the despair of feeling worthless. That change in focus reflects what Christ was modeling when he donned a towel and washed the disciples' feet.

I'm reminded of Frank, who handled his insecurity by bringing the spotlight to himself and becoming jealously angry if anyone else was getting attention. After seeing the truth about himself, he stepped out of the limelight. He quit wearing flashy clothes and jewelry. He actually changed his child's diaper for the first time, helped wash dishes with his daughter, went to his son's Little League game, and took out the trash.

He went on to help in an inner-city soup kitchen in which nobody knew who he was. He discovered the joy of self-giving service rather than self-serving performance.

- Name sin. Not long ago, a pastor and I were talking about Jesus' response to the woman caught in adultery: "Then neither do I condemn you. Go now and leave your life of sin." I had to confess to this pastor that saying "Neither do I condemn you" was much easier for me than to say "Go and leave your life of sin."

While we're called to say both, the subtle pressure is to shy away from proclaiming the harder truths of the gospel. But pastors don't have that option. To link the healing process with genuine biblical discipleship, we must name sin. We cannot be complicit in one of the glaring errors of secular psychology.

In my counseling, I occasionally have to say, even though it cuts across my grain, "Cut it out. You've got power; you can control your behavior. You don't have to be a slave to these things." While empathy is important, sometimes the call for repentance is more urgent. At some point we've got to say that certain behavior is sin, that God is more powerful than that sin, and that repentance is required.

Ask the Right Questions

One skill that helps us link a person's behavior to God's Word is asking the right questions. Our questions help people discover their deeper motives, to explore what's going on inside.

I ask people questions like "What's the payoff for how you are acting?" or "What's in this for you?" I want to help people discover their underlying motivations and the results of their behavior. When they do, they sometimes discover the payoff is decidedly negative.

Many pastors, for example, come to Marble completely frazzled and burned out—they are workaholics. Most workaholics never stop to consider the end result of what they're doing. Questions like "What happens when you do this or don't do that?" force them to evaluate the consequences of putting so much time and energy into their work and so little elsewhere. Often they discover their drivenness originates in someone's comment that they're not good enough. They overlook three hundred compliments and become obsessed with one criticism.

So they push on to prove otherwise. Often they're amazed to discover the bottom line of their workaholism: they *are* inadequate! Our questioning can hold a mirror to their lifestyle and help them toward spiritual growth.

A common story for pastors who come to Marble is that of Tim. He constantly had to prove his value, doing so by maintaining rigid control of programs and people. Though he pushed countless tasks to completion, he left many hurting people in his wake. He was unaware of what was happening and couldn't understand why his critics called him cold and insensitive.

We explored his attitudes about himself and how that affected his attitudes toward others. As Tim began to recognize that his sense of worth was completely wrapped up in his productivity and projects, he began to realize that he often felt irritated with people who got in his way.

Now, with a new foundation of self-worth in Christ, he can take time to really hear others. He wrote that it feels so good to be able to listen to his parishioners, to understand them rather than give them a quick answer to get them out of his hair. He has a whole new vision for ministry, which now includes loving people and not just completing projects.

Cautions for Caregivers

Finally, let me add two caveats necessary in a church culture of gaping wounds and infinite needs.

First, make sure you're helping people for their benefit, not yours. I entered medicine with a deep need to help others. Much of my makeup came from my mother's temperament. She is a natural caregiver who was trained as a nurse. To this day, she still loves to hover over us kids and attend to the needs of her children. (And we all love having her mother us.)

Sometime during my medical internship, I realized a lot of my caring was for me, not for the person I was helping. I needed to be needed. That is a hazard for all caregivers, including pastors. We need to keep asking ourselves, *For whom am I doing this?*

Second, set limits on what you'll do for people. This is as much for their benefit as for yours. At Marble, the couples who stay for two-week stints live together in a lodge a hundred yards or so from my home. Often the couples will ask my wife, Melissa, and me to come over in the evening and visit.

Early in our ministry, we took them up on their offer. But we soon discovered on those evenings that the group deferred to me, the leader, and the group dynamics changed. The group stopped interacting and doing the hard work of processing the ideas they had been exposed to earlier in the day. When I stayed away, they had to depend on themselves and on each other.

Likewise, if pastors become too involved in support groups and other recovery ministries, participants will look to them as the experts. In the end, the group loses. People need to struggle to find answers; this hard work is necessary for healing.

We'll need to watch closely the number of hours we invest in certain individuals, or the time spent with a couple in marital counseling. The best thing for them may be for us to back off, letting them learn to fly on their own.

The recovery movement has nudged many in our churches for the first time to take a hard look at their lives. Skeletons are being evicted from dark closets, and compulsions are being brought under control. Many are feeling a new sense of emotional and spiritual freedom. The problems that propel many people into counseling and support groups are, in effect, wonderful opportunities for discipleship.

Meanwhile, as pastors, our mission hasn't changed. Our job is to steer people in the direction of the Cross.

6

Why Pastors Make Great Counselors

I'm not just a professional; I'm an extension of the love of Christ, a channel of his grace.

—Robert J. Morgan

I love it, and I hate it. It's exhilarating, and it's exhausting. Pastoral counseling—it's part of who I am and what I do, yet it often feels as if it's an invasion into my life.

No one does pastoral counseling better than a pastor. Not a psychiatrist, a psychologist, or a psychotherapist.

Professional counselors, the good and the biblical ones, have an important role to fill. I don't understand much about schizophrenia, repressed memories, cyclothymic disorder, or the treatment of ADHD, OCD, or PTSD. Mental illnesses are complex, and I'm not equipped even to recognize some of them. My parishioners and I have benefited from good counselors, and I consider them my allies.

But they are not my replacements. I'm not prepared to yield to a society enamored with Sigmund Freud, B. F. Skinner, Carl Rogers, Albert Ellis, or Joseph Wolpe. Pastors can still do things that professional therapists can't.

After all, the prefix "psych" means "soul"—and pastors are tenders of the soul. That's our job.

Pastoral counseling, as I'm using the term, is helping people resolve their problems, facilitating positive changes in their lives, and helping them grow toward greater wholeness. No one does that better than pastors. Here's why.

Pastors Care As Friends

When people come to me with problems, they come to someone who loves them. I'm not just a professional; I'm an extension of the love of Christ, a channel of his grace. Many professional counselors, of course, exhibit genuine concern, perhaps even love, for their clients—but not as only a pastor can.

When I began pastoring twenty years ago, I studied *shepherding* in the Bible. The Hebrew word is closely aligned to the Jewish word for *friend*. That's what people need. In its essence, Christianity is nothing more than personal relationships—with God and each other. Within these friendships comfort is best proffered, advice best taken, rebukes best accepted, and corrections best made.

I may not have all the answers, but I can love and listen. I may feel I'm doing little good, but I can pray. Recently, I sat in my office absorbing the laments of a young couple. I felt a tide of frustration rising in me, and my inner voice muttered, "How in the world can I help them?" My outer voice took them to the Scriptures, shared an anecdote from my own marriage, and prayed with them.

When they left, I sighed, feeling the session had been wasted. But the next week, the wife called. "Thanks for seeing us," she said. "John said he wouldn't talk to anyone else, but he likes you. He said you'd understand, and things have been a little better. He said he'd like to see you again."

Pastors Build on Existing Relationships

Recently, a Bible study leader called and said, "I'm about to leave my wife. I've gotten involved with a woman at work. But I want to talk to you about it." We met, and after several chin-quivering, heart-throbbing, plain-talking sessions, he repented.

I referred him and his wife to a trusted marriage counselor, but it was the friendship of years that laid the cobblestone path he followed to my door. We had long joined in worship every Sunday. We had butted heads in meetings and prayed and planned and consoled one another. I had baptized his children, buried his father, and visited his hospitalized sister at all hours. The connections were already in place.

A therapist recently told me, "You pastors have a real advantage because you're part of a person's life more than I can ever be. Counselors get intimate with people quickly; then we're gone. You are in a person's life consistently. My role is short-term; yours is long-term, and it's the long-term role that usually proves most valuable."

Who but pastors can do informal, incisive, on-the-spot grief counseling at funerals, marriage counseling at weddings, bedside counseling in hospitals, conflict-resolution counseling at committee meetings?

Pastors Preach Care Every Sunday

The apostle Paul said to his elders, "You know that I have not hesitated to preach anything that would be helpful to you but have taught you publicly and from house to house."

Our house-to-house, person-to-person ministry doesn't stand alone. It rests on a public role of preaching the Word, correcting, rebuking, and encouraging with great patience and careful instruction. One of the boons of a long pastorate is the accumulation of encouraging letters that testify to this, like this one:

> I wanted to drop you a note to let you know how much I appreciated your message Sunday morning. . . . I learned Saturday night that my younger brother in Idaho attempted suicide after drinking all night Friday. I badly needed your words about troubled loved ones. I want you to know I'm keeping two copies of the message in our file with important papers, one copy for each of our two sons so I can share it with them when they are older. . . .

Pastors Give Biblical Solutions for Spiritual Issues

Most people who approach pastors expect us to speak of spiritual realities. Many would be disappointed if our Bibles remained closed and our knees straight. I can't reduce everything to an oversimplified, black-and-white, wave-the-Bible-at-it problem. Human complexities can be as impossible to untangle as a child's ball of string. Yet I sometimes wonder if such an over-simplified reduction might, in the final (psycho) analysis, prove more helpful than much of the jargon dispensed all over town at seventy-five dollars an hour.

Ever wonder what a psychoanalyst would have said to Cain? *Let's talk about your childhood. How did you feel when he bragged on Abel's mutton stew instead of your vegetable soup? And your mom's apple pies—what was that problem all about?*

The Divine Counselor told him, "Sin is crouching at your door."

What would a modern therapist have said to the unraveling King Saul? To the woman taken in adultery? To shy young Timothy? To the demoniac of Gadara? To Paul, the driven man?

There is no better tool than Scripture for penetrating soul and spirit, joints and marrow, thoughts and intents. It is the Bible in all its authority—specifically the promises in all their sufficiency—that revives that soul, makes wise the simple, gives joy to the heart, and light to the eyes.

Pastors Are Accessible and Affordable

I have the privilege of sacrificing more. Few professional therapists remain on call twenty-four hours a day. Maybe I don't either, for over the years I *have* learned to build some safeguards into my schedule and some hedges around my family. But I'm still generally more accessible than a listing in the Yellow Pages under PSY. I have the capacity to hurt more, to care more, to weep with those who weep, and mourn with those who mourn. For these reasons, I think I am better at counseling than . . . well, than I think I am. And the final reason why?

My fees. I'm free, so to speak. Even that counts for something.

PART 2

Caregiver Issues

Part 2

Caregiver Issues

7

Appropriate Affection

In the face of many emotional needs, let us not shrug off completely the ministry of touch.

—Michael E. Phillips

I couldn't have painted a better scene of missionary life. Small, native children ran alongside, urging me to take their picture. Scraggly dogs yapped in rhythm. The air was heavy with rain, the smells rich and primordial. We walked a tree-lined road that was overgrown yet stately. As we walked, the pastor of the local church was explaining the move of God's Spirit in his country.

Then he unconsciously broke the marvelous mood. As a show of affection, this African pastor took my hand and firmly held it as we walked. The action took me by surprise. Every nerve in my arm screamed to my head, "Pull away. Fast!"

I looked around to see if anyone could see us—two men holding hands on their way to the next village. I hoped my sweaty palm would make further hand-holding impossible, but the pastor ignored the squishiness and retained his warm grasp. In my discomfort, I learned something about myself: I am a child of my culture.

Even though all of us are learning to break through "macho" stereotypes, which prevent many men from showing much affection at all, on that African path I forgot all notions of the liberation of the changing modern male. As the seconds collided together, I planned my escape.

"Look at that!" I said, pointing my sweaty hand at a child holding a scorpion by the tail. It happened to be the hundredth one we had passed in the last mile, but it gave me an opportunity to slip my hand out of his and firmly secure it in my pocket for the rest of the trip.

I was safe from my hang-ups for that day, yet the incident began a trail of thought that I would walk many times. Why had I reacted with such alarm? Why is intimacy such a dark closet in my mind, while others have acquired such holy freedom to express emotions outwardly?

Several years have passed, and I have tried to answer those questions in the context of my own ministry. As a pastor, I have also noticed the dilemma as perceived by men and women in my congregation: To hug or not to hug? It's a haunted house with many rooms and few guides.

Intimacy Prevention

I notice a secular world fidgeting more and more at the idea of being close to others. Back in 1984, *Ms.* magazine was calling intimacy a "turn on," and *Harper's* was warning society of "Enemies to Intimacy." But since affection and sexual attraction are rarely divorced in the secular mindset, sexually transmitted diseases are closing the door to intimacy, public or private. Now the world feels it will survive only if it shows the cold shoulder. And by its definition of intimacy, perhaps rightly.

However, the fidgeting is not restricted to singles bars. It's also found behind the pastor's desk. I can recall a half-dozen tragedies that involved pastoral colleagues' being removed from ministry for adultery. Each one of those moral failures steels my resolve to avoid the situations that wreaked such havoc.

But what is improper affection? And how do I avoid it? I've encountered several situations where I've decided strictly to avoid any show of affection.

When my emotions are unstable. Affection is proper under certain emotional conditions, but when I am emotionally unstable, a powder keg of problems is lit.

When my dad died close to my sixteenth birthday, I suffered an emotional letdown of mammoth proportions. I began to respond to dates in uncontrollable ways. The emotional strain was leaving me vulnerable to the dark side of affection: attachment without self-control. That, of course, was not good. I needed to still my raging emotional life before I subjected others to my misguided affections.

Several years ago in ministry, I came face-to-face with another potentially dangerous situation. A young woman came to me with a deep need to be released from alcoholism. We spent several sessions together, which resulted in both the alleviating of her drinking problem and her becoming a Christian.

During that same period, however, my wife and I were struggling through the stress-filled early weeks of having a new baby. We were getting very little sleep and were not as close as we should have been. One afternoon while preparing mentally for a session with the woman with the alcohol problem, I found myself floating into a sensuous daydream—involving her. I realized what was happening and invited a deaconess to join us for that session, which became the last.

I have no idea how close I was to the emotional precipice of infidelity, and I don't want to know. I do know, however, that I was in no condition to show or receive any affection in relation to that counselee.

When the person pulls away. We've all seen the romance movies where the hero pulls the petulant damsel into his arms. She fights him at first but eventually succumbs to his charm, melting into his embrace.

A forced churchly affection, however, will never turn warm someone who doesn't want it. At times, some people simply don't want affection of any kind. It comes across as an unwanted commitment to an equally unwanted emotion. They need the security of distance. We've all known occasions when an overly familiar touch on the shoulder sends a shock wave of recoil.

When I sense a growing gap between me and someone in the body, my immediate response is to attempt to bridge that gap with affection. I tried it last year, and I learned my lesson.

The elders had rebuked an older couple for an impropriety. During a particularly warm Communion service some weeks later, I sought to embrace them both during our time of greeting one another, but they decidedly pulled away from me. The wife summed up their feeling: "Pastor, we are no longer that close to you. Hugging us will not solve the problem."

I realized I was using affection as a quick-fix substitute for the gradual rebuilding of a relationship. The one is not interchangeable with the other.

When it means nothing. A recent article in a well-known women's publication bore the auspicious title, "Have You Hugged Your Dry Cleaner Today?" At various times in the secular world as well as in Christian circles, affection becomes the latest fad. The indiscriminate hugging of a dry cleaner points out that affection can be emptied of meaning through random and meaningless gestures.

But are there holy hugs that can be dispensed with integrity and surety of purpose? In the face of many emotional needs, let us not shrug off completely the ministry of touch.

Appropriate Intimacy

How do we know when to express affection in appropriate ways? Some situations lend themselves to brotherly shows of affection. Here are situations in which I'm willing to step out on a limb.

In the face of loss. I often think of the story I heard about a young boy and an old man. A family of three moved into a two-bedroom house. The boy, five years old, loved to play outside because his new house was too small. Across the lane lived an old man and woman whom he loved to visit.

The old man and the boy talked and played together every day. One day, however, the old woman died. The old man would not be consoled, and his neighbors left him alone with his grief. The boy's mother repeatedly warned him to stay away from the old man and under no circumstances to bother him.

However, children have insatiable curiosities, and the boy eventually crossed the lane to talk to his elderly friend. When the mother looked out the window, she saw the old man weeping uncontrollably. She urgently called her son home. As he came in the door, she scolded him, "What did you say to the old man to make him so sad?"

The boy lowered his head. "I didn't say nothin'," he stated. "I just climbed on his lap and helped him cry."

I cannot hear that story without thinking of my friend Joe. Although he is a well-respected member of our church, at times he can be an enigma, for he is sometimes caustic, sometimes comical. He loves the Lord Jesus, and he loved his wife, Edie.

She died one night after a lengthy illness, and I fought with myself over what I should say to Joe. I hated sounding insincere with words of comfort, especially to a good man like Joe. The moment I came into the room, however, his posture helped me know what to do. He sat slumped in his chair and looked ten years older and six inches shorter than he was.

I walked over, helped him up, and embraced him for twenty minutes. He cried and then talked till late evening. It's been over a year now, and every time we greet it's with a warm embrace.

When someone is hurting, affection is much more than a warm fuzzy or a mild turn-on. Intimacy is the bonding of comfort, the balm of closeness, the first and greatest expression of understanding. There are very few who will misunderstand its intentions, and fewer still who will misappropriate its vulnerability.

Remember when all cameras were turned to a small-town school in 1986? The space shuttle had exploded, and a beloved teacher was dead. How would the students react? The television cameras revealed a disheveled group of kids holding one another, embracing each other's hurt. In the face of loss, genuine affection is definitely needed.

Yet even the embrace of comfort is not automatic. God's people need reassurance that intimacy is not an enemy. Unless people have been trained to do so, most will not react to sorrow with physical closeness. More likely, they will speak some awkward, ill-chosen words. As a pastor, I take responsibility for bridging the affection gap.

I recall a delicate situation where affection was helpful. The man of the house had been killed in a plane crash. Since there had been very poor communication in the house before his death, the family had very little they could say to one another. In the middle of a visit to their house, I decided to instruct them about affection.

I voiced their inner anxieties about putting their grief into words, and I suggested they skip the words and enter into the intimacy that heals. I started it all by raising the oldest son to his feet and hugging him. Almost immediately they began to embrace one another and share their mutual hurt.

I left at that point, but I heard later that the affection had opened the floodgate of speech. Today, the family is closer than ever.

In the face of discouragement. Our denomination requires that each candidate for pastoral ministry complete a stint as a parish intern. I arrived on the scene of my internship with excitement and plans. This would be where I would cut my pastoral wisdom teeth! However, my enthusiasm was no match for my inexperience. I had to deal with a string of ideas that never developed. That's when God brought into my life a strange type of affection meted out by a beautiful human being.

His name is Bob. God gave me healthy injections of Bob just when I felt my spiritual reserves reaching empty. Bob would saunter over in my direction after a worship service and place his firm arm around my shoulder. Then he would grab someone and say to him, "Tell me something nice about my friend Mike." As forty other people listened, I had something nice said about me. All the time, the ever-present arm of Bob lingered. I couldn't have survived without those times of encouragement.

It's tough to define discouragement accurately. A slumped shoulder, a shattered voice, or a war-worn smile may be the only clues of a friend's discouragement. But we pastors know that discouragement can be a killer, draining the last vestiges of personal goals and dreams. Warm, bear-hug affection can cut through discouragement faster than anything else.

We have an exercise in prayer meeting that we call "the filling station." If someone is discouraged, we invite him or her to stand in our circle. Then we all lay hands on that person and begin to pray in turn. We thank God for this person, for the person's Christian life and testimony, for past, present, and future ministries. The prayers ask God to fill the person with encouragement, but one of the keys to the exercise is God's working through the laying on of hands.

Jesus loved to touch those who labored under discouragement. Touch became the signature of his healing ministry. A woman whose body had been tormented twelve years with hemorrhaging reached out to touch her Healer. As he asked who had touched him, the woman fell at his feet in fear that she had violated some law.

People in churches today also hesitate to touch lest they break some law about showing their affection. I picture Jesus raising the woman to her feet and holding her hand gently as he speaks a word of comfort: "Daughter, your faith has healed you. Go in peace."

Caroline, a woman I know, has suffered for years from kidney disease. She had undergone months of preparation for dialysis, and her kidneys were giving her immense pain. Yet insensitive people had chastised her for lack of faith. Just months after dialysis began, she was rushed to a nearby hospital for a kidney transplant. Her heart was full of hope and praise. The kidney was rejected by her body, however, and had to be removed.

I came to her bedside not knowing what to say. She lay there despondent and worn out. All my words of comfort sounded hollow. I asked if I could hold her hand. She took both my hands in hers and held on tight. Then I began to sing songs of worship to God.

I was singing on behalf of her wounded spirit. For two hours I sang like that. My hands were holding hers, my spirit responding to the low condition of her spirit. As I left, her eyes caught mine. "God touched me through your hands," she quietly told me.

In the face of rejection. I read a newspaper advertisement that totally caught me off guard. They were advertising for people who could work as deodorant testers. Every morning the testers would be expected to put on a prescribed amount of deodorant, work up a sweat during a one-hour workout, and then report to the laboratory. A paid "sniffer" would bury his nose in their underarms to see if they—and the deodorant—passed the test.

I could never be a tester. I'm sure the sniffer would flunk me, and I couldn't handle the rejection.

The pews are populated with burdened believers. Many Christians feel so frustrated and inadequate because of past sin, failure, and doubt. And to finish them off, there are always plenty of "spiritual sniffers" to let them know when they aren't making the grade. Therefore, to avoid rejection, people retreat into a world of don't-touch-me-because-it-hurts-too-much. They are afraid to be touched, and they won't touch.

A good way to bring people out of this cocoon of rejection is to show them through affection the warmth of unconditional acceptance. God's people, however, must be subtle and sincere with this kind of warmth. Few things are more distasteful than a Christian who goes around handing out affection insincerely. People instinctively know when they're victims of a spiritual cheerleader.

Ted had two qualities that made him as popular as fungus. In conversations, he did *all* the talking. But people could have accepted that quality if the other weren't so obvious. Ted weighed 360 pounds. He had tried every diet and was on the mailing list of every weight-loss clinic in the Western Hemisphere. Even an amateur psychologist could see that Ted was carrying around a ton of rejection, which he tried to hide with food and words.

I tried to show affection to Ted, but he wasn't easy to get close to (no pun intended). He kept pushing me away.

One day he phoned me and he was frantic. I rushed over to his house to find him in a pool of water. His pipes were leaking, and he knew nothing about plumbing. He couldn't afford a plumber. And to top it off, he was too big to get under the sink himself.

I'm no plumber's apprentice, either. But I asked the Holy Spirit for some Noah-like advice and then rolled up my sleeves. I got the water turned off and the tap disconnected. Ted and I drove with the cracked faucet to a local plumbing supplies store, and we returned with a new faucet, which I paid for. A mere four hours later I had it installed, like a true professional.

At the end of this ordeal, I put my arm almost around Ted's shoulders and said I was glad to be of some assistance. At that, Ted began to cry like a baby. He said, "No one has ever cared enough to put an arm around me." We spent the next two hours in talking and healing, crying and hugging. That day, Ted gave his life over to the control of Jesus Christ.

When I saw Ted a month later, he had lost sixty pounds. My embraces became increasingly more effective as they covered more territory.

Perhaps one reason there are so many untouchables around us is that they've rarely been touched by an accepting hand. My spiritual plumbing exercise opened a door to Ted's heart, which could then accept my heartfelt emotions. I've learned I must build a foundation of acceptance first, and then I can erect a structure of affection.

Affection Ambivalence

My closest friend shuffled nervously as we waited in the airport to say goodbye. As college freshmen unsure of whether we would return to school the next year, we sensed this could be our final time together. Blaine was leaving for his home, and I would head home in a car later. The terminal was teeming with people, which made our final moments more hazardous. *To hug or not to hug?*— we both felt the awkwardness of the situation.

"Why do guys find it so hard to show friendship with a hug?" Blaine asked. I didn't have an answer. All I could think of was the possibility of a thousand eyes focused on us. But as I looked around, I saw many people embracing as a token of a fond farewell. That emboldened us to do the same. We exchanged bear hugs!

Affection reacts to genuine love the same way forgiveness reacts to confession: it's the suitable reaction. Still, I am cautious, wary of those times when I might be out of line with a warm embrace.

But through my friends who have cared enough to hold me close, I am beginning to feel release from the bondage of remaining distant. In the face of my own insecurities, I'm learning to sort out the time to embrace from the time to refrain.

8

The Need to Be Needed

Perhaps God brought Mark into my life to show me
secrets of emotional health that I'd unwittingly neglected.

—Robert J. Morgan

I found my buddy drunk and dazed, parked on the shoulder of a Tennessee back road. It was 2:30 in the morning. His eyes, wild with cocaine and alcohol, darted toward me, then to his ignition. As he drove off, I jumped on the hood of his car and shouted at him through the windshield.

"Mark, we love you! I just want to talk."

"Get off the car, Rob!"

"Mark, listen to me. We love you."

"Rob, don't make me hurt you!" he shouted. "Get off the car!"

"Not till you talk to me," I yelled. "Stop the car and talk to me!"

"Rob, get off the car! Get off! Get off the car!"

I didn't think he'd hurt me, but I knew he wouldn't listen. I slid off his moving vehicle and watched the taillights vanish in the night. I felt the emptiness of the darkness swallow me.

Trail of Tears

I was Mark's pastor, but he had become more than a parishioner. My wife and I had taken him into our home to help him overcome his addictions, and for months we watched him grow. He loved the Lord and devoured his Bible, memorizing key verses with the enthusiasm of a child. He became like a son to my wife and me, like a brother to our three daughters.

Then one Sunday he disappeared.

We weren't emotionally prepared for Mark's relapse, and when it came, it unearthed a problem in my life that lay buried like a leaking gas line—a tendency to become badly overinvolved.

"I'm unsuccessfully struggling to retain—regain emotional perspective," I scribbled in my diary. "I spent hours yesterday searching for Mark in bars all over town. Last night I found him, but he wouldn't talk to me. I actually rode on the hood of his car, clinging to the windshield wipers, trying to reason with him through the glass as he drove down the road. A throbbing depression has hit me."

My journal tracks the next several months:

December 19, 1990 Mark charged from his girlfriend's apartment last night so drunk and doped and frightened that we feared for his life. Called police to be on the lookout. We knelt around the sofa and prayed through tears.

December 22, 1990 Mark came dragging in today, drunk and high. He's sitting in his car, trying to decide whether or not to let me check him into a treatment center. It's our daughter's thirteenth birthday, and my family is all here. It's a real mess.

January 15, 1991 Today is the deadline for peace in the Persian Gulf, and war seems at hand. My greater attention, however, is with Mark. I repeatedly awaken in a sweat through the night to pray for him. My heart literally hurts. Katrina and I feel he's probably going to leave, to run away, to relapse, perhaps to die a miserable, lonely death. I can't stop him.

February 4, 1991 Mark's gone again, didn't come home last night. His girlfriend called about 10 P.M., crying. She had found him buying cocaine. My girls sobbed themselves to sleep.

March 27, 1991 Mark's relapsed again. He comes in to sleep, about four or five in the morning. Spends the rest of his time drinking and drugging. The counselors tell me I've got to evict him. I can't continue to "enable" him by giving him a safe haven.

March 28, 1991 I went to Mark's room and sat on the edge of his bed. I told him what I had to tell him, and he said he'd be out by April first. I went on to the health club but didn't have much of a workout. I returned to my office and cried.

March 29, 1991 Mark asked to borrow some money for a deposit on a new apartment. I refused, and he grew furious. He cursed. He told me he'd never again ask me for anything. He said he never wanted to talk to us again. He stormed from the room. I sat on the bed and wept.

April 29, 1991 Mark came back yesterday, exactly one month after bolting. He was humble, hurting, pitiful, broken, and determined to get better.

May 11, 1991 I can't continue to live like this, always on edge and full of apprehension about Mark. I see another relapse coming.

July 7, 1991 Mark didn't show up. . . . I have galloping anxiety.

July 9, 1991 Another relapse. When I heard about it, I lay on my office floor in terrible pain. What's wrong with him? What's wrong with me?

On August 31, I found Mark in a seedy apartment, badly depressed and ready to die.

"Rob," he slurred, "just look at me. I can't stop. I'm hopeless. I'm a hopeless reject from society. I've lost my job. Lost my friends. I've hurt so many people and broken so many promises. . . .

"Rob," he continued, eyes unfocused, "I've got enough cocaine in this apartment to kill an elephant, and my body won't take much more. It'll only be two or three days. You'll forget about me in a month. I read somewhere that when you die, your friends adjust to it in a month or two. It's just meant to be. Let it be."

After an hour of pleading, I finally choked back my tears and moved toward the door. Turning, I took a last look at him and walked away. There was nothing more I could do. He would be dead, I knew, within forty-eight hours.

The Pain of Love

Looking back, I see that many of my reactions were appropriate. Portions of my agony were legitimately for Mark. We loved him as part of our family. Our tears were like those of the Savior who wept over Jerusalem. How can you watch another person self-destruct—especially a loved one, especially at close range—without anguish?

Paul wrote of his lost kindred, "I tell the truth in Christ, I am not lying, my conscience also bearing me witness in the Holy Spirit, that I have great sorrow and continual grief in my heart." G. Campbell Morgan said, "Men only pray with prevailing power who do so amid the sobs and sighing of the race."

But too much of my grief was for me. I had become a textbook example of overinvolvement. Melody Beattie wrote that those who become overinvolved "aren't crazier or sicker than alcoholics, but hurt as much or more. They haven't cornered the market on agony, but they have gone through their pain without the anesthetizing effects of alcohol or other drugs. . . . And the pain that comes from loving someone who's in trouble can be profound."

Somewhere down in my heart, I had needed Mark. He was the brother I didn't have, the son I've never been given. He was siphoned into my soul to fill a hole of unknown origins. I had become dependent upon him—on his friendship, his love, his companionship. Our relationship, which began with his being dependent on me, had turned into my being dependent on him.

Funny how that happens.

Beattie continues, "So we become dependent on them. We become dependent on their presence. We become dependent on their need for us. We become dependent on their love. . . . A certain amount of emotional dependency is present in most relationships, including the healthiest ones. But many men and women don't just want people—they need people. Needing people too much can cause problems."

Fallen Lines

My needing Mark caused problems in my pastoral ministry. I became so obsessed, so numbed with pain over Mark, that I wasn't good for anything or anyone else. I'd grope through each day in a sort of daze, unable to focus, unable to give myself to those who needed me. My study time deteriorated, and I hadn't the energy for even routine administrative duties. I was a basket case at home, unable to provide emotionally for my family.

Late one night it dawned on me that my obsessive pain resulted from violating a basic teaching of Scripture. I was seeking to draw from Mark the emotional support that should have been provided only by other God-ordained sources.

The psalmist wrote, "The lines have fallen to me in pleasant places," and those words assumed new significance that evening. I came to understand that God had drawn a triangle around me, ordaining a trio of friends to meet my deepest needs:

My Master. It's so tempting, as one writer put it, "to impoverish life at its center for the sake of its ever-widening circumference." My drive for an ever-growing ministry had fatigued my center, making me vulnerable; and rather than resting in the Father, I was relying on a rickety brother.

A man's character is often unmasked by observing where he goes to replenish his morale. I decided to view God as my best friend. It may seem irreverent to think of God as a pal, but Abraham was called "God's friend," and the Lord spoke to Moses "face-to-face, as a man speaks to his friend." Jesus frequently said things like: "The Son of Man is a friend of tax collectors and sinners" and "No longer do I call you servants, but I have called you friends." Most shocking, he said, "Friend, why have you come?" to the greatest traitor in history. I reasoned that if Christ could call Judas his friend, there might be hope for me.

A good friendship involves trust, so I began turning Mark's problems over to the One who can do the impossible. I stopped praying, "Lord, my best friend's killing himself!" Instead, I learned to pray, "Lord, you're my best friend, so please deal with our buddy Mark."

Some problems we can't solve, despite our best efforts. I shouldn't destroy myself worrying about problems that only God can solve.

My mate. My wife, Katrina, had mourned for Mark, too—we had wept together for him—yet she was baffled by my preoccupation with his condition. I slowly realized that perhaps Mark had been claiming a lot of time and emotional energy that should have gone to her.

We took off for a few days, flew to a resort city, rested and sunned and shopped and prayed together. I thought of God's wisdom in creating Eve. Alone in his utopia, Adam could soak up emotional strength from many sources—his divinely given occupation, his animal friends, his physical vitality, his lavish environment—but none of those could compare with God's gift of Eve.

Not everyone would agree, but for me, my wife—and only my wife—can be my earthly best friend. For me, seeking deep levels of emotional support and intimacy outside of my marriage is dangerous.

For those without a spouse or an intimate friendship with their spouse, I think of my friend Agnes Frazier. For fifty years she and her husband, Emit, had morning Bible reading and prayer at the breakfast table. On the day he died, she went to bed thinking that she could never again start the day with devotional exercises. But the next morning she bravely sat at the kitchen table and opened her Bible to the spot where she and her husband had quit their reading twenty-four hours before. The verse that stared up at her was "For thy Maker is thy husband."

She smiled and said, "Thank you, Lord."

Me. There is one other person I claim as a best friend.

Me. As Mark's insanity engulfed me, I realized I needed to care for myself, to withdraw for my own protection. H. W. Boreham once wrote, "Very few of us treat ourselves with courtesy. Many a man behaves toward himself as though he and himself had never been introduced. He is at no pains to cultivate his own acquaintance. He never wishes himself a jovial good-morning on waking; he never has a good laugh with himself in the course of the day; he never says an encouraging word to himself when things are going badly; he never shakes hands with himself or pats himself on the back when things are going well.

"He simply tolerates himself. He would not get the best out of a horse or a dog if he treated it in such a way; how, then, can he hope, under such impossible conditions, to get the best out of himself?"

How, indeed?

I'm learning to spend more time alone. More time walking. More time secluded. More time talking to myself, saying, "Bless the Lord, O my soul." I'm learning to take trips occasionally by myself, a night now and again in a lodge on the mountainside—just me, my Bible, my journal, a good book, and my walking shoes.

Solitude in moderation deepens the soul and protects me from the seduction of being needed.

Burdened No More

Perhaps God brought Mark into my life to show me secrets of emotional health that I'd unwittingly neglected.

God was also at work in Mark—without me.

As I left his dimly lit apartment that bleak afternoon, I left behind the phone number of a trusted counselor. Three days later, Mark called him. That was three years ago, and today Mark is married, sober, and the regional manager of a famous ice cream company.

Do I still worry about his relapsing? All the time. But I continually commit him to God. Just last week, we rendezvoused in Atlanta for a Braves game. He's still my buddy, but I no longer encumber him with the burden of my own emotional health.

9

Counseling the Seductive Female

*The therapeutic art of counseling is far more than
advice; it's a relationship between the
counselor and counselee.*

—Andre Bustanoby

S he was a very attractive woman, by my estimate about thirty-
five years old. (She turned out to be a well-preserved forty-five.)
I introduced myself in the waiting room and told her I would be
her counselor.

"I'm Colleen," she said. Then, lowering her head slightly, she
looked me intently in the eye. It was one of those looks that
needed no words. I got the message, even though I don't normally
attract the instant attention of women.

Colleen then fluffed her hair, pulled her sweater tightly over
her well-endowed figure, and looked back at me coquettishly as
if to say, "Do you like what you see?" I knew at that moment that
Colleen's sexuality and my reaction to it would be a primary dynamic in the counseling to follow.

If counseling were mere advice giving, her sexuality and what
I thought about it would be immaterial. But the therapeutic art of
counseling is far more than advice; it's a relationship between the
counselor and counselee. It deals with deep emotions. It draws
both parties into an intimate bond. Sometimes sexual feelings are
discussed—and legitimately so, for sexuality is an important part
of life, a gift of God to be under his control.

Admittedly, this kind of encounter is fraught with danger.
While some naïvely say that truly Christian counselors should have

no problem working with members of the opposite sex, experience shows that we do. Not only do we have problems handling the counselee's sexual arousal, but we may also have difficulty controlling our own sexual feelings.

As a pastor for twelve years and a counselor in clinical practice for the last fourteen, I also know that pastors in large churches may encounter someone like Colleen as often as once a month, especially if those pastors are attractive and have charismatic personalities. And while I recognize that not all counselors are male, I will refer to them that way here because this article is specifically about male counselors working with seductive female clients.

The Old Safety Strategies

Seminaries have long recognized the problem of sexual attraction in pastoral counseling and have advanced a number of safety strategies. Although these approaches help, they have shortcomings.

One strategy frequently recommended is *the open door*, the policy that pastors leave the study door ajar when counseling women, so someone in the outer office can monitor what's going on. The problem with this is that counselees want privacy. They won't be honest about their problems if they think someone is eavesdropping. In fact, often they don't even want other members of the church to know they're seeking counseling. If someone else has to know what's going on, the counselee prefers that person be present in the room.

What's more, the pastor who doesn't have his own sexuality under control may not make any sexual advances in his office anyway. He may instead develop a relationship with a woman in a more private setting.

Another strategy often suggested is *referral*. A counselor *should* refer a counselee to whom he is becoming sexually attracted. But too often this strategy doesn't work because the counselor isn't willing to admit to himself the extent of his attraction until it's too late. By that time he's not willing to give it up and make a referral. What's more, he may be afraid the counselee will tell another counselor about the tryst.

A third approach is *team counseling*, which may be a workable alternative if the counselor has access to trainees who are willing to team counsel for experience. But to staff a church with two fully trained, fully paid counselors does not make economic sense if the primary objective is to provide the counselor a chaperone.

Even if the counselor should have an unpaid intern or be able to afford a fully trained team member, the system's theory of counseling must be taken into account. This theory says that a counselee's response to two counselors will be different from her response to only one. Not all counselors make good team people, either. And then there's the question of whether the counselee will accept an intern as an equal member of a counseling team. The intern's value to the effort may be reduced by the counselee's attitude.

In defense of team counseling, an analogy sometimes is drawn to a physician's protocol with a member of the opposite sex. It's argued that a gynecologist doing a pelvic exam uses a nurse as a chaperone, as does a plastic surgeon who does cosmetic work on the female breast.

The realities of medical practice, however, don't always make this possible or even necessary. A shortage of nursing staff may require the physician to use judgment about when a chaperone is really required. Often a busy office routine may not make it practical. The physician must determine whether rapport and a professional attitude already have been established with the patient. The age difference between the physician and the patient might also be enough to settle any question.

Even if the chaperone system should be observed rigidly, however, the counselor/counselee relationship is not an exact parallel. The presence of a chaperone in a physician's examining room doesn't change the condition of the tissue being examined. But in counseling it's another matter. The presence of a chaperone may well keep a basic problem from coming to the surface, particularly when the issue is the counselee's use or misuse of her sexuality.

Some may ask, "What's wrong with that? Aren't we trying to avoid sexual abuses in a counselor/counselee relationship?"

That is an important consideration, but avoiding danger is not our only goal. Our principal responsibility is to help the counselee.

And if the counselee's basic problem is using her sexuality to control men, the problem must be dealt with in a setting that is most likely to yield positive results.

When We're Alone

Often a woman with this problem is not aware of it. All she knows is that she experiences disastrous sexual encounters with men without knowing why. Indeed, in a chaperoned setting the counselee may be the paragon of purity and innocence. I have seen counselees with this problem function quite differently in group therapy as compared to individual therapy.

This is what was happening with Colleen. Besides seeing her in individual counseling, I also worked with her in group counseling. In individual therapy, she behaved seductively, often pressing me to tell her or show her that I found her attractive. In the group she came across as a man hater and took great pleasure in putting me down.

Her man-hating façade was a cover for how she really felt—ugly and unloved, desperately desiring to be affirmed by a man. In the group she came across as a strong, competent woman who didn't need men.

My task in counseling Colleen one-to-one was to help her see that she was trying to do with me what she did with other men. The only way she knew how to relate to men was sexually, and she always wound up being used. I had a responsibility to her not to let this happen in the counseling setting. Indeed, by keeping it from happening, I likely would be the first man who attempted to have a relationship with her on some basis other than sex.

My prayer was that this would open the door to new and successful relationships with other men as well. I knew I would be under constant pressure from her to become involved sexually. The key for me would be having my own sexuality under control and understanding that a sexual relationship with Colleen would have devastating consequences: It would destroy my marriage and my fellowship with God, and it would put me in danger of professional censure. Further, sexual involvement would do a terrible thing to this woman who had come to me for help.

All the safeguards in the world will not help the counselor who has not come to terms with his own sexuality, who does not loathe the idea of sex with a counselee, and who does not feel the terrible responsibility for helping, not hurting, that soul who comes for assistance.

As counselors, we must face two realities. First, transference is not bad. It's natural and acceptable for counselees to develop feelings of affection for the counselor. Second, no safeguards will work if we don't come to terms with our countertransference, if we allow our own affection for the counselee to go in the wrong direction and lead to improper behavior. Having come to terms with our own sexuality, however, we can establish a professional relationship with the counselee.

The Professional Solution

The sexually seductive counselee needs help. She can be helped by the counselor who understands that her seductiveness is not just a "sin problem" but evidence of being terribly unsure of herself. She doesn't feel like a whole woman, and the only way she knows how to relate to men is sexually.

She needs to learn that sexuality is not only what we do but also what we are—male and female. Our gender affects our behavior and our feelings. We all need a sense of wholeness as a man or woman, as the case may be, and not just the ability to perform sexually.

My job as a counselor is to bring the counselee to that place, so far as I am able. Colleen probably could perform quite adequately sexually. But this was the *only* way she could relate to men. I needed to help her find better alternatives.

Counselors of all schools recognize that healthy feelings of worth are supplied through the affirmation of significant others. This is basic to child development, and it continues throughout life. The parent who maintains an attitude of respect toward himself and his child raises a child who believes in his own worth and the worth of others.

Thoughtful parents affirm not only the child's worth as a person, but they also affirm boys as boys and girls as girls.

There's a parallel between the parent/child and the counselor/counselee relationship. To affirm the counselee involves affirming both personhood and gender. But—and this is crucial—gender can be affirmed in a way that acknowledges both the counselee's sexuality and biblical morality.

Affirming Gender and Godliness

And how *does* a counselor affirm a woman's gender? By being empathic, warm (what the texts refer to as "unconditional positive regard"), and genuine. The problem comes with the woman who stirs the sexual feelings of the counselor. With this kind of woman, there is so much attraction that countertransference takes place.

The counselor meets the counselee in the reception room, and immediately his inward reaction is a combination of "Wow!" and caution. The woman is gorgeous and extremely provocative in manner and dress. His sexual response is entirely involuntary, as is his professional response of caution.

As the session begins, the counselee unfolds her story. The counselor learns that in spite of her assets, the woman is in crisis over her identity as a woman. The counselor may respond to her unprofessionally with a stated or implied, "Baby, let me affirm your femininity." Sadly, this kind of response happens even among Christian counselors.

A second, more professional response is one of curiosity: "How is it that a woman who obviously draws all kinds of male attention should be in a crisis over her identity as a woman?" The answer to this question will not come quickly or easily. Eventually the counselee will almost always turn it around and ask the counselor, "What do *you* think of me as a woman?"

The responses can range from an inappropriate "Let me show you, Sweetheart" to the opposite extreme: "I think it's time to make a referral." Or the counselor can do the hard work of dealing with his countertransference in a professional way. The scenario might go like this.

Counselor: "I'm surprised that a woman who is so feminine in appearance and manner should think so little of herself as a woman."

Counselee: "You find me attractive?"

This is a difficult question to avoid, but it can be answered with a clinical, rather than a seductive, "Yes, I do." The counselee is sure to explore this further, and if the counselor maintains a professional attitude, the discussion can be used therapeutically.

The counselor's candid admission of attraction makes him genuine. But he'd better be ready for the next question: "How attractive do you find me?" The implication is, *If you're sincere, you'll show me how attractive you find me. If you don't show me, you're not sincere.* This is a common ploy by women who manipulate men through sex.

But the counselor can bring the manipulation to light, without making the counselee feel condemned or endangering himself, by saying something like this: "I feel caught in a bind. I'm getting the message that if I'm really sincere about finding you attractive, I'll prove it by becoming sexually intimate with you. And if I don't, it's because you really are a washout as a woman rather than because of my Christian and professional convictions. I'm wondering if you don't miss some good friendships with men because you need to have them prove that you're a sexually attractive woman. What I'm trying to say is that I'd like to be able to see you as a sexually desirable woman without having to go to bed to prove it. I'd like to be something other than your bed-partner. I want to be something better: your friend."

Such a frank expression from a counselor raises an important question: Should a counselor really admit to finding a counselee attractive?

Assuming the counselor has already come to terms with his own sexuality, the answer is yes. The principle of genuineness is at stake. But genuineness does not require that we act out our feelings.

The genuineness of the counselor may be the very thing that provides a therapeutic breakthrough. If the counselee uses her sexuality to triumph over males, or if the only way she knows how to relate to males is sexually, a counselor who is both honest and professional can do her a great deal of good. His genuineness reveals that he has the normal sexual instincts of a male, but his conduct reveals that she doesn't need to use her sexuality to have a close relationship with a man.

Another situation can arise that requires some maturity and finesse: when a woman behaves seductively, but the counselor does *not* find her advances tempting. In this case, an entirely different problem presents itself. When the verbal or nonverbal "Do you find me attractive" question arises, how do you affirm the sexuality of a woman you do not find sexually attractive?

The key is to find an honest way of affirming her *femininity*. If the counselor has developed an unconditional positive regard for her, out of genuine feelings he ought to be able to tell her what he likes about her as a woman.

"One of the things I find attractive about you is your sensitivity to the inner feelings of others."

Or, "The thing I appreciate about you as a woman is your vivaciousness." Note: the word *vivacious* is not used of lively men. It's used of lively women. The very choice of word sets her apart as a woman. What's more, a *man* has said, "I appreciate you as a woman."

Obviously, we must avoid gimmickry here. Ours must be a genuine response or we'll wind up doing more harm than good. But the principle is the same here as for the sexually attractive female: my job is to affirm her attractiveness as a woman while maintaining my moral and professional standards.

The Verbal Touch

Sometimes a counselee is affirmed as a person by a nonsexual touch or hug. But in opposite-sex counseling, isn't there a danger that touching will be invested with sexual meaning?

Some counselors believe that a counselor should never touch a client of the opposite sex. And many pastors, with good reason, feel that hugging and touching are inappropriate in a church context because these are too easily misunderstood—both by the person being touched and by others who observe it happening.

A counselor doesn't have to touch a counselee physically to find sexual titillation, however. Some counselees have reported some heavily sexual conversations with other counselors, conversations I felt had nothing to do with counseling. A counselee has a right to feel angry when her head clears later and she feels she has been exploited. We have to ask ourselves continually, *Do the sexually oriented conversations have a therapeutic purpose, or are we engaging in conversational voyeurism?*

We have to be totally honest with ourselves. Motive is the key. Do we touch (physically or verbally) out of sexual attraction, out of an inner desire to exploit the situation, or out of a spontaneous expression of care for that person, quite apart from gender? When you touch with sex on your mind, you set the stage for sexual exploitation, whether you touch with words or with body contact.

Direct Sexual Advances

I am not so naïve as to think that a sexually seductive client will be discouraged by my determination to maintain a professional relationship. Indeed, as a counselor, I may be considered a challenge, and she may be all the more determined to seduce me.

Colleen was that kind of woman. At the end of a session in which I had made it clear that I didn't want a sexual relationship, she said, "Well, the least you can do is hug me." Before I could decide how to answer, she put her arms around me and hugged me with a full frontal hug, being sure I could feel her entire body. She then stepped back and looked at me as if to say, "Now, didn't you enjoy that?"

I took the initiative and said, "Colleen, there are friendly hugs and seductive hugs. That definitely was more than friendly."

Though she snapped at me for "rejecting" her, she made another appointment. In the next session I dealt with what happened in the previous one. Colleen wasn't happy about my reaction to her and my resistance, but she said she understood. When the session was over, she asked if she could give me a "friendly" hug. Once again, however, it was anything but friendly.

We had reached an impasse, and I didn't trust myself alone with her any longer. I told her that if I were going to be of any help to her, we would have to do something different. I wanted a female colleague of mine to come to the next session, evaluate where we were, and make some recommendations about where we should go.

Colleen was dead set against this. She said she would continue in my group, but she would not be part of a session with another counselor.

In our next group session, I understood why she wanted to stay in the group. She used it as a forum to attack me more viciously than ever. I knew she was angry and hurt that I didn't respond to her sexually, and it would be only a matter of time before the group would realize something was wrong.

Finally it happened. After several weeks of Colleen's outrageous attacks on me in the group, one woman demanded, "What is it with you, anyway? You act like a rejected lover, Colleen. What's been going on between you and Andy?"

This was the breakthrough we needed. After much hesitation, Colleen gave me permission to tell the group what had happened. In the security of the group, she was finally able to take off her mask and show that she felt like a frightened, unloved, little girl. I was then able to go on with her in the group and establish the first wholesome relationship with her that she had ever had with a man. If my first concern in counseling had been my safety, Colleen would never have tipped her hand and revealed her fundamental problem with men.

The way the group responded to Colleen's attacks points to yet another principle worth bearing in mind. Namely, there is no failsafe way to protect yourself completely from allegations of impropriety, no matter how professional and careful you might be. However, because I had a consistently credible record of treating female clients properly, with respect and professionalism and genuine Christian concern, the group recognized that any problem in my relationship with Colleen would not be because of impropriety on my part. That kind of consistent track record is the best defense against such allegations.

Helping the seductive female is difficult, but it can be done. It requires that we control our own sexuality. We mustn't need female sexual advances to reinforce our own faltering egos.

But most of all, we must recognize that such women have needs that require a mature, nonexploitative love. It is the love of a father for a daughter, which on the one hand enforces a taboo on sexual activity and yet on the other hand affirms her as a woman.

When we offer that kind of love, tremendous healing can take place.

10

Transference: Loosening the Tie That Binds

What we do with the attraction is what is important.

—Archibald D. Hart

I f you were hungry for love, wouldn't it be nice to find someone who was well-educated, mannerly, articulate but also a good listener, respected in the community, occupationally powerful, yet unselfish, and willing to spend time alone with you for free?

Numbers of counselees think so. They come to a church office and find themselves in the presence of the kindest, most receptive, admirable, gentle, wise person they've met in a long time. The solution to their turmoil, they gradually realize, is not so much what the pastor is saying as the pastor himself.

In my classes for working clergy who are pursuing the D. Min. degree, I talk about this hazard, technically known as *transference*. (The client is projecting feelings and desires into the counseling relationship that belong somewhere else.) Each term the students write a response paper on how the course has related to their situation. Every time, 20 to 25 percent of them report transference as an actual problem they have faced in their ministries.

Countertransference, the even more distressing corollary, is when the *counselor* projects feelings and desires into the mix that belong elsewhere.

The Problem

At the outset, let me stress that an intimate relationship between a pastor and a church member does not always involve physical sex. Although such relationships have the potential to become sexual, they may remain as emotional attachments for a long time.

"I've been lonely," wrote one pastor, "and I cannot communicate with my wife. She doesn't understand how I feel. All she wants to talk about are the kids and her mother. I want to explore ideas, thoughts, and feelings. So I began to spend time with ____ after we finished our counseling sessions. She understands me. I can share myself with her. I hope this doesn't go further—I'd hate to have to decide whether to leave my wife or not."

This pastor is kidding himself. The relationship will go further if he does nothing to stop it. All sexual affairs begin in this benign way.

Although most liaisons emerge out of counseling relationships, some start when a minister has to work closely with someone on a committee or project. Since more and more younger women have assumed church responsibilities in recent years, male ministers are now in closer working relationships with women where feelings of warmth and affection can easily arise. Sometimes the relationship develops with a secretary or another work colleague.

Male pastors are typically attracted to younger women, although it is not unusual for ministers to be attracted to older ones as well. And attraction does not require extensive contact. Glances from the pulpit to someone hardly known, or a chance encounter in a corridor or on a hospital visit can find the pastor obsessed with a strong attraction to someone else.

Sexual responsiveness is fundamentally instinctual, even though it is heavily influenced by factors of learning. It is based in biology, with hormones that can powerfully control behavior and emotions. So the basic attraction to others should not concern us. It is quite normal.

What we do with the attraction is what is important. Whether we succumb to it, deny or repress it (which is often the gateway to a state of increased vulnerability at a later stage), or honestly and courageously confront and deal with the attraction will be determined not only by our spiritual maturity but also by our level of self-understanding and the professional competence derived from good training.

The apostle Paul, in 1 Thessalonians 4:3–5, says, "It is God's will that you should be sanctified: that you should avoid sexual immorality; that each of you should learn to control his own body in a way that is holy and honorable, not in passionate lust like the heathen, who do not know God."

In essence, Paul is telling us to understand our bodies and know how to control our urges and drives. Since much attraction gets out of hand in avoidable situations and rises out of needs the average pastor does not understand, better training about the counseling process can prevent the catastrophe of ministerial affairs.

How Transference Happens

I believe the main source of church-related sexual affairs is the counseling relationship.

Over the past decade, the topic of sexual intimacies with clients has received considerable attention in the helping professions. In California it is now illegal (not just unethical) for a psychotherapist to have sex with a client, even if evidence shows the client was the primary seducer and a willing participant. Psychotherapists are required to report all cases of clients who have had sexual encounters with previous psychotherapists.

These professions readily acknowledge that in the interactive, personal relationship of psychotherapy, warm, friendly, intimate feelings are bound to develop. Just as surgery produces blood, therapy produces a closeness that can easily be mislabeled "love." The competent therapist recognizes these feelings as a by-product of therapy and is trained to deal with them. His or her own hang-ups and unmet needs are not allowed to enter the picture.

True, not all psychotherapists are adequately trained, or follow their training. But some ministers are not even aware of these issues, let alone have any training in dealing with them. Both need help.

Although a minister's personal family and married life is a basic deterrent to deliberately searching for an illicit affair, it does not guarantee safety in the counseling room or in the more subtle encounters of committee or project work. I have always believed, despite protests from unsuspecting pastors, that a minister's vulnerability has nothing to do with his marital happiness. For many centuries Scripture has warned us to be on guard when we feel most safe! Sexual attraction can occur as easily when one is happily married as when one is not. You may more deliberately *seek out* an affair when you are not happy, but you are not necessarily safe when all is bliss at home.

Contributing Factors

All ministers are vulnerable to affairs for the following reasons:

The counseling relationship. It provides an opportunity to explore the feelings of another person. People not involved in counseling don't get the same opportunity and probably can't grasp how deeply satisfying a true empathic understanding can be.

I know some ministers who deliberately do not do one-to-one counseling; they want to avoid the closeness either because they perceive themselves as too needful of intimacy or because they are physically very attractive to the opposite sex and constantly have to fight off their advances. This is a sensible decision in these cases.

The pastoral image. Male ministers can be very attractive to women simply because of their role. They are perceived as caring, concerned, and helping, yet with a power that is exciting. They can attract pretty women who in other settings would not give them a second look. Many ministers confuse this attraction to their role with attraction to their person.

They are also perceived as "safe." Intimate experiences with ministers do not typically create as much guilt in women as would other affairs: "After all, if the pastor is willing, it can't be that bad." Many are misled into believing they can allow their warm, loving feelings to develop with a minister because he will know where and when to set limits. When they find that no such limits are set, they often panic. In other words, the minister, having stepped out of his role, is no longer seen as attractive; he has destroyed the very reason for his attractiveness. He suddenly finds himself facing an accuser.

The denial of sexual urges. It is an unfortunate consequence of our Christian aspirations to holiness that we create a sexually repressive subculture. Many ministers (and Christians in general) are afraid of their sexuality and see in it a tremendous potential for sin. And they are right. The healthier way to deal with the sex drive is to bring it into the open and courageously confront and master it.

The majority of ministers enter their profession with the highest ethical intentions. They have a deep desire to be genuine and spiritual. But they are often also confused about their sexuality, and rather than confront their feelings, they repress or deny them. Believing they are immune to sexual temptations, and often denying the emotions that are staring them in the face, they increase their vulnerability. When the inevitable finally happens, everyone is shocked. But they have marched headlong into trouble, their traditional role and high moral standards fortifying them not at all.

The home situation. Although a happy marriage does not guarantee safety, an unhappy one certainly doesn't help. "The pain of having a lack of intimacy and free flow of conversation in my marriage was too much for me to bear," one pastor wrote to me. "I longed to love with abandon, to feel feelings and share intimacies with someone else." He went on to describe a series of seven affairs over ten years.

Although such excessive needs for affection can be neurotic, the fact is that if a marriage is satisfying, a minister should be able to focus even his neurotic needs on his spouse. An affair can easily be encouraged when the need for intimacy is great and the marriage does not provide an opportunity for close sharing.

Life stages. It is quite clear that men, in particular, are more vulnerable to affairs when they pass through critical stages of life. One of these is commonly called the mid-life crisis, but there are other critical stages also. Almost every decade brings its own period of crisis, demanding a major adjustment of values and behavior.

Ministers do not escape these. If their work is not satisfying, or if they are having problems in the church, they are more prone to a crisis period. In times of burnout, interpersonal conflict, or when major life decisions must be made, the desire for comfort and emotional closeness increases dramatically.

Danger Signals

Since an intimate affair can develop during counseling almost unnoticed, a discussion of the danger signals is crucial.

1. One early signal of countertransference is when a pastor begins to look forward to the counseling sessions with a particular parishioner. He ruminates about the appointment and cannot wait for the time to arrive. His pulse rate increases, his palms become sweaty, and his voice develops a slight tremor when he sees her.

2. Very soon he begins to extend the session time and may even grant her extra counseling sessions. He cancels other appointments (often without even realizing he is doing it) to please her.

3. Hidden or oblique messages are sent both ways. The message, which on the surface is innocuous, means something more personal at a deeper level.

4. Counseling sessions may occupy an inordinate amount of time on sexual matters. The client may begin to share sexual history or previous affairs that are quite unrelated to the problem for which counseling has been sought.

5. The pastor may begin to notice his own marital frustrations more. He begins to complain about petty things, often because he is feeling guilty and can alleviate this guilt by transforming it into anger.

6. He begins to fantasize excessively about his client. Sexual fantasies may focus on her exclusively.

7. He makes excuses to call her and have extra conversations with her. Luncheon appointments in a remote setting may then follow. These are rationalized as "additional counseling sessions."

8. Casual touching becomes more frequent, and the sessions end with embraces that become more prolonged or intense.

One particular personality type, the hysterical personality, is a very high risk for a minister to counsel. It has long been recognized in psychiatry that the difference between a brilliant psychiatrist and a less skilled one is that the first recognizes the hysterical personality and runs away faster. This should also be true for ministers!

The hysterical personality is typically shallow, overly reactive, even vivacious, uninhibited in displaying sexuality, given to flirtations, coquetry, and romantic fantasy. Such a person is also impressionable and craves excitement, but is naïve and frigid. She is, in essence, a caricature of femininity, drawing attention to herself to obtain admiration.

Because this personality is extremely prone to transference, the pastor who falls prey to her seductions is bound to be destroyed. He may be embarrassed by public displays of affection and the discovery that her initial attractiveness was only superficial.

Dealing With Transference

The average pastor cannot afford the time and energy demanded by a counselee with a high propensity for transference. Training in dealing with transference problems requires extensive supervision, far more than is typically provided in a course on counseling. If this training is available, you should take advantage of it.

In the meantime, the safest way to deal with transference is simply to receive it as one would receive any feeling of a client. This is done without encouraging the transference any further. The counselor helps the client see that the feelings reside in her, not in the counselor.

The counselor may ask clarifying questions to increase the client's understanding of her feelings. "You feel you're in love with me. Why do you suppose this is so?" In other words, the full expression of feelings is allowed without either condoning or rejecting them.

At a later stage, and only when it can be done without offending the client, the transference feelings are interpreted directly. For example, "Sometimes when people share their innermost secrets with someone else, they feel drawn and very close to that person. Do you think this is what is happening here?"

Always stay professional. I don't mean you cannot be friendly and personable. I do mean that you keep to your appointment schedule and avoid stepping out of your professional role.

Don't hesitate to make a referral to a trusted Christian psychotherapist if the transference gets out of hand. A mark of professional competence is knowing your limits.

The Pastor's Protection

But what about countertransference? What does a pastor do with those warm, loving feelings toward a client?

First, never share these feelings with your counselee. Never talk of them or even hint that they are present. They are your problem, not your client's. If you do, you will either encourage the development of an intimate relationship, or you will be rejected. You lose both ways.

Second, understand the difference between countertransference and simple attraction. In simple attraction, which is quite normal, you can walk away from the person to whom you feel some attraction. You are free to leave. You can choose to leave. But when you are obsessed with someone, allowing yourself to think about her constantly, you have problems. You must learn to redirect your thoughts and avoid fantasizing over the person to whom you feel attracted.

Third, be aware of the power of your position, and pray that God will help you use it wisely. If you neurotically need excessive intimacy, praise, or admiration, get help for your problem.

Fourth, develop a system of accountability. Not only are you accountable to God, but you need someone to share with honestly, a person to whom you can be accountable and talk frankly about your feelings. Such a person could be a work colleague, a pastor from another church (where the accountability can be reciprocated by yourself), or even your spouse.

The Pastor's Spouse

In fact, the spouse's role is extremely crucial in helping a pastor develop a safe position from which to counsel. Many wives find it difficult to understand how their husband, a pastor, can be attracted to another woman. How can a man so prominent, so respected, so intelligent, be subject to vulgar temptation?

As Paul Tournier points out in his book *To Understand Each Other,* this attitude in a wife only increases a pastor's guilt feelings and prevents him from sharing with her his innermost struggles over sex. To him, she becomes the incarnation of moral law. Tournier says, "This is the driving force of much adultery, so severely denounced by the virtuous . . . wife once she discovers it." She thinks that if he really loved her, he would not think of other women.

What she doesn't know is that her pastor/husband desperately wants to confide this struggle to her. He wants to channel his arousal back to her, where it belongs. But her veil of silence, resistance, and condemnation only increases the emotional distance.

From the viewpoint of Christian morality, this woman is right. But she has done nothing to help build a safer, more secure marriage from which her pastor/husband can minister to the fears, sufferings, sorrows, guilt, and misery of a lost world. The same is true from the woman's perspective when she encounters a husband who is not receptive to her feelings.

Tournier goes on to provide the soundest advice I have yet discovered on preventing illicit affairs in the ministry (or, for that matter, in any Christian marriage). He says, "The best protection against sexual temptations is to be able to speak honestly of them and to find, in the wife's understanding, without any trace of complicity whatsoever, effective and affective help needed to overcome them."

Coupled with a dependence upon God's Holy Spirit to provide help in time of trouble, this sort of transparency can prevent affairs. It can also build a depth of love, understanding, and oneness that I doubt can be experienced any other way this side of heaven.

11

Staying Close to Your Enemies

There is something positive and healing about face-to-face contact with people at odds with us.

—Gary D. Preston

I was in my new pastorate for less than three months when one of the founding laymen took me to lunch.

"It seems to me," he started out, "and I've confirmed this with a number of other key people in the church, that you may not be the right person for this job after all." He pointed to a couple of insignificant (at least to me) changes I had made in the worship service and how that had offended some people involved in our music program.

"In fact," he warned, "there are a growing number of people who just plain don't like you or where you're leading the church. I'm not sure those people will remain in the church if you stay."

As a pastor, I must maintain healthy relationships with all the people in the church, even those with whom that is difficult. Put bluntly, "How do I shepherd people who don't like me? And whom I don't really like?"

Resist What Comes Naturally

In ministry, doing what comes naturally is often the best approach. When I am at the bedside of a hospital patient, with families at a funeral, or sharing the gospel with a nonbeliever, my pastoral instincts usually guide me in the right direction.

However, that's not true when it comes to pastoring difficult people. One of my natural responses is to distance myself from difficult people. I've learned to make it a point to seek out difficult people and spend a few moments talking together.

Recently a woman in our church let it be known that, in her opinion, I had acted out of anger and harshness. She voiced her criticism after she had sent me a letter apologizing for her role in the issue and commending me for the way I handled it!

When I saw her at a community event a few days later, she walked past me without saying more than "Hello." I could have let it pass and said that her coldness was her problem. Instead, I decided not to do what comes naturally. I practically had to chase her down the hallway. When I caught up with her, I didn't confront her about her actions or anger toward me; I engaged her in friendly conversation to make sure she knew I wanted to connect with her.

It was amazing what those two minutes did. We ended up laughing about something one of her children said that week. She hugged me as I left and gave me a look that said, "Thanks for talking to me; I needed that."

Even if our contact with the person doesn't solve the problem, it builds a bridge rather than a wall between us. There is something positive and healing about face-to-face contact with people at odds with us.

Invite Talk About Sensitive Subjects

The next time I saw this woman, we were able to talk with more ease, so I broached the subject of our conflict. My purpose wasn't to make a point or add another thought about the subject. I simply said, "I've been wondering how you are processing your frustration. I want you to know that I care."

This second contact was easier for both of us, and it communicated to her that we could talk about this issue. The subject didn't need to be avoided.

It's important to let people know that even subjects of conflict can be discussed; they don't end the relationship. I've had ongoing differences with one couple over the style of our worship service. I've met with them on a couple of occasions to talk specifically about that issue. We continue to disagree.

We see each other regularly, and sometimes, when we are talking about something unrelated to worship, I will intentionally bring the subject into our conversation. I might casually ask, "I've been wondering if you have noticed any positive changes in the worship services lately?" or "Did you enjoy the extra hymns we sang today?" I'm not trying to stir up controversy; I simply want them to know it's okay to talk about something we disagree on. We can disagree and still work together.

Keep Private Battles Private

One of my bigger relational mistakes came at a church meeting.

One person had battled me repeatedly about my emphasis on evangelism. At a business meeting, the subject of evangelism came up, and several people expressed their excitement about how the church was finally reaching out.

I took the opportunity to say, "Of course, there are some in the church who tell me that we are losing more people than we are gaining because of this strong focus on evangelism."

Almost everyone recognized that I referred to the "no evangelism" proponent. The majority of the people supported our evangelism philosophy. It was clear my critic was part of a shrinking minority. I had scored a major victory on this issue, and a public one at that—or so I thought.

Ultimately, the statement came back to haunt me. Just as a negative political ad campaign can generate sympathy for the opponent, so too can a public attack against someone in the church. Throughout the week following, I heard comments like, "I don't think it was fair to say what you did about Ed. He can't be as opposed to evangelism as you implied."

Someone else said, "That wasn't appropriate to raise an issue about Ed's position when he was not present to respond."

I could support every statement I had made about Ed's opposition to evangelism. That didn't seem to matter. Even though people didn't agree with his position, they disagreed even more with my public attack of him.

The moral is, some things are best left unsaid. Don't make private battles public.

Practice Kindness

There is a bumper sticker that adorns the chrome of numerous cars in my community. It reads: PRACTICE RANDOM ACTS OF KINDNESS AND SENSELESS ACTS OF BEAUTY. It's a good reminder of one of the most helpful lessons I've learned about pastoring people I find difficult to love.

I look for opportunities to be nice to them. It is amazing what acts of kindness can do to build bridges to people. A man in a former church let me know every time I failed to fulfill some expectation of his. Whether returning a phone call within his prescribed time limit, reciprocating a lunch invitation, or giving him an equal number of compliments to the ones he gave me, he seemed to keep score in a way that made me the perpetual loser.

I found him increasingly difficult to be around. After the Lord convicted me of my attitude, I began to look for ways to show him kindness.

I stopped him after church one Sunday and said, "I was wondering if you might be available this next week to help me work on my fly-fishing." He was an avid fly-fisherman, and I could hardly catch a weed in a stream. In the weeks after our fishing outing, often he referred to our fishing lesson in conversations with me and others.

Fishing on my own sometime later, I finally caught a fish big enough to keep. On the way home, I stopped by my "instructor's" house and presented him with my first big catch as a gift for helping me learn to fly-fish.

Another time, I invited him to go skiing, and he asked me to show him how to canoe. On some outings, we talked about his need to keep score of people's behavior to make himself the winner. He eventually admitted this was negatively affecting his wife and his oldest son. I offered some help on how to deal with it.

When Best Efforts Fall Short

Of course, no approach to dealing with difficult people will be successful with all the people all the time. In Romans 12:18, the apostle Paul said, "If it is possible, as far as it depends on you, live at peace with everyone." Paul recognized that not everyone will want to live at peace with us.

What do we do when our best efforts still come up short?

In a former church, one woman seemed never to be fully satisfied with anything I did. Seldom would she tell me directly of her displeasure; I usually heard it through an intermediary source.

I met with her and told her, "I'm unable to live up to your standards of performance and expectations for my ministry. I feel as though I can't please you." I told her that since I couldn't, I was going to stop trying.

Of course, she assured me I didn't have to please her.

I responded, "So you won't mind if I no longer concern myself with pleasing you with every action and decision?"

She said she wouldn't. This took the pressure off and diffused some of her constant complaining. I shared with our elders my conversation with this woman so that if her carping continued, they could address the issue with her directly and decisively.

Sometimes, of course, people decide they can no longer be a part of my life or ministry and leave the church. I've learned even here to open the door of communication as much as possible.

One couple told me they could no longer support my ministry or sit under my preaching. My natural response was to let them leave and not to contact them. Instead, I picked up the phone and asked if I could stop by for a brief visit. They reluctantly agreed.

When we met I told them I was not there to talk them out of their decision. I asked them if there were specific incidents where I had wronged or offended them personally. I wanted to apologize if there were.

They said the issue was more a difference in philosophy and direction, so they decided it was best to find another church. I thanked them for their years of ministry at our church and invited them back anytime. Before I left I asked if I could pray with them.

As I walked toward the door, the wife took my hand and said,

"I was surprised you wanted to visit us, but I'm glad you did. Now when I see you at the supermarket, I won't have to avoid talking to you." The door of communication was still open. They may not come back to the church, but at least they didn't leave with a bitter spirit.

Not only are these approaches helpful in building good relationships in general, they yield personal growth in my relationship with Christ. The more I seek to love difficult people, the more God uses them to refine me into the image of Christ. After all, learning to love people is one of the ways we become like Christ.

PART 3

Care Systems

12

Keys to a Family-Friendly Church

Americans are desperate for a sense of community.
Eventually many of these lonely people search for
fellowship in a church setting.

—James Dobson

The church I grew up in was the center of our social life; I felt loved and accepted by this extended "family." That little body of believers provided an unshakable foundation of values and understanding, which I still hold firmly. I was three years old when I knelt and gave my heart to the Lord.

I'm still grateful for the teachings I received in those early years.

The *greatest* contribution the church can make is to draw families to the person of Jesus Christ in an attitude of genuine repentance and renewal. Nothing brings husbands, wives, and children together more effectively than a face-to-face encounter with the Creator of families. In fact, it is almost impossible to stand in his holy presence without recognizing our pettiness and resentment and selfishness with those closest to us.

Each size of church has its contribution to make to the family. Some people thrive better in a crowd; they need the programs and specialists that can be provided only in a large church community. Adolescents, for example, are driven by this "urge to herd," and they feel more secure with larger numbers of their peers.

On the other hand, some people need the intimacy and personal touch of a small church family. In my life, this sense of being known and cared for in a small church hooked me into the fellowship. The warmth I felt there compensated for the lack of sophistication in program and personnel.

Whatever the size of your church, you can become more family friendly.

What Families Need

The local church is the *first* line of defense for the family. The pastor is there when sickness occurs and heartaches abound and needs are expressed. Furthermore, the vast majority of people who come to Christ do so by the efforts of organized churches, which nurture and feed them as babes in Christ.

We need fellowship with believers, we need reinforcement from those of like mind, and we need biblical exegesis from someone trained to explain the Word. We *need* the church.

On the other hand, the church cannot substitute for the role of parents in the lives of their children. Boys and girls look deep into the eyes of their mothers and fathers to see if they *really* believe what the pastor and youth leaders are saying. Any ethical weak spot, any indecision is discerned instantly and magnified by the next generation. That's why home Bible studies and immersion in the gospel provide the foundations of faith in children. This is a responsibility of the home.

I once conducted a poll on our radio program, asking people if they felt their churches were supportive of families. We received 1,440 responses: 61 percent were decidedly positive, while 39 percent tended to be negative.

The first group of respondents focused on the pastor himself. People said, "He teaches us about the importance of families." "He is a family-oriented man." "He models good fathering for the men of the church." "He obviously loves his wife."

There's nothing quite so forceful as a pastor getting up in the pulpit and stating, "You won't be able to find me on Mondays or Saturdays, [or whatever day] unless there's been an absolute emergency. I will not be here; my home phone will ring, and no one will answer it. What I'm saying to you is 'Go thou and do likewise.' No one should work seven days a week."

Those who responded positively to the questionnaire also

compliment their churches for conducting programs on marriage, communication, and adolescence.

Finally, they appreciated the spirit of love expressed to their families by the entire church—not just the pastor.

The most frequent complaint of the negative 39 percent, however, surprised me: They criticized the church for fragmenting families. They regretted, for example, that children don't worship with (or even see) their parents while at church. Even at picnics and informal activities, the children have separate activities while the adults play softball or whatever. Most felt that families should not be together all the time, but there should be *some* common experiences to unite them spiritually.

I agree.

I believe it is possible to minister effectively to a transgenerational audience. The key is storytelling. Children love to hear stories, and surprisingly, adults listen to them, too. Obviously, we can't gear the whole preaching ministry to a preschool level, but we can certainly come together *occasionally* for meaningful worship. Even when a message is beamed to adults, children hear and understand more than we suppose. If nothing else, they see their parents responding to the worship, the music, and the pastor. They need this experience.

Targeting the Key Life Stage

Adolescence is the great turning point, perhaps the key stage in family development. At this point, teenagers who have been raised in the church are either strengthened in their faith or lost to the world. During this difficult and risky time, beleaguered parents desperately need the church's support. Not only are wholesome activities and biblical teaching necessary, but instruction is needed to counterbalance the un-Christian experiences young people are exposed to every day.

For example, most students now encounter sex education in school that undermines (or at least fails to reinforce) basic Christian standards. Who will set the record straight, if not the church? Who will have the courage, in a day of sexual revolution, to say, "Abstinence is God's commandment"? Who will address the social and sexual questions posed on television and offer biblical arguments and scriptural underpinnings?

My point is that the Western world has moved away from the Judeo-Christian heritage, and no one is more vulnerable to that departure than teenagers, who live on the cutting edge of culture. The family that holds to traditional understandings needs all the help it can get to preserve the faith and morality of its children. Unfortunately, many churches offer no formal sex education programs and seem to feel their ultimate objective is merely to socialize the youth.

Our purpose in the church is not merely to give kids something to do on Friday night. I agree with Tony Campolo that we must give teens something worth living and dying for. When we introduce them to Christ and give them a passion to serve him, we draw them to the Lord—and from there to their families.

That doesn't mean we can keep adolescents from going through adolescence. The low self-esteem and the inner conflicts won't be entirely eliminated, no matter what we do. The turmoil is rooted in the hormonal changes of those years. As soon as puberty becomes apparent, the personality becomes more volatile and irritable. I believe those factors are directly linked. They result from an ongoing glandular upheaval, similar to premenstrual tension or menopause or a severe mid-life crisis.

No amount of church activity and counseling will eliminate that. Nevertheless, youth pastors can help teenagers cope with their stresses during this time. They can also facilitate communication between parents and adolescents. Of course, there will be times when even the most competent and dedicated parents are unable to relate to their children. Their situation reminds me of the early days of our Apollo space programs, when astronauts were blasted into the sky aboard small capsules. As they reentered the earth's atmosphere, there was a period of about fifteen minutes when the buildup of negative ions prevented ground controllers from communicating with them. We waited anxiously, wondering about the ship's safety. Then, Chris Craft in Houston would say, "We have reestablished contact, and the astronauts are safe!"

Something similar often happens to parents and teens as they go through the negative ions of adolescence. During this eerie phase, a youth minister or a pastor *can* sometimes get through, can establish contact, and influence the spaced-out cadets. Hopefully, the time will come when parents will be able to heave a sigh of relief and say, "Thank God, they're safe!"

Wounded-Family Care

More than a third of our population is unmarried, with an increasing number of single-parent families represented in our churches. Those families, almost without exception, have enormous needs. Women who are working and raising children alone are often desperate for help—financial, mechanical, educational, and spiritual. Just getting through each day is a major accomplishment.

There are exceptions to this pattern, of course, but most single parents of small children are struggling for survival. If I understand biblical imperatives correctly, it is the task of intact families to extend a helping hand. The Lord has a special place in his heart for widows (including rejected husbands and wives) and fatherless children.

The churches that best serve these wounded families usually offer these kinds of assistance: Fathers invite children of divorce to recreational activities; mothers do the same for the increasing number of children being raised by single fathers; educational programs are provided; loans and gifts are offered, especially at Christmastime or when illness strikes; houses are painted and cars repaired; meals are brought over for the working mother.

Perhaps most importantly, single adults are made to feel accepted and loved by the church—part of the mainstream instead of the periphery.

Related to care for wounded families is social action. The pro-life issue is the most important cause now on the scene. Someday, the killing of unborn children will be as evident as the killing of Jews by Nazis. When that day comes, the church will be judged by its record on the abortion question.

The primary reason for the controversy today is that Christians don't know what goes on in abortion clinics, and they've been deceived by the rationalizations laid down by the abortion forces—

"A woman has a right to her own body." "We're only removing a 'product of conception,' a blob of protoplasm." In reality, we are killing *babies*, and the church must find a way to defend these innocent little ones.

That's part of building a family-friendly church.

Reaching Peripheral Families

I'm concerned about the number of families that come through our churches each year and give us a fleeting opportunity to introduce them to Jesus Christ. Typically, it's not our theology that brings them to our door. They're not even primarily motivated by our facilities or our program or our pastor. One thing is uppermost on their minds: Are they needed here? Can they find acceptance? Will they be included? Could this be the place where they will fit in and find friends and fellowship?

I'm convinced Americans are desperate for a sense of *community*. Eventually many of these lonely people search for fellowship in a church setting. But what happens when they arrive at the sanctuary? Often they encounter busy, harassed people who are focused on their own needs.

Now certainly Christian people have been trained to be friendly to newcomers, but their response is superficial. "Sure glad you came today" will not suffice for follow-up phone calls and invitations to dinner and lasting friendships. That's why visitors often attend services for a while but eventually conclude "we're not needed here" and then fade away.

I wish I could convince my fellow Christians that the most productive form of outreach is right under our noses. Nothing links families to Christ like linking them to the established community of faith.

Sunday can be an exhausting day for Shirley and me. We work hard to reach those whom we feel need our involvement. Sometimes it's a couple standing alone in a Sunday school class. Perhaps they've attended the church for five years or more, but the social awkwardness is evident on their faces. Even though we attend a friendly church, I occasionally become irritated by the lack of dedicated workers in this critical task of *caring* for people. It is, in my opinion, the most important family ministry a church can implement.

But this does not come easily. The problem involves the self-concept of established members; they don't see themselves as part of the in-group, being needed by the out-group. They are struggling themselves to find a sense of community.

How often do we hear established members generalize about "them"—the rest of the congregation: "They never call us. They don't seem to care whether we come to church or not. They're snobbish to us." What these people don't realize is that each family in the "they" *also* tends to see itself as being left out. The tragedy is that commitment to Jesus Christ and to the church is lost because of these unmet needs and expectations.

True commitment to building strong families requires strategic action. Here are some specific concepts a church might implement in its setting:

1. Mandate a vigorous premarital counseling program. The best ones provide a trained person to do at least six sessions before the wedding and two or more "check up" sessions six months afterward.

2. Assign couples as department heads, teachers, and other workers. The idea is to get families involved together instead of further fragmenting their time.

3. Be diligent not to overwork the more dedicated members. Families of the committed are vulnerable. The wise pastors I know keep track of how many nights per week families are expected to attend church activities.

4. Provide free baby-sitting whenever the church doors are open. Many mothers desperately need relief from constant child care. Some of them may not be able to attend if childcare isn't offered.

5. Target young mothers. One of the best forms of family outreach I've seen is a program called MOPS (Mothers of Preschoolers). It is an educational, recreational, artistic, and spiritual program each week for young mothers, who can be some of the most harassed people on the face of the earth. While these moms are engaged in Bible study and craft activities, the children have an interesting program elsewhere in the church. Mothers love this

program and will come even if they have no interest in or knowledge of the church. Then, if the program is conducted properly, they usually begin attending the Sunday services.

The Most Important Family

If you don't have your homelife in good order, you have no business teaching others how to handle theirs. But *no one* is perfect at home. You can no more be a perfect father or husband than you can be a perfect human being. You may know all the rules for good family life, all the biblical principles—and yet simple fatigue will affect your ability to implement them at certain times.

After a sermon it is *always* possible for a pastor's wife to say to her husband on the way home, "I guess you know you don't live up to what you preached today." That is the nature of human imperfection.

Shirley is generous to me because she loves me, but it's not difficult for her to identify my faults. That's why I frequently talk publicly about my shortcomings at home. In one of my books I describe our classic "umbrella fight." I'd come home from a trip exhausted. Shirley wanted me to clean the backyard umbrella that Saturday, while I felt entitled to watch a football game. After all, I'd been working hard and deserved a day off. But while I was out of town, she had been taking care of our children and managing the family. Now that I was home, she felt it was high time I offered her some relief. We had a three-day collision of wills over that.

I think it's important for family specialists to reveal incidents like that. I have also tried to describe times I did not father our children properly. We need to admit we're not perfect at home. Honesty demands it.

And people love it.

At Glen Eyrie in Colorado, we were filming one of our series, and I told about a frustrating day when I rode the backs of my children. I said, "That day I violated everything I write about." The audience applauded! They need to hear about times I haven't measured up to my own standard.

I've struggled through the years to balance family and career. My most difficult decision was to quit accepting speaking engagements, regardless of how influential or interesting the setting. I reached this decision in 1977, after I began to feel I was not at home with my family as much as I should be.

I had never abandoned my wife and children, but most speaking commitments occur on weekends—prime family time. I began to agonize over the contradiction: The Lord had given me a message about the family I wanted to convey, but how could I do it without sacrificing mine?

The dilemma continued for more than a year. Finally, a day came when a decision had to be made. Auditoriums had to be scheduled for the following year, and the booking deadline had arrived. One evening, we prayed together as a family and asked the Lord to make the decision for us. Then we went to bed. Shirley and I decided to read for a while. I picked up a book, and after about twenty pages, I came across a reference to the eighteenth chapter of Exodus, where Moses is visited by his father-in-law, Jethro, who is concerned because Moses was accepting too many responsibilities. As I read the first verse, the Lord seemed to say, "This is your answer." I continued reading as Jethro told Moses to stop counseling all day and get some help. *The Living Bible* quotes Jethro as saying, "If you follow this advice, and if the Lord agrees, you will be able to endure the pressures, and there will be peace and harmony in the camp."

I met the next morning with Mac MacQuiston, my representative, and told him I would not be speaking in 1978. Unfortunately, Mac represented only three speakers; he needed each of us to keep his business solvent. I had just jerked one leg of that stool out from under him. He stared at me for a full minute, until finally I said, "For Pete's sake, Mac, say something!"

He said, "I'm shocked. I don't know what to say."

"I don't either," I said. "All I know is that the Lord does not work on half an equation. If he is telling me to do this, he's got something for you as well."

As it turned out, Word Publishers videotaped one of the last remaining seminars, which became the "Focus on the Family" film and video series. It has since been seen by 50 million people, while I've stayed home. In the meantime, Mac became vice-president of Focus on the Family and later went on to other important Christian service.

I put my family first, and the Lord did the rest. What I thought was the end turned out to be the beginning. Even our Focus on the Family radio ministry grew out of that decision, and it now reaches more people than I could have spoken to in a lifetime of travel. But most importantly, I now have the memories of my children as they walked through the teen years, which would have been lost to me otherwise.

The problem of balancing career, church, and family is a constant struggle. It is rarely possible to realign priorities once and for all. An imbalance can occur in a matter of days. The moment I relax and congratulate myself for having practiced what I preach, I tend to say yes a few times when I should have said no—and suddenly I'm overworked again.

Nevertheless, I am determined to fight the dragon of overcommitment tooth and nail.

13

Support Groups May Be
Worth the Trouble

*Before starting a support group, a church
should count the cost.*

—Randy Christian

O ne man's face began to redden. His jaw muscles bulged. Another said, "You can't be sure they haven't already sexually abused someone themselves. Once they cross that line, they're not safe. They can't be trusted alone with kids."

Eight men, most of them professionals in their late thirties or early forties, sat in my office, part of a support group for the husbands of women sexually molested as children. They were voicing their fears about my suggestion: "What do you think of starting a support group for adult male victims of sexual abuse?"

The idea was clearly not a popular one.

Months earlier, a young man had talked with me after church. This likable, wise believer had been involved in several ministries in our church. Having been sexually abused as a child and having endured a lot of inner torment, he had asked, "Can we start a support group for men abused as children? I'm really struggling with this, and I need some help."

I thought about it for six months. Research says most child abusers (90 percent men), have suffered abuse themselves as children. Once an adult slips into the cesspool of child abuse, it's nearly impossible, without God's intervention, to reclaim them. If we could bring healing to those abused as children, we could break the chain of exploited innocents.

As the idea simmered, I sat down with a woman who leads our support group for women molested as children. As I described the need, her face tightened and a hint of fear flashed in her eyes. Finally I asked, "What's going through your mind as I talk about this?"

"We need to help those people," she answered, "but frankly, they're the ones we're most afraid of."

Later I mentioned the idea to our children's ministry director. She asked, "What about security for all the kids around here? If we bring such people into the church, parents will want complete assurance that we have safeguards to protect their children."

Meanwhile, others expressed excitement about the value of such a group. Our divorce recovery group leader said, "That could prevent so much heartbreak."

One of the psychologists to whom we refer clients heard my idea and bubbled, "I've got people for your group. When are you going to start it?"

So I did my homework, and when the time came to present the idea, I was ready. At a meeting, our senior minister, Clark Tanner, an easygoing leader who enjoys turning qualified people loose to lead, asked, "Randy, what are the support group ideas you have for the upcoming year?"

I proposed the AMAC (Adults Molested as Children). After presenting the merits of such a group, I concluded, "If we want to make a unique impact, this is where we've got to go. There is no other church in the area that's doing it."

A seasoned administrator, Clark asked several pointed questions. We talked about congregational fears, how widespread the opposition was, and what the probable fallout would be. Finally, he said, "This isn't the time. I'm going to have to tell you not to start that group this year."

But he didn't slam the door. We went on to discuss what would have to happen to bring church-wide consensus on such a ministry, as well as what costs we should anticipate. We agreed to discuss it again after one year.

As my senior pastor knows well, support groups cost something. They tax the entire system of the church. A church may be flush with excitement at the prospects of helping a needy group, but if a church is not ready, a new support group can do more harm than good. We are wise, then, to count the cost of support groups before we start them.

After starting more than two dozen different support groups in our church, I've learned what costs to anticipate and how to deal with them.

Yet I don't want simply to identify costs; that one-sided approach would make me too timid. Before I survey the costs, I remind myself of the benefits.

The Payoff

Just as a house or car has a high cost with a significant benefit, so support groups have proven to be worth our while. As our divorce recovery groups illustrate, they foster:

Healing. Larry was hurting when he came to our divorce recovery group. His wife had abruptly pronounced their marriage over, and soon he found himself divorced. The members of divorce recovery groups are, by definition, gashed and wounded. Their grief is as real as any cut or bruise. Over the following weeks, the group gave Larry the support, acceptance, and living skills that brought hope and the beginning of health.

Evangelism. Although she didn't have a church background, Angela came to one of our groups. In the course of the sessions, she saw faith at work in others and sensed her own need for Christ. She began visiting the church on Sunday mornings and was baptized approximately a year after beginning with the group.

While our groups are open to anyone—without pressure to attend the church or to believe in Jesus—our caring enough to offer the group often earns us a hearing. It's not unusual for group members to begin attending the singles fellowship, Sunday morning worship, or other activities, and eventually commit themselves to Christ.

Deeper faith. Once wounds begin to heal, group members experiencing the grace and forgiveness of Christ often find their faith increasing.

Strengthened family members. Many recovery group participants have family members who are also hurting. When Ginger attended the divorce recovery group, she was concerned about her two children, both in elementary school. She wanted similar support for them. We provided that in the Children of Divorce group, which we offer periodically.

The Cost

Other pastors frequently ask whether I believe they should start this or that support group. I have two responses: First, I know of no more effective ministry than support groups. Second, before starting one, a church should count the cost. To estimate the cost of a group, I ask these questions:

How will this group affect other church ministries? One church, well-known for ministry to the divorced, has been so effective that divorced people now account for approximately half of the church. And a majority of the children in the church now come from divorced homes.

These children need extra attention and individual help; they often struggle with major emotional problems. This puts a heavier load on the children's ministry and the church's counseling services. As discipline problems increase, recruitment of children's ministry workers becomes more difficult. The church now finds itself drained of both financial and human resources.

Had the church considered the effects of such an outreach, it may have made the same decisions, but it would have better prepared for such difficulties.

When we considered offering a group for male sexual abuse victims, we projected an increased demand for counseling services, as well as a need for airtight security around the children's ministries. In our case, we weren't administratively prepared to deal with these costs.

What church tensions might emerge? Our congregation offers three different support groups for sexual abuse victims. As a result, such people perceive us as "safe," meaning they think we'll be sensitive to their traumas and needs. Consequently, as a percentage of our congregation, we have more abuse victims than do most churches.

The presence of such victims in our church, however, puts other members on edge. Each support group attracts a unique population, and each population causes the congregation unique anxiety.

In addition, if a church is successful with such a ministry, its demographics may shift, and that can lead to resentment among (or loss of) long-time members.

One church in a university town developed support groups for students away from home. Within a year, many new young people were attending the church. The church found itself starting other ministries for these new members; in fact, the number of programs literally doubled, as did church attendance. However, as some established members noted, although the new members received much support, they gave back little money, time, or leadership.

Can we deal with well-intentioned but troubled volunteers? One couple came to our church after they saw a public service announcement for one of our groups. One day in the hall the woman told me, "God has led us here to work in your counseling ministry. My husband and I can do a lot to train you and your workers for this ministry."

We explored what she meant, and then I asked, "Can you name other churches you've worked with?" Later I called one pastor whose name she had given me, and I learned she had previously approached him in the same manner. Sensing she was unstable, he had her meet with a church counselor, who later recommended, "This couple will have to deal with some personal issues before they can be considered for church leadership."

So she and her husband left that church and, as I later discovered, moved rapidly from church to church for several years before landing in ours.

I decided to meet with them for lunch to discuss their past and to see if we could help them build a credible foundation for ministry. I told them what I had learned. I haven't seen them since.

Hurting people often avoid their pain by trying to heal the pain of others. Such people need the church's help but too often reject it when they're not allowed to become leaders. Well-meaning church leaders looking for willing volunteers often fail to see the dangers such people represent to the church and to themselves.

What church resources will the group require? A local church told me they were starting a *therapy* group (versus a support group) for abused women. They envisioned a group of ten women who would meet at the church; in addition, a program for their children would be provided and individual therapy for group members offered.

Their vision was wonderful but not terribly realistic. I suggested they think about what would be required for the group:

1. *Leadership.* Such a therapy group requires at least two trained therapists to lead it. Most churches will have to pay the therapists' fees, generally between $15 and $40 a person per session.

A support group, on the other hand, does not delve deeply into psychological issues. It's more concerned with the sharing of experiences and mutual care. It doesn't require a professional psychotherapist and thus is less expensive.

2. *Oversight.* If a professional therapist leads the group, he or she should in some way be accountable to the church, usually through a staff member. If a lay volunteer leads the group, the church should provide trained supervision. In either event, group leaders need administrative oversight from either a staff person or key layleader.

3. *Curriculum.* Therapists themselves set the format of many therapy groups, so many groups do not need a curriculum. However, this church wanted to provide a related program for children. Such curricula is difficult to find; the church would have had to develop one or hire a specialist to do so. Each option demands substantial time and money.

4. *Childcare.* A church will want to provide facilities and staff to care for any children of participants. Without childcare, a church shuts out many would-be participants, especially single and lower-income parents.

5. *Facilities.* A therapy group requires a private and comfortable meeting room. Since the group experience could spark trauma in an individual, it's good to have private rooms nearby so that people can be individually counseled on the spot. In addition, childcare facilities should include cots or mats for children staying up past bedtime.

What problems might be exposed in the group? One church formed a support group for parents of troubled youth. As a result, that problem received some attention in the congregation. Whether you call it concern or gossip, it brought out the problems of one leader's family, who were not attending the group and whose teenage son was involved with drugs.

Many considered this a positive thing; a problem was finally out in the open and could be handled. However, some people didn't like the way the problem was brought out, nor did they think it right that it was not dealt with until some group members began talking. The friends of the family began to distrust such a group. Many thought the group was "dragging people through the mud."

What expectations might be raised? The more any church gives its people, the more they expect. When I served a small rural church, I was grateful for the chance to use an IBM typewriter on a mimeograph master to produce a handout. Today, I expect the quality of a laser-copy printed from a computer, duplicated on a high quality, multicolored duplicator. The same dynamic can occur with support groups.

When I first came to my current ministry, the idea of *any* group excited the congregation. Shortly after we started our first group, a member of the church timidly asked whether we could start another. When the answer was "Not at this time," they were happy the answer wasn't "No!"

Four years and numerous groups later, people ask me almost weekly to start new groups or provide new services. When I cannot begin a new group, or when counseling requests are referred or put on a waiting list, people are offended. The more we offer, the more congregants expect, and the more upset members get when something cannot be provided.

If the Cost Seems Too High

Sometimes the price will be too high. At such times I remember three things.

1. *"Not now" doesn't mean "never."* When considering a new ministry, I'm sorely tempted to feel, *It's now or never.* The crying need and my excitement to help combine to create in me a sense

of high urgency. But I'm finding that good ideas can stand the test of time.

2. *More resources are available than we're now aware of.* If lack of resources is the main roadblock, that may not be enough reason to say no. When beginning our divorce recovery ministry, we needed to inform the community of the new ministry, but we couldn't afford advertising. I mailed public service announcements to the cable television "bulletin board." We received several phone calls, but I noticed that the cable station aired the announcements erratically.

I phoned the cable commission and was told, "The announcements are put on by volunteers, and we don't have any." I began sending my secretary to the cable commission two hours a week, and we soon not only received regular phone calls from the community regarding our groups but were also asked if we owned the cable company, our name being so frequently on the air!

3. *We are not the Messiah; we only work for him.* A church is tempted to think needy people will be lost without this or that potential ministry, and that there is no substitute for what the church can offer. That may be true in some instances, but in others it simply is not.

At one time we sponsored a "Freedom Group" for people recovering from chemical dependency. We ran into several crippling problems: there was competition from other organizations, such as AA, and we found that if people can get help from some non-religious organization, they tend not to come to the church.

We also lacked leadership; chemical dependency groups usually want leaders who have overcome the problem themselves, and we didn't have a former addict who wanted to lead our group.

Finally, our policy of confronting those who showed no indication of repentance alienated those accustomed to AA, where no "cross talk" is allowed.

We know that many of our people struggle with chemical dependency, but we finally faced the fact that we weren't providing an effective group. We closed it down. Within weeks, however, the participants found other groups in the community, some of which I didn't know existed. The Lord provided for their needs when we couldn't.

Janet, a member of our church, was talking to a friend at work when the subject of churches came up. When Janet mentioned she attended ours, her friend exclaimed, "Oh, you go to the support group church!"

When she told me about this episode, I thought, *That's not a bad way to be seen.* People in our community view us as champions of the cause of the weak and needy, an image that well fits the church of Jesus Christ.

14

Caregiver Care

*Church leaders can be viewed either as workers to fill
slots or as fellow ministers who need special care
commensurate with their added responsibilities.*

—Bruce Larson

My first church out of Princeton Seminary was in Binghamton, New York, where I was associate pastor. My wife, Hazel, and I had been married during my last year of seminary, and ten months later our first baby arrived. Four months after that, a second baby was on the way. All the changes in our lives took a toll. Mad and frantic, and with our marriage in serious trouble, we reached out in desperation to two laycouples in the church who were also new parents. "We're going through a terrible time," we confessed.

They surprised us by saying, "So are we!"

So we decided to meet with them to pray and read the Bible. Those meetings turned us around and saved three marriages. Beyond that, genuine new life broke out in the church, and within a year, a number of groups were meeting. By the next year, there must have been a hundred such groups gathering out of that little church in downtown Binghamton. People were drawn to the kind of intimacy and caring we distressed couples had stumbled upon.

We went from Binghamton to Boston, where I studied psychology at Boston University. After earning a master's degree, I was called to pastor a church in Pana, a small town in the lush corn and soybean fields of central Illinois. I tried to impose on those dear folks what I had learned. Not knowing that the conspiracy against intimacy can be enormous in a small town, I experienced little success, and I began to feel lonely and disheartened.

I'll never forget lying in bed in our tiny, unair-conditioned bedroom late one sweltering summer night. A Rock Island train was crossing the sultry prairie, and we could hear its distant whistle. Hazel turned to me and sighed, "I wish I were on that train going anyplace."

"Me, too," I replied in frustration. "Me, too."

By the time we left a few years later, we did have a couple of groups functioning, and many lives were changed by Jesus Christ. I am grateful for our years in Pana, for they taught me that intimate support groups—and especially getting church leaders into such groups—won't always be a popular thing.

Later, after twenty-one years in parachurch ministry, I was offered the pastorate of University Presbyterian Church in Seattle. At least one friend, who knew the size and scope of the ministry at UPC, advised, "Don't go. It will kill you." But I went anyway.

Once I was there, however, I discovered that my four predecessors had left under unhappy circumstances. I panicked and called out for help at an elders' retreat.

"They tell me this church can be pretty hard on senior pastors," I said, "but I hope to leave here someday in my right mind and still praising the Lord. To do that, I need your help. Who would like to volunteer to meet with me once a week for ninety minutes on Friday mornings?"

Six men came up to me during the retreat and offered to join me. For ten years we "Seven Dwarfs" met quietly out of the flow of church traffic to talk about our lives, our families, our Lord, our finances—anything but church shoptalk. To put it another way, they were my pastors during those years.

Through my years in ministry, I've recognized my need for continuing care as a pastor. And if *I* need it, so do the other leaders—the staff and elders. Ministry is too tough to go it alone. Lay leaders and staff need pastoral care as much, if not more, than men and women in the pews.

A Model for Models

In churches as large as University Presbyterian or the Crystal Cathedral, obviously I cannot be available to every person who walks in off the street. But I've had a policy that members can always see me. If it's not urgent, it may take a couple of weeks to get an appointment, but I am available. I need to be, if for nothing else than to be a relevant preacher, one who is aware of the hurts and needs of the congregation.

But for me, pastoral care centers on the staff and church officers. They're the ones I pastor first; they get the major part of my time and attention. For example, at UPC we had thirty-six elders on Session and twelve program staff members. Those forty-eight people were my primary responsibility.

Modeling, we're told, is the most effective teaching method. Early on, I learned that if I want a tithing church, I have to tithe. If I want a praying church, I must pray. And if I want a small-group church, I need to be in a small group.

So in my ministry, I strive to model how an authentic leader relates to other people. As the elders and staff observe my ministry style, my priorities, my way of approaching life, I hope they will see certain qualities: openness, vulnerability, the ability to put people ahead of assignments, a steadfast commitment to the Lord, and a genuine relationship with him.

If the staff and elders take up this style of ministry, they in turn become models for the church. People are watching them and observing their lifestyle to discern what this Christian life is all about. That's why I tell our elders, "Your primary job is not to draw up budgets, spend the money, and run committees. Rather, it is to demonstrate how the family of God behaves. We need to be upfront if we're angry (instead of carrying resentment), preferring one another in love, quick to support and help one another. The people of the church are watching us closely. They see the quality of our relationships with the Lord and with one another."

One phrase seems to sum up that philosophy for our Session: Elders are not simply big-E elders, who serve Communion, spend money, and decide programs; we are also small-e elders, who are ministers who care for people, beginning with the other elders.

This kind of mutual caregiving between the church staff and elders is bound to permeate the entire congregation.

Caring for Staff

What are my pastor-care concerns for staff members? I want to encourage them to be real people, not super saints. My first concern isn't that they produce tremendous amounts of work (which, of course, I wouldn't discourage), but that I help leaders realize they can cry, they can say no when there is too much on their plate, they can take a day off without guilt. Mainly I want them to remain genuine and spiritually healthy.

For instance, one associate pastor leading worship began the prayer of confession: "Lord, I'm sorry I put my fist through the wall this week." We could all picture that much better than vague generalities about falling short of God's best and not doing some things we ought to have done.

There is no power in confessing that we are generic sinners. But when we say something like, "Lord, I was preoccupied with selling my house this week and neglected you," that's specific confession. That helps people grow in their understanding of godliness. And that's the kind of staff attitude I want my pastoral care to enable and encourage.

Staff members have a great deal of responsibility in any congregation, so the weekly staff meeting is an important time that ought to include more than job-related problems. Staff members need personal support as well.

One former associate just came through a divorce. His wife left him and their four children after twenty years of marriage. He continued on staff through this trauma, and the church wept with him and grew with him. It was tough for him to be a homemaker and father and pastor. But at his time of heartbreak, he had a pastor and a church to share his hurt and share his ministry.

This kind of pastoral relationship within a staff doesn't come automatically because offices line the same hall; it has to be developed—usually by the head of staff. When Hazel and I arrived at UPC in 1980, we invited the four other pastors and their wives to our home for dinner. I made my two-alarm chili, and we talked and dreamed the evening away. When they left, Hazel said,

"Didn't that feel good! Let's do it again."

"We can't make a practice of this," I protested. "I may have to fire someone, and I can't do it if we're the best of friends."

"Oh, let's just try it," Hazel urged, not willing to let me off the hook.

So twice a month we met at our home for dessert and sometimes dinner. We met as a family. We laughed and cried and weathered tough times in some of our lives. What we did was blur the image between the professional and the personal.

I know that may fly in the face of some management advice, but it worked for us. I sometimes had to lay down the law as head of staff, but when I did, I had the advantage of knowing the staff members, and they, in turn, knew and understood me. We became intimate friends; even family. Sure, we were competitive and insecure sometimes, but we were family, so when one scored a goal, everyone cheered.

I sometimes consider how different this is from some church staffs. One senior pastor I know hasn't spoken to one of his staff members for five years. I can't believe this kind of strain doesn't show up on Sunday mornings, when both stand before the congregation to lead worship.

A church is not a clinic in which a faceless and interchangeable staff services the clientele by showing up and handing out pills. I believe the staff of a church is a living, breathing family. We may wrestle at times. We may injure one another sometimes and rescue each other other times. But we're in it together and we need one another. Ministry is not my profession; it's my *life*. My colleagues are not mere co-workers; they're my brothers and sisters.

Caring for Layleaders

My plan for pastoral care of the leaders begins with an emphasis on the three essentials of the Christian faith.

1. *An encounter with the living Lord.* Basic to Christian life is an experience of God's power and presence. Many churches are full of unconverted believers who assent to right theology, down to the last "I believe" in the Apostles' Creed, but who nevertheless wonder deep down, *What good does it do me?* They've given their

money and their time to the church, but they've never met Christ Jesus.

As a pastor, I need to begin by ensuring that each elder has actually had an encounter with the living Lord. Some elders with forty years of service in the church have just begun to learn to talk with Christ and listen to him and know his presence.

One elder tells a memorable story of how he became a Christian. He heard an evangelistic team speak about the new life, and, as the meeting ended, Pete said to a team member, "I can't give my life to Jesus with integrity. I have commitments for the next three years."

So the evangelist asked, "Well, how about next week? Is that free?"

"No, it's not," he replied. "I'm already committed."

"Then how about the next twenty-four hours? Would you turn your life over to Christ for the next twenty-four hours?"

"Well, I guess I can do that," Pete replied, and he did. He never took it back.

2. *The experience of koinonia.* I'm convinced people want and need to know others on a deep and personal level and be known by them, but they're terrified of rejection. They've been rejected so many times, they're afraid of reaching out again. They are determined to avoid anything personal. They'll do Bible studies, take on projects, bring in speakers, and discuss Christian books—anything but talk about their lives, their failings, their needs.

Yet, however much some tend to avoid it, church leaders need to be a part of the body; they need to experience *koinonia.* Jesus' commandment was, after all, to "love one another as I have loved you." Intimacy is scary, but Jesus first modeled it for church leaders when he gathered the Twelve.

My need for *koinonia* led to those weekly meetings with the Seven Dwarfs. And to meet that same need for all the leaders, we divided the Session at UPC into "families" of six or seven who gathered at the beginning of Session meetings to catch up on one another and share joys and burdens. The members of these families soon began to take on the pastoral care of one another.

I remember a typical Session meeting with an enormous docket, which ordinarily would have kept the Session until after midnight. With the Session families meeting first, however, we were finished with the entire meeting by 9:40. Why?

There's an obvious reason. People come to such meetings with baggage—a rocky marriage, a job in jeopardy, health problems. They may arrive angry or guilty or anxious. But meeting first with six other caring friends, they can work on those issues; then elders don't veto somebody's initiative in the business meeting because they're mad at the world.

Session retreats are another way to build *koinonia*. Several years ago we used the book of Galatians as the basis for our retreat. In that letter, Paul tells his story in the first two chapters, declares his beliefs in the second two, and shares his ministry in the last two. I suggested we divide our retreat into thirds and cover those same three topics.

On the first night three elders told their stories, and the next day, all the elders told their life stories in their Session families. By telling and hearing such touching, intimate histories, that Session experienced *koinonia*.

Koinonia promotes accountability. Pastors and elders can sometimes get out of line, but when structures like our Session families are in place, there's someone to say, "Hey! Just what do you think you're doing?" In this setting, people care about us— enough to keep us from error. Even better, the pastor doesn't have to do all the "straightening out." Each staff member and elder has a Session family to hold him or her accountable.

For instance, when one man from my small group suddenly walked out on his wife of twenty-seven years, I talked with him. But mine was only one of nearly a dozen contacts from fellow group members. All lovingly listened to him, prayed with him, and asked him pointedly, "Can this really be what God wants?" He had a whole lot of "pastors" caring for him.

3. *The exercise of ministry.* Most church leaders have some ministry within the church. They may head up the Sunday school or coordinate the ushers or lead Bible studies. These activities are almost a given. But an additional ministry I encourage these people to do takes place outside the church walls.

I make a point of visiting all my elders in their workplaces. When I first began doing this, they suspected I came to solicit their help for the church. After touring the workplace and greeting colleagues, we'd go out to eat, and my lunch partner was invariably wondering, *Okay, when's he going to ask me to do something?*

They were surprised to find I was not there to recruit them. "I just want to know how your ministry is going at work. How do you see your ministry here at Boeing? (or Nordstrom? or Swedish Hospital?)" When conversation turned to Session assignments, I'd underscore that I was there to talk about the ministry at work and at home with the family.

Ministry takes many forms, but there is nothing more rewarding than being the one through whom lonely, desperate, drowning people find new life and purpose in the person of Jesus Christ.

A chemist friend tells this unique story. A man at the laboratory approached him one day with a confession. "Earl, I envy you. My life is a mess, but obviously something is different about you. I figure it has something to do with Jesus, because I've heard you talking about him. But I have a problem with Jesus." These two Ph.D.s discussed the Christian faith at length without a breakthrough. Finally, Earl turned to his friend and asked, "Can you make a turnip?"

"Of course not," the fellow replied, a little surprised. "No chemist can make a turnip."

"Then would you be willing to turn your life over to the Great Turnip Maker?" Earl pressed.

The fellow chemist thought a minute and replied, "Yeah, I could do that," and they prayed together. It wasn't long before Earl's friend discovered that the Great Turnip Maker was none other than Jesus Christ himself. He read in John's gospel, chapter 1, "All things were made by him, and without him was not anything made that was made." And Earl had the joy of seeing his friend find what proved to be genuine faith.

Ministry takes place all week long in all we do at the workplace, yes, but also in our homes and in our neighborhoods. A developer and his wife, both in their late thirties, moved into a new home in an area he was developing. It was a neighborhood with enormous homes surrounded by big lots, so it wasn't easy to get to know neighbors.

Unhappy with that situation, these two opened their home during Advent for a beautiful, candlelight dinner for about a hundred neighbors. The fellowship was so warm and genuine that they decided to keep the meetings going. Now they have regular gatherings there, and in addition to dinner, they invite a guest speaker to share his or her witness. Thus this young couple ministers to the whole development.

Church leaders can be viewed in two ways: as workers to fill leadership slots or as fellow ministers who need special pastoral care commensurate with their added responsibilities. I, of course, choose the latter.

But this pastoral care is not the job of the senior pastor alone. Church leaders, lay and clergy, can learn to pastor each other. After all, we need one another, not just to perform ministry, but to be the body of Christ: mothers, fathers, sisters, and brothers to each other.

15

Preaching for Life Change

We need to know what to say no to. But above all, we need to know what to say yes to.

—S. Bowen Matthews

I n late winter 1988, I preached on divorce from Mark 10: "What God has joined together, let man not separate. . . . Anyone who divorces his wife and marries another woman commits adultery against her."

"Our first reaction to Jesus' words," I said, "is to look for loopholes, to bargain, to soften the blow of his words. That's why we don't hear him speak and race to confess our failure and restore to honor God's will for marriage."

In the next breath, I said, "Many of you here are divorced. Some of you are remarried. What's done is done. It is not my responsibility or my wish to lash divorced and remarried people with Scripture and send them away feeling guilty or aggravated. I suspect all of you who have experienced divorce have had more than your share of guilty feelings. Divorce is not the unpardonable sin. But it is sin. If you have confessed and repented of that sin, then let's get on with your life."

Within hours, a woman from our congregation sat in my office. "You just don't understand what I've been through," she said.

She proceeded to tell a horrible story of what her ex-husband did to her. Given her circumstances, my well-intentioned sermon seemed harsh and uncomprehending.

It would be easy to dismiss her complaint. She may have simply refused to own up to her contributions toward the failure of the marriage. But I find that callous. Pastors need to be tough, but toughness without spiritual discernment deteriorates into spiritual abuse. She had come to the service seeking bread and found a stone.

Why?

The Tension

In retrospect I trace that sermon's failure to haste and the lack of passion with which I handled the tension between compassion and conviction. The entire sermon was about divorce and remarriage. But only six short paragraphs developed the tension between the eternal will of God and the experiences of people whose failed marriages have marred that will.

Issues around this tension abound. I can talk (have talked) for hours about some of these issues. Books about them fill a short shelf in my library. I passed over them that day in haste.

But haste had a more devastating partner in the failure of that sermon. Those six paragraphs were entirely cognitive. Rereading them now with that woman's heart-cry in my ear, they seem cut and dried, distant from her pain. She heard no hint of how I had at times struggled to admit that in some marriages divorce actually made more sense than staying together. My words had no taste to her soul; no salt from my tears seasoned them.

If I could preach that sermon again, I would take half the sermon to develop the tension in my commitment to God's eternal plan and my commitment to the people who have marred the plan and who have sometimes been broken in the process.

I'm grateful for that woman. She was one of God's instruments to reshape my heart so I could grow more consistent in preaching God's Word without compromise, but also with compassion.

The following principles maintain the balance for me.

Make No Apologies

Conviction-driven sermons need no apologies. I make no apology for holding before people in a clear light—but not a lurid light—the sins of our generation and calling us as Christ's people to turn away from them.

For example, our congregation stands squarely as a pro-life congregation. On Right to Life Sunday this past January, I stated as clearly as I knew how that being pro-life did not mean that we support in any way the killing of abortion doctors. I had heard a few people in our congregation talking about the killings with an unexpected sympathy. People needed to know where I stood.

In mid-April I said that Leviticus 18:22 "doesn't strut, but it strikes with dispassionate accuracy at our culture: 'Do not lie with a man as one lies with a woman; that is detestable.' Despite homosexual propaganda to the contrary, the Bible from beginning to end declares that homosexual behavior is detestable to God."

Every pastor who says that sort of thing stands, however humbly, in the company of the prophets of Israel, the apostles of the church, and Jesus Christ himself. He is declaring the eternal will of God.

But he'd better be willing to take the heat. In one church I served, two high school girls got pregnant at about the same time. Each carried her baby to term. One gave her child up for adoption. The other kept hers. Neither married the father of the child she bore.

The parental support for those girls throughout pregnancy and delivery took my breath away. Both sets of parents stayed in the church. Neither defended their daughter's action. Both welcomed their daughters at home. Both showed uncommon courtesy to the boys, each of whom was well known to the respective families. Both suffered in unique ways after the birth of the babies: one by helping to rear the child their daughter chose to keep; the other by grieving as the child their daughter chose to place for adoption was taken from them (and into a Christian home).

That spring I stood before our congregation and acknowledged those births outside marriage. Without going into great detail, I told the congregation I thought those parents were heroes for the way they loved their girls through one of the most difficult times a parent can pass.

Not everyone appreciated the tack I took. One person complained that there was "no mention of the offense against God that sin is. Also no mention that when we strike out in rebellion against God's protective mandates, we reap a bitter pill. Your singular emphasis was on how we should be supporting those now reaping the consequences resulting from ignoring God's laws."

True, I did not mention those matters on that occasion; I thought it would single out people who were already embarrassed and desolate. It would hit them while they were down. It is also true that my emphasis was on how to support those girls and their families.

I responded by saying to that person, "You need to put yourself in the position of a mother with a pregnant teenager and ask yourself what you would want to hear from your pastor in the pulpit of your church. There was no question about those families' knowledge of the sin of their daughters.

"There is a very large question whether this or any congregation knows how to relate to faithful church members who find themselves in that terrible position. I tried to offer such help to the congregation as well as comfort to those grieving parents."

I would gladly take the heat for it again. I would also repeat what I said a few weeks later (with the two families present in the congregation): "There is a lot of talk about educating people, especially young people, about human sexuality. Most of this so-called education is an attempt to educate people, especially young people, to honor and practice sexual immorality with impunity. The wreckage of that lie litters our national landscape with teenage pregnancies, venereal disease in epidemic proportions, precipitous medical costs, and death of a particularly horrible kind."

Take the Test of Satisfaction

Too many conviction-driven sermons will make a congregation self-righteous. Nothing makes us feel so righteous as exposing another person's glaring evil, especially if it is an evil we are never tempted to do. My righteous indignation at computer hacking is as pure as the arctic snow, because I have as much interest in the subject as I do in soil samples from Bangladesh.

When pastors preach often and strongly against specific sins, their preaching becomes predictable: It focuses on sins that do not tempt most of the congregation. If it focused on sins they were tempted to commit, the preacher might have a revival on his hands; or more likely, a riot. Since that is usually not the focus, the congregation goes away satisfied, congratulating themselves on how upright they really are.

Furthermore, that kind of preaching raises a question about the pastor and his people: What are they hiding? Is all this predictable condemnation of someone else's sin a ruse to keep them from facing up to some awful truth about themselves?

To counter this danger in myself and in my congregation, there is a small test by which I gauge our spiritual health: If we leave church feeling satisfied with how upright we are, we are flirting with the devil.

I don't ever want to go away from church feeling satisfied with myself. I want to go away feeling satisfied with our Savior, who restores my soul, who leads me in paths of righteousness for his name's sake, and at whose right hand there are pleasures forevermore. Too much preaching against someone else's sin compromises this.

That small test encourages me to remember compassion even when I denounce sin.

Add Yes to No

Conviction-driven sermons tell only half the story. "Put off," says the wisdom of the New Testament, "your old self, which is being corrupted by deceitful desires . . . and put on the new self, created to be like God in true righteousness and holiness."

Denouncing sin has a place in pastoral ministry. But in order of intention, it is not first place. Yes, we need to know what to say no to. But above all, we need to know what to say yes to.

In the Ten Commandments series, I pictured each commandment as a doorway in a large wall. We say no to the behavior each forbids in order to pass through that doorway to the other side. There we find paths that lead to joy and union with our God— what older theologians called "the beatific vision."

With this in mind, I preached two sermons on each commandment. The first sermon expounded the meaning of the commandment. The second said, "Let's assume that we obey the commandment. What possibilities for holiness does it open up for us?"

For example, in the second sermon on the First Commandment, I said, "You and I have obeyed. We are keepers of the First Commandment. We have renounced all pretenders to our ultimate loyalty and affection in order to embrace and be ravished by the living and true God. What is that like?"

I then quoted five statements from the Psalms—for example, "My soul thirsts for God, for the living God. Where can I go and meet with God?" I asked, "Is there in your experience anything that approaches such passion for God, such delight in God himself?" The rest of the sermon pointed to one path of how to do that.

These first three principles, faithfully applied, restore my perspective when confronted by the evils of our time—and the temptations to become rigid and uncompassionate about people caught in those evils. They restore in me the realism to focus primarily on our God and not on our evil. They restore in me the realism to consider more carefully the actual people listening to my preaching and what might be going on in their souls as they listen.

I even have the realism to remember that strangest of all creatures in the congregation—me, and my part in the world's evil and my aspirations to holiness. The hills and valleys become a plain, and compassion joins conviction on level ground.

Know Your Sinfulness

Balance comes from assuming the position of adulterer. John 8:1–11 tells the story of Jesus and the woman taken in adultery. Every preacher in whom conviction and compassion are to marry and bear fruit must stand in the position of the woman taken in adultery.

Paul Tournier wrote of her, "This woman symbolizes all the despised people of the world, all those whom we see daily, crushed by judgments that weigh heavily upon them, by a thousand and one arbitrary or unjust prejudices, but also by fair judgments, based on the healthiest morality and the most authentic divine law. She symbolizes all psychological, social, and spiritual inferiority.

And her accusers symbolize the whole judging, condemnatory, contemptuous humanity."

Corky was my childhood buddy. We grew up in a day when car tires had inner tubes. Several disused ones hung in every garage. We would take them down, lay them out flat, and cut from them wide strips of tubing. The strips looked like giant rubber bands. Next, we cut each strip in half, laid it out lengthwise, and nailed one end to a piece of wood that had a handle. Then, we would walk around and slam those long pieces of rubber down on the street or sidewalk. The sound was louder than a rifle shot.

One day, Corky hit me right across the back with one of those things. I grabbed mine, crying and swearing, and chased him down the street. I hate to think what I would have done to him if I had caught him. I had lost control.

But he was faster. He got to his house and locked the door. I didn't see him for a long time, but I looked for him. I meant to make him pay for what he had done to me.

Many years later, it struck me: What if Corky and I had lived in New York City and had been members of different gangs? Gang wars have been started for less than that. There were no gangs in my neighborhood, but all the passions that start a gang war or a world war were fully operational in my little boy's heart.

Whatever human evil I preach against, I find it easy to imagine myself succumbing to that very evil, if the circumstances were right. I find it easy to see myself in place of the woman taken in adultery: guilty, accused, waiting the final condemnation from him who has all authority in heaven and earth.

Standing there in her place does wonders for balancing conviction with compassion.

Use First-Person Stories

Balance comes by using first-person stories. First-person stories from real life put a human face on convictions, and that face invites compassion.

Genevieve was a twentysomething-year-old woman who suffered from Marfan Syndrome, a hereditary disorder that affects the connective tissues of the body. Her mother had the disease before her. She and her husband consulted a world-class authority on the disease about her becoming pregnant. He strongly cautioned her against it. That very week, if not that very day, they received word from their obstetrician that she was pregnant. An abortion was indicated.

No one in our congregation would have blinked if she had gone through with the abortion. Her life was at stake. Genevieve, with the knowledge and consent of her husband, made the unexpected choice of carrying the child to term. About seven months into the pregnancy, Genevieve was hospitalized for tests. Her doctors suggested she be transferred to Philadelphia for more sophisticated tests. She was loaded on a helicopter for the short flight. Just before the helicopter lifted off, Genevieve sat up on the gurney. The arteries of her heart, weakened by the disease, further weakened by the pregnancy, detached from the heart. Death was instant. The doctor, who had just put her on the helicopter, rushed back and delivered a beautiful baby girl, who today is nearing graduation from high school.

Many would say she was unwise, unthinking in allowing the pregnancy to continue. We might also say, "Greater love has no one than this that one lay down his life for his friends." I do not say this to praise her. What she did transcends praise. I do not hold her up as an example to be imitated. What she did does not invite imitation. Rather, like some new sun in our sky her act of love serves as a flaming center of gravitation by which the rest of us may in some decisive way be drawn away from the gathering darkness of the old creation.

A story like this moves the sermon beyond the cognitive. Instead of head to head in an intellectual battle, we go heart to heart with our people. The story mediates to the congregation our passion for truth and our compassion for people.

Do I have a story like that for every confrontation between conviction and compassion?

Yes, but only after twenty-nine years in pastoral ministry. And I have a lot more as a result of being perceived as someone who cares for people in the jungle of life.

The moral McCarthyism of the Christian right and the Christian left distort reality. We who wrestle to preach with conviction and compassion in proper proportion need to look faithfully beyond these distortions to a better way.

On that better way, we see Jesus Christ rising from his doodling in the dust and towering up over the centuries to utter to the adulterous woman before him the most redeeming words ever to pass human lips: "Neither do I condemn you. Go now and leave your life of sin."

16

Customizing Personal Ministry

*Church members form the core of a congregational
care system.*

—Dale S. Ryan

W e hate to leave," wrote Nancy the day before the moving van
arrived. "You have been such a caring church family, and we
thank God for you!" I sat in my office and read and reread that
letter. It felt good to be a church that cares.

In the middle of the tenth reading, the telephone rang. It was
Fred. He, too, was leaving. "We haven't been to church in six
weeks," he said, "and no one called us. No one seems to care. We
won't be back."

I felt sad and angry and guilty all at once. I knew there was
some truth to Fred's complaint. Our church seemed unable to care
for him in the ways he needed. I felt the failure, and it didn't feel
good.

Why did our congregation care so effectively for Nancy's family
yet lose Fred through the cracks?

Primarily, I realized, because we had developed care strategies
to respond to Nancy's kinds of needs, but none of our caring structures fit Fred's situation.

Every church wants to be known as "a church that cares." Most
congregations realize this won't happen merely by employing a
caring pastor. The "that's what we pay the pastor to do" strategy
is doomed to failure. Church members form the core of a congregational care system, so the key to effectiveness is having lay-

people respond to a wide variety of needs. But how? Which structures work best?

Below, I've grouped lay-care strategies into six general categories. Some you'll recognize as your own, but if you feel as frustrated about your "Freds" as I feel about mine, you may find the other strategies worth considering. I've found that a mix of care strategies best meets the diverse needs we confront.

Friendship

When Nancy and her family moved here, her husband, John, wasn't a Christian. His first involvement with our church was playing on our softball team. He made several friends, and six months later, when he was injured in an auto accident, the first people to visit the hospital were his softball teammates.

He had established relationships with Christian friends, and when he needed care, they responded. They mowed his lawn. They took care of his children when Nancy went to the hospital. John experienced Christian fellowship at a deeper level, and he began to pay attention.

Such care illustrated the social-network or friendship strategy. Any program that develops social relationships (Sunday school classes, sports teams, choirs, small groups) increases the availability of care.

There are some clear advantages to this approach. Because people already have a relationship with the person providing the care, they recognize the care as genuine and natural. It may be easier for them to ask for help. Also, friends are sometimes able to recognize needs before people can bring themselves to ask for help—a major advantage.

Care provided by a friend also helps build long-term relationships. The care John and his family received from the softball team led to lasting friendships, which led, in time, to John's willingness to consider making a commitment to Jesus.

The limitations of this approach? First, friendships don't always make it easier for people to share their needs. Some people find it easier to ask for help from a person they don't know, such as a counselor.

In addition, this strategy works only for people with established social relationships in the congregation. People who are new to the church, who have relatively low social skills, who are on the fringe, or who have had relationships disrupted through divorce or death of a spouse may not find care.

Finally, a friendship strategy is rarely adequate for major or long-term traumas. When a child dies, when a person is diagnosed with a chronic disease, or when a young father is killed in an auto accident, the needs almost certainly exceed the care available within social relationships.

No congregation can thrive without a friendship-care strategy. Every congregation will need, however, to develop additional strategies to respond comprehensively to the needs of the congregation and community.

Shepherding

Another approach is the shepherding strategy. The care providers are official representatives of the congregation (usually elected, such as deacons and deaconesses), and the congregation is divided into care groups (often on a geographical basis) with each group assigned to one representative. The representatives contact the people on their care lists to inquire about needs and to offer help.

Bill used this approach better than anyone I've met. After being elected a deacon, he was assigned a list of families to shepherd. He prayed daily for each member of each family. He called them at least monthly. He sent cards on birthdays and on other special occasions. He regularly visited each home and in turn invited families from his list into his own home. This regular contact, combined with Bill's sincere and direct style, resulted in many opportunities for ministry.

Bill tells of a man unresponsive to his phone calls for over two years. Every offer to meet personally had been refused. However, when the man found out his father was dying of cancer, he called Bill and shared his concerns. Bill's persistence made it possible for him to care when the opportunity came.

This approach boasts several advantages. Because the care providers are an identifiable group, they can be trained. Bill's training as a deacon raised his skill level and confidence. He knew his limits and that he could take advantage of other resources.

Bill identified another advantage: some people responded differently to him after he became a deacon. He visited one woman in the hospital who said, "Thank you for coming. Now I feel like the church has visited me."

Finally, because a shepherding strategy is more organized than the friendship strategy, it's easier to ensure accountability. A care provider can be held responsible for caring for his or her people.

The limitations to shepherding strategies are also fairly easy to identify. First, since congregations typically include only members on their shepherding lists, the approach isn't outreach oriented. Also, few congregations recruit enough shepherds to ensure consistent, quality care. One reason for Bill's success was that he insisted on limiting to eight the number of families on his list; he felt unable to do a good job with more.

Finally, if the care providers have management responsibilities in addition to their shepherding, care easily gets lost among other priorities. Many deacons are expected to make personnel decisions, do long-range planning, and oversee other programs. Shepherding strategies rarely work well under these circumstances, since care tends to be postponed until other tasks have been completed.

If care providers are not overburdened or distracted by other concerns, however, a shepherding strategy can work well.

Counseling

Six months after Fred left our congregation, he called again. He was eager to let me know how things were going, and he wanted to apologize for the combative sermon he'd delivered when he left. "I realize now," he said, "that I was not ready to be helped." He explained how he had been helped in many ways by the lay counseling program of a nearby church.

"It was the kind of help I was willing to receive," he said. "I don't know why I couldn't receive yours, but I didn't want to go to that support group."

Many others, like Fred, find counseling a lifeline in times of need. A counselor may be lay or professional. There are, however, common features of all counseling care systems. The care provider

has a well-defined role—neither friend nor institutional representative, but counselor. The agenda for the relationship is therapeutic rather than social or institutional. In addition, typically care is
provided at regularly scheduled times, and people needing care
must take the initiative to make an appointment.

The advantages: the care providers are usually far better
trained than in most other strategies. Another major advantage is
that a person needing care doesn't have to be part of the congregational social network. Anyone can make an appointment. This
approach, therefore, is more outreach oriented than either of the
first two.

The limits: many people resist help provided by a counselor
because of the social stigma. Economic circumstances present additional barriers to receiving care, since counseling can be expensive.

Counseling can be an excellent addition to the care strategies
of a church. It cannot make up for inadequate friendship opportunities or the absence of shepherds, but counseling has an important place in any comprehensive care plan.

Body-Life

After his sermon, Pastor Smith invited the congregation to join
him in prayer. "While you continue to pray," he said, "I want to
give you an opportunity to respond to what God has been saying
to you today. If you need to receive God's healing love this morning, I'd like you to indicate your willingness by raising your hand.
Then I'll pray for you." As people responded, he acknowledged
each hand. After a few moments he prayed publicly for those who
had identified themselves and invited them to come forward after
the service to continue in prayer and to receive counsel.

This is the kind of care provided by a body-life strategy. Unlike
other strategies, which provide care in a private setting, this offers
care in public, community settings.

Some churches use this strategy as one of the central features
of their care system. They often provide a section of the worship
service or a special service dedicated entirely to the sharing of
needs and to public responses to those needs. A person in such a
service may come forward and explain that she has lost her job.

The pastor thanks her for sharing and asks several people from the congregation who have experienced the loss of a job to come forward to pray for her. They lay hands on the woman and pray. The service may move on to other concerns while a small group of people continues to pray about the woman's specific needs. The entire caring event is public, a response of the whole community to individual needs.

Advantages? First, care is immediately accessible. You don't need well-developed friendships or lists or counseling centers. Second, care and worship are clearly connected. Care stands as an integral part of church life. It can, therefore, shape a community of faith in profound ways. It's difficult to maintain an unreal image of ourselves if week after week we publicly acknowledge our needs and our struggles.

The primary weakness of body-life strategy is providing continued care. Needs expressed in a meeting may require more than a short-term response. It will be difficult, for example, for someone to come forward every Sunday to say, "I still have cancer." Because this strategy is more responsive to acute than to chronic needs, it functions best in conjunction with other strategies better suited to long-term care.

In addition, care organized in this way can be dependent both on the emotional climate of the congregation and on the worship leader. A consensus inevitably forms as to what is acceptable to admit, and people whose struggles violate the social or ethical norms of the congregation may not want to voice their problems. Since care is available only to those who state their need in public, it often limits care to those who are new to the congregation (they have little to lose if rejected), those who are extremely well integrated into the church family (they have built a level of trust), and those whose personality allows them to go public with their needs.

Body-life strategies can be effective. Even congregations that don't use them as central elements can occasionally use this strategy to develop a climate conducive to care.

Support-Groups

When Mary made an appointment to see me, I was afraid it would be a difficult session. She'd been through a series of struggles in the six months since I'd last talked with her. Our previous conversation had consisted of my listening to her explain how no one understood her problems.

To my surprise, her first words this time were, "I've found a group of people who understand me." She had acted on my suggestion to attend our Adult Children of Alcoholics group. There she discovered people who had experienced what she was experiencing and who were able to care for her.

Our congregation has many support groups, and I can't imagine how we'd survive without them. Alcoholics, victims of sexual abuse, people with fragile sexual identities, people with cancer, people with physical disabilities—the list of people whose needs could be responded to with a support-group strategy is long.

On a recent Sunday, three people came forward after our service to commit their lives to Christ. Our senior pastor found that one person recently had been diagnosed with cancer, one was a victim of childhood sexual abuse, and one had a chemically dependent spouse. In each case we had a support group to respond to these needs. As a consequence, these people began their Christian life knowing God's family could help in the most difficult of life's struggles.

A second advantage is that people often will come to support groups who will not accept care extended in any other way. Because care is offered by people who share the particular struggle, people see support groups as safe places to receive care.

Finally, support groups are usually outreach oriented. As their existence becomes known in the community, support groups provide easy access to care for the unchurched, who are introduced to Christian fellowship at the point of felt need.

A minimum number of participants is necessary for a viable group, of course, and that is one limit to support-group strategies. Forming a support group for people with cancer, for example, may not work if you can identify only one or two people with cancer at any given time. So support groups may better suit larger congregations. Smaller congregations, however, can cooperate with other congregations or aggressively seek participants from the community.

In contrast to a counseling strategy, a support-group strategy puts people into leadership who are publicly needy. If you want to form a support group for alcoholics in your congregation, the group will need to be led by recovering alcoholics. Some church leaders may be concerned at the prospect of giving leadership positions to people who have experienced major struggles, especially if the group is responding to socially stigmatized needs. Sensitivity to people's anxiety as well as a clear understanding of the gospel will be needed to overcome resistance to ministry of this kind.

Even with these limitations, support-group strategies have enormous potential for outreach.

Teams

"I blame myself," Ralph said after a year on our deacon board. "I guess I just can't do it. Even when I make the phone calls, I can't do it often enough to get to know the people. I feel like I haven't gotten anything done. I'll be glad when my term is over."

It wasn't easy for us to hear Ralph's discouragement. His honesty, however, was just what we needed. It stimulated us to make the transition from a shepherding strategy to a team strategy.

Some ministry was happening using a shepherding strategy, of course, but congregational growth made it increasingly inefficient and frustrating for many of the care providers. We were burning out some of our most gifted members by using a strategy that no longer fit our congregation.

The solution was to divide the deacons and deaconesses into teams. We no longer assign an individual to a list of church members; a team now shares the responsibility to respond to a specific kind of need. One care team takes care of shut-ins. Another responds to families experiencing medical crises. Other teams focus on new members of the congregation, people at risk of leaving the congregation, and several other recognizable pools of people.

The team approach is common in other areas within the church (Christian education, for example), but it hasn't been emphasized as a care strategy. One of the best-known examples of a team strategy is the ministry of The Church of the Savior in Washington, D.C. In this case, all the ministries of the congregation, not just caring, are organized around what they call "mission groups." To be a member of The Church of the Savior is to be a member of one of these groups. The target populations of these mission groups vary from residents of substandard housing to members of Congress. Each mission group, however, begins with the interests and calling of a group of people. Team members commit themselves to each other, to a set of spiritual disciplines, and to a set of ministry tasks.

Part of the potential of a team strategy comes from the singleness of purpose of these groups. Team members aren't easily distracted because they are responsible for only one clearly defined ministry area. Another advantage is that team members can support each other and hold each other accountable. That greatly improves the motivation and enthusiasm of care providers.

Because of natural turnover, a team strategy requires attention to management. One team is often needed simply to administer the others. A second potential limitation is the impossibility of forming a team for every conceivable need. The decision to target certain needs will mean that other needs won't be targeted. For this reason, a team strategy needs to be coordinated with other approaches. Most congregations, however, can readily identify needs that can be dealt with effectively by a team.

Customizing a Plan

Clearly no single lay-care strategy is free from limitations. A congregation that uses a single strategy limits its response to the needs around it. Here are some of the things I've learned about developing a comprehensive care plan.

Keep working on your system. Congregations change. A mixture of strategies that works today may not be as useful in five years and could need major overhaul in ten. Care systems need regular self-examination.

I've found it helpful, for example, to keep a written guilt list. Great ideas for ministry often come from looking for patterns in the things I wish I had time to do. Our support group for people with cancer didn't get started until I noticed how regularly "visit cancer patients" showed up on my list of "things I felt guilty about not getting around to doing." Now we have a team that ministers more effectively, more regularly, and to more people than I ever could have reached personally.

Include community needs. If I want to care more effectively for widows, why not include widows from the community rather than just those from within the congregation? A care plan is an opportunity to declare God's love in practical ways to people who do not know of his love and grace.

Do what you can. An emotionally difficult part of developing a strategy is that in defining the kinds of care we can provide, we become aware of many needs we're unable to meet. A lengthening guilt list is frustrating. That should neither surprise us nor stop us from doing what can be done.

Careful planning and creative thought, enriched by consistent prayer, can produce a mixture of care strategies that touches lives in a variety of ways.

Who cares? The church does, in more ways than one.

PART 4

Crisis Situations

17

Called Into a Crisis

The question is not if *a crisis will come, but when.*

—Gary L. Gulbranson

The day I candidated at Glen Ellyn Bible Church, following the Sunday morning service, we were having lunch at the home of the chairman of the board of elders.

Suddenly, in the middle of the meal, the phone rang, and when our host returned, his face was pale. We immediately knew something was wrong.

He quickly gave us the facts: the son of one of the church families, a college-age man who had attended church that morning, had left the service before my sermon, gone home, and apparently taken his own life.

We dropped our forks and drove together to the grieving family's home. As others gave comfort to the family, I listened, offered what I could, and avoided treading on their grief.

As the afternoon went on, my thoughts turned to the evening service. What I had planned to preach would now be out of place. This was a crisis not only for the immediate family but for the whole church.

After we left their home, I spent the next few hours planning how to lead that service. I chose a different sermon text, Second Corinthians chapter one, and outlined a new message. My ministry that night, by necessity, addressed the pain and grief everyone was feeling.

It was not a typical candidating Sunday. But years later, one of the church elders observed, "When we came to vote on Gary's candidacy the next week, it wasn't a matter of deciding whether or not to call him as our pastor. He already was. We'd been through a crisis together, and he had already proven to be our pastor."

Crises don't come at convenient times. I can't schedule them into my calendar. But they are a critical part of my calling, as much as preaching or administration. Not only do people need care for the devastation already experienced, they need help handling the ongoing effects. Crises have the potential to worsen and expand, like the fires and aftershocks that follow a major earthquake.

All pastors live squarely on a fault line. The question is not *if* a crisis will come, but when. Even though I can't schedule them, I can, like residents of San Francisco, learn to be prepared.

Separate Crises From Problems

First we must know what truly is a crisis. If we treat every problem as a crisis, we will be full-time crisis managers. Every pastor has had calls in the middle of the night from someone who wants immediate attention for a relatively minor problem. The key is to be available to such people, helping them deal with their own problem, while not overresponding.

If the person calling considers his or her situation a crisis, then I treat it as one, at least initially. I give such people my full and immediate attention; I respect the feelings and validate the pain they feel; I show I care. And I'm available like this until I can see where things stand.

Empathy at this point is critical. I try to react not based on how I feel about others' problems but on how I would feel if I were them. Their mountain may be a molehill, but if they see it as a mountain, I need to help them work through those feelings and get a better perspective.

Communicating such care while assessing the situation may take only five minutes. Then, depending on the need, I can set an appointment or make other plans to attend to them. In this way, I can manage the problem without dismissing the person's pain.

And if it's an authentic crisis, I can take more immediate action.

Manage Your Reaction

I once received a call at 3:00 A.M. to come and help the family of a man who had just killed himself with a shotgun.

Initially, all they knew was that a shot had been fired and the man was hospitalized. It was my job to drive the wife and her three children to the hospital and then, when I discovered exactly what happened, inform them that he had taken his own life.

In situations like this, my first challenge is to manage my own reactions.

I typically face two kinds of crises: those I feel confident and qualified to manage because of my experience and training, and those that intimidate me. Each has its own temptations.

When I feel comfortable, I get impatient. I know the nature of the problem before the person stops talking. I know what needs to happen. I know how people tend to respond. And I know how to fix things. I want to start giving advice prematurely.

When I'm intimidated by the situation, I want to do something, anything, because I'm the pastor. I feel like if I don't take control, I'll appear feckless. Under that pressure I usually blunder.

To manage my reactions, I keep two things in mind:

Stay calm. I won't be much good to people if their crisis becomes my crisis. In a situation where I can neither touch bottom or keep my head above water, I have to remain calm. If I over-identify with the people's fear, panic, and insecurity, I will be unable to minister. I want to be able to feel what they feel, to tell them those feelings are normal, but I want to keep a clear head. How?

My answer is to acquire skills and training. I must have something to offer people. Burnout hits pastors who repeatedly face situations that outstrip their competence.

When I was in seminary, I also worked as a real estate agent. One day my partner put me in an uneasy situation. A woman who had worked with his daughter was dying of cancer. The doctors had told her she had only a few weeks to live. She didn't know Christ.

He said, "You have seminary training. Would you call on her?"

"Yes, I'll gladly see her," I replied. Inside, however, I felt queasy, dubious of my ability to say anything that would help her.

Later I sat in the parking lot of the hospital, marshaling my strength, thinking, *Nothing I have done to this point has prepared me for this.* I prayed and decided the one thing I could do was listen. If nothing else, I could give an attentive ear and pray with her. With that in mind, I walked into the hospital and took the elevator to her room.

It didn't take much small talk to get down to her real need. I said, "I don't know what you're going through, and I really want to hear."

"It started as ovarian cancer," she said. "Then it spread throughout my lower tract. The pain is like the harshest pain a woman goes through in labor, but this one never stops. At first I fought against taking pain medication because I wanted to be clear-minded when I visit with my thirteen-year-old daughter. But then the pain got to be too much."

By the time we finished talking several hours later, she had prayed to receive Christ. When I walked out of the hospital, I was totally spent. I got in my car and slumped in the seat with my eyes closed. I knew the Lord had helped me minister to this woman, but I also knew I lacked the competence to handle all the issues involved in helping people in crisis. Then and there I decided to pursue all the crisis skills possible.

Though I have followed through, I don't always have total control of my emotions, and at times I feel uneasy and at a loss. That's good. It keeps me depending on the Holy Spirit for effectiveness. I never enter a crisis with the idea I'm going to solve it. I use the skills I've learned. Yet only as the Holy Spirit applies them to the person in need can they take hold.

A crisis is an opportunity. In a sense I've learned to look forward to crises—not to the harm they cause, but to the good that God brings as a result:

1. People grow. One night a member, Mary, called to tell me

her thirty-nine-year-old husband was dead. While they were on vacation together, he had suffered a massive heart attack.

She had no one to help her. My wife and I stepped in, and over the next few days we became extremely close to her. Until then, she had been only marginally involved in the church. As she experienced Christ's love through us and the church, she began wanting to share it with others. Now Mary has become heavily involved in caring for others in need. Her crisis was a tragedy, but she emerged a stronger person and a more committed believer.

2. Relationships deepen. Most people never forget that the pastor was there in their hour of deepest need. Our family is now as close to Mary as to anyone in the church, although before her crisis I knew her only as the red-headed woman who sat with her husband in the third row. After pastors leave a congregation, the people who keep contact are often those whom they helped in crisis.

3. A sense of satisfaction fills me. Since crises are part of my calling, and since I have invested considerably in crisis training, I get fireman-like satisfaction from entering the burning houses of people's lives and walking out with them on my shoulder. This isn't the Messiah complex at work but a legitimate sense that I am doing something significant, doing what God called me to do.

I can't immediately see the fruits of other pastoral labor, but when counseling in crisis, I often see tangible results very quickly.

Decide Your Steps

I may not be able to plan for a specific crisis, but I can decide ahead of time what steps I will take once a crisis presents itself. Here is what I try to do:

Offer appropriate touch and presence. In the midst of the suicide tragedy on candidating Sunday, one woman from the congregation came to the family home and simply sat on the couch with her arm around the shoulder of the grieving mother. For the entire afternoon, I don't think she said ten words. But the mother later told me, "I drew more comfort from that than anything."

Presence is powerful.

Pain and trauma isolate a person, particularly in medical crises. A patient is in alien surroundings, often treated by personnel as a problem rather than a person. People in pain want to withdraw, like a turtle into its shell. But isolation intensifies the pain.

So those in crisis first need others to be with them. Meaningful touch helps pull crisis victims out of isolation. Although sufferers can dismiss our words, touch—the language of crisis—has innate authority.

Resist giving advice. One of the biggest mistakes a pastor can make is to prescribe answers and solutions in the initial stages of a crisis. At this stage, crisis victims need description, not prescription. So I let them fully describe what has happened, what they're feeling, what they're going through. Few things communicate compassion and concern more than unhurried listening.

This means resisting the temptation to offer even good advice. We all know that clichés usually cause more pain than comfort. When crisis victims hear pat answers, they feel we don't understand the depth of their trauma.

Even truth, given prematurely, can do more harm than good. Although this may be the fiftieth person we've counseled about grief, to the person going through the grief, it feels like a unique experience. So if you tell a widow, "You are not the only one who has experienced this; others in our church have gotten through this, and so will you," you are only belittling her loss. Later, the person may want to get in touch with others who have gone through the same thing, but in the beginning, the person needs to simply express how this experience is like nothing else.

Sometimes I don't listen well because I prejudge the situation or the person. I did this once with a couple in a marital crisis. They were not a part of the church, so I didn't know anything about them when they came to see me. But the wife, a seething volcano of anger and bitterness, made it difficult to like her from the start. She even made fun of the church, calling our worship a "dog and pony show."

I felt she was a lost cause, and frankly, I wanted to get rid of them gracefully. As counseling continued, however, I discovered some of the roots of her anger. She had suffered sexual abuse as a child. The more I learned, the less I wanted to write her off.

Rarely are counseling situations clear from the first session. The longer I counsel, the more I know about human nature, and ironically, the less I feel I can prejudge people. More than ever, I listen for the factors that make this person and problem unique.

Clarify the situation. Medical crises require quick decisions about procedures to be done, organs to be donated, life-support systems to be used.

A death forces kin into dozens of decisions about funeral arrangements, the distribution of possessions, living arrangements, financial planning, and legal matters.

Unemployment requires reassessment of retirement, education, self-identity, where to live.

Crisis victims make handfuls of life-changing decisions, and usually in a compressed period of time. One of these decisions alone is stressful. Add them up, and it's bewildering. Tack on emotional shock, and it's crushing. Not surprisingly, decision-making can cause people in crisis to freeze. They desperately need someone who can objectively identify the issues, sort the priorities, and clarify values.

When a person in church loses a loved one, I drop everything to be with the family. I also accompany the family at the funeral home and inform them, "I want to help you understand what the funeral director is doing." We go into the casket room, and I help them clarify what it means to buy a casket, that their feelings for their loved one don't have to be expressed in a lavish casket. I help them assemble documents.

I've learned a key principle about how assertive I can be in helping a family deal with doctors, funeral directors, and lawyers: If these professionals are not making sense to me, they are almost certainly not making sense to the crisis victim, who is normally too intimidated to ask many questions. So I ask on their behalf. And because I've gone through these things before, I can help interpret the technical language and procedures and decisions.

These aren't the only things I clarify. People need help interpreting their feelings. Is anger the fountainhead of this man's marriage problems, or is anger masking guilt over some failing? Is the broken person at a funeral simply grieving the loss or resenting the increased responsibilities? The job of clarification and interpretation is one of our most important.

Do damage control. Crises can easily get out of control. Most people can deal with only one crisis at a time, but every crisis has the ability to spawn other emotional, financial, occupational, family, and identity crises. Victims can quickly lose hope. When a person is vulnerable, when everything is already shaky, the "offspring" of crises can do incredible damage.

Take marital arguments. One couple came to me right after the wife learned of her husband's adulterous relationship. He had been involved for three years with his secretary. I knew I wasn't going to save their marriage in one session, but I did need to contain the forest fire.

First, I wanted to keep them from tearing each other apart. In addition, they had three kids. I knew she probably wanted to march home and say, "Look what your father has done." She probably wanted to call up the other woman, whom she knew well, and tell her off. She could have kindled an inferno. She could have moved out of the house and cut herself off from everyone. Each of these could have created additional crises, and that was the last thing they needed right then.

So in that first visit, we addressed the bare minimum. I needed to hear their story, trace how the adultery developed, and let her initial anger and his defensiveness blaze in a place where they couldn't incinerate each other. She needed to hear me say, "It's right for you to be angry at him." He needed to hear, "What you've done has not irreparably harmed your marriage or your life. There's still hope for you." And we tried to contain the flames to the smallest possible area.

Today, they are holding their own. They're still clearing away some of the charred timber, but they're making it.

Show the next step. A woman called me, sobbing, and said, "I have to see you today." I agreed to see her immediately.

When she came in, I learned she was suffering intolerable guilt over two abortions she had had before committing her life to Christ. In a single day, due to a conversation she'd had with a friend who didn't know her situation, it became a crippling issue.

In that first meeting I assured her of Christ's forgiveness and began to walk her through the grieving process. As we finished that session, I assured her, "Let's talk again next week." Her emotions were so tender, I knew she would require consistent support to keep her from tumbling back into debilitating guilt.

People in crisis, who tremble before a dark future, need light shed on the next step. They need to look forward to care and attention in the immediate future. So I always conclude my initial care with "I'll call you tonight" or "We'll meet at my office on Tuesday at three o'clock." I specify what I'm going to do next, and I don't put that too far in the future. How far depends on how they have responded to my initial attention. I don't overwhelm them with a detailed plan for solving the crisis. I tell them, "We're going to take this one step at a time."

Most can't see much beyond the next step anyway.

Identify Unique Cases

All crises require a similar approach, but not all are alike. Each type of crisis requires unique skills, attention, and focus.

Death: In addition to listening and empathy, I find people are helped by knowing the stages of grief. That way their mercurial emotions aren't so baffling to them.

Domestic violence: Over the years several abused wives have called me, saying they've been beaten and they're scared it could happen again. We don't waste time scheduling an appointment for this afternoon at three. Instead, I tell her to call the police and get to a shelter, where I will make contact with her.

I give immediate and specific direction with domestic violence because the participants have a confused, skewed understanding of their situation. Wives often feel responsible. In addition, after being hit, they assume, *Well, this was an isolated thing. It won't happen again. Things will get better.* But things usually get worse.

Child abuse: The law requires I report any abuse I have witnessed or heard about. But when it comes to relaying second-hand information, I only report what I have witnessed or heard: "A woman reported to me today that her child is regularly beaten by the woman's husband," not, "I know a child who is being beaten by his father." It's the legal system's job to figure out exactly what's going on. It's my legal responsibility to report what I've heard.

Marriage conflict: Anger is often the biggest roadblock to progress. After letting a husband and wife vent their anger at each other, I try to get them to take a step back to see a long-term solution to their crisis. Only then can we begin working constructively.

Loss of job: For the unemployed, a large part of the crisis is self-identity, especially for a man. He assumes all the family's financial responsibility is his, and he's dropped the ball. Since society says, "A man is what a man does," he feels like a loser. He may even be hearing that from his wife or kids.

I have two immediate objectives in these cases. First, I help the person feel worth outside of his or her ability to provide financially. Second, I find the immediate financial pressure point—a mortgage payment, a tax penalty—and help the person figure out how to deal with it.

Threatened suicide: Most people who threaten suicide feel they've lost control of everything—except death. So the last thing you want to do is wrest control from them by saying, "Don't do it. It's wrong. Think of all the people you would hurt." That only reinforces their despair.

I let them take control, even in the conversation. "Tell me what's going on in your life." I affirm the one positive action they've just taken—calling me: "It was great of you to reach out to someone. It's important for you to do that." I let them feel they've taken some control of their lives already, that calling someone was a good thing.

Life-Defining Moments

Since the early days of my ministry, I have intentionally sought opportunities to help people in crisis. I have volunteered as chaplain of hospitals and with the police and fire departments. I have gone out of my way to build a network of relationships outside of the church in organizations such as Rotary Club so that people in the community with a crisis but without a pastor can call me. I emphasize to the congregation that despite the size of our church, I am available to them in a crisis.

Why bring more problems upon myself? Crises are life-defining, path-setting moments for people. If someone stands at their side, representing Christ and offering compassionate help, they often will draw closer to God. And that, finally, is what my ministry is about.

18

When to Intervene

Without some kind of personal relationship, intervention is difficult and risky.

—Marshall Shelley

A pastor encountered one of life's little dramas playing itself out as he entered the YMCA: a toddler wearing a wet bathing suit was coming out the door from the swimming pool area, and her mother was saying, "You are such a coward!"

The child was shivering, and her cheeks were wet—from tears or the pool? The pastor couldn't tell. She simply stood there shaking as her mother continued, "It's the same every week. You always make your daddy and me ashamed. Sometimes I can't believe you're my daughter."

The pastor found himself thinking, *I wonder what the penalty is for hitting a woman?*

"What she was doing was more hurtful, more brutal than a beating," he reflected. "It was emotional child abuse, and if it continues, that toddler will grow up feeling worthless, which will lead to all kinds of destructive behavior."

If that woman had been a member of your congregation, what would you have done? Most pastors feel the urge to do *something*, either immediately or eventually, to help the mother realize what's at stake, to help her be a better parent. Even if she isn't asking for help.

When is intervention appropriate? How do you enter a situation uninvited? It's not an easy decision.

Recognizing the Risk

Sometimes pastors step in—and later regret it. Despite pure motives and a deep desire to help, their well-intentioned intervention can at times do more harm than good.

Earl and Edna Waring were in their forties, and they were childless. David Lindquist, their pastor, also noticed—along with everyone else—their penchant for public bickering.

In the adult Sunday school class, Earl would joke about looking forward to the church potluck "so I can finally get a decent meal." Edna would counter, "I'm just glad the church has a full-time janitor to clean the floor after you've eaten." The rest of the class would laugh nervously. The humor did not quite cover the barbed intent.

David wondered how he could help Earl and Edna relate to each other without continual put-downs. One day he stopped by their house and asked point-blank: "Sometimes you two seem unhappy with each other. Why is that?"

"We're not unhappy," Earl said.

"Around the church, people perceive you that way, and so do I," said David. "You bicker about money in Sunday school. You publicly ridicule each other's appearance. Last Sunday, Earl, in front of your wife, you told me, 'Edna can't cook worth a lick, which wouldn't be so bad if she'd only make the beds, but she never does.' It's wearying. But even worse, I worry about what it's doing to your relationship."

Earl and Edna didn't seem to take it seriously. David left, but he was determined to try again. He knew that often people needed time to get used to the idea of dealing with a problem. Over the next few weeks, he visited Earl and Edna two more times, and each time he'd ask, "How are you two getting along?" Each time they'd reply, "Fine."

But David didn't give up. On the next visit, he pressed harder.

"There must be something underneath that's rankling you two. Earl, tell me, what attracted you to Edna in the first place?"

As Earl retold the story of their meeting, Edna remained strangely quiet, seemingly preoccupied. When he was done,

David pressed her to open up, to describe her relationship with Earl.

After a long pause, she said, "Earl, I need to ask your forgiveness." She seemed to stumble for words. She began to talk about her past, revealing several rather sordid sexual experiences with various men before she had met Earl.

"I was quite a floozy," she said. "Maybe that's why I'm the way I am now. I've never been very domestic. Of course, I'm saved now, and that puts everything away, but sometimes I still feel guilty."

Earl listened wide-eyed. "I never knew that before!"

"I appreciate your sharing that," said David, feeling that at last he'd made a breakthrough. "Earl, how about you? What experiences in the past may be continuing to influence the way you relate to your wife?"

Earl hung his head and admitted that he, too, had been rather promiscuous in his young adult years. He admitted he still was attracted to other women, although he had not actually been physically unfaithful.

David talked about forgiveness and about accepting each other. Before he left, he prayed with them that they would be able to support each other rather than tear each other down.

Unfortunately, the approach was a mistake—at least in that particular encounter. Now, ten years later, David wishes he had handled things differently.

"I got them to confess all this dirt to each other," he says. "But all it really did was create suspicion and distrust. 'Will she do it again?' 'Can he ever really put his past behind him?' They had been married about eight years at that point, and though they bickered, they had stayed together. But within another year, they were divorced."

Of course, they might have divorced anyway, but David feels his unwise, or perhaps untimely, intervention contributed to the failure of the marriage.

"Given their patterns of communication, I had simply added to the ammunition they could use against each other," he says. "They had learned to live with the bickering about cooking and unmade beds. That was a comfortable—and safe—way of fighting. But sud-

denly I'd introduced the heavy artillery, and even when it wasn't
used overtly, it was always in mind, and that proved too weighty
for the relationship to bear.

"For me," he reflects, "it raises the question of whether we
really need to know everything in the past or not. Isn't the forgiveness of God sufficient not to raise those questions again?"

Seeking disclosure for disclosure's sake, he now feels, is a mistake.

David Lindquist's experience also raises another issue: At
times, trying to help only hinders. If even well-intentioned intervention can prove destructive, when should a pastor intervene,
and when should a bad situation be left alone?

Obviously, even in small churches, there are going to be more
fires flaring up, more problems in people's lives, than any pastor
can personally stamp out. How do you decide which ones to take
on?

When *Not* to Intervene

There are occasions when it is probably best *not* to try to help
those who don't want help.

When you don't know the person. Without some kind of personal relationship, intervention is difficult and risky. In these
cases, the better strategy is an indirect approach.

"At the shopping center, I often see harried mothers ready to
strike their toddlers or scream at them for simply being young and
dropping their ice cream or whatever," said one woman, a co-min-
ister with her husband. "Since I don't know them, I don't feel I
have the right to directly intervene, but one time I walked by and
said, 'They're a handful, aren't they? I'd forgotten how much patience it takes to be a parent. Even so, I wish my children were
that age again. Yours are so cute.' It knocked the props out from
under the mother. Suddenly she said, 'Yeah, they are kind of cute.'
I was simply trying to be a little salt of the earth. We never exchanged names, and we may never meet again, but that compliment kept her from throttling her kids."

When you're beyond your depth. When a situation demands
more skill or time than you have available, the best thing you can

do for yourself *and* for the person is to bring in someone else.

One pastor found himself facing an impossibly complicated marriage triangle. Initially the wife came to the pastor complaining about poor communication patterns. When the pastor met with the husband, he discovered the man had been having an affair for over a year.

The problem was that the wife was pregnant, and so was the mistress! The husband didn't want to lose his family; he wanted to keep his wife. But he was not only emotionally attached to his mistress, he felt a moral responsibility to help her through the pregnancy and delivery of *their* child.

The pastor was stumped. "Normally, I'd tell a man to stop seeing his mistress as a prerequisite to rebuilding his marriage. But what could I do in this situation?"

When the husband started bringing the mistress to the pastor for counseling, the pastor knew it was time to call for reinforcements.

"I was in over my head," he said. "I think I know how to help couples repair their marriages, but I can't do that and help the husband and his lover at the same time."

Since the husband and wife were members of his church, he continued to see them, but he referred the mistress to another Christian counselor.

When is it time to refer? Another pastor offers a helpful image: "I give it my best shot in two or three meetings to see if there are any indications of healing. I'm a counselor, not a psychotherapist. The difference: Counselors put bandages on the wounded so natural processes can help them heal. But when a person is continually ripping the bandages off the wound so it will never heal, it's time for the psychotherapist."

Perhaps the best most pastors can do is clean out the dirt to prevent infection, apply bandages, and set up the situation where normal healing processes can work. When the person persistently sabotages that treatment, it's time to refer.

When your motivation isn't right. Motives are always mixed; elements of fear/love/worry/altruism/reputation all get tangled together when confronting a volatile situation. And yet, pastors have found that some of their most counterproductive confrontations take place when they've gone in with the wrong motivation. So they identify warning lights that occasionally tell them their motives are not right for intervention.

"I was once tempted to confront a husband about his misbehavior, but I realized the only reason was because I liked his wife. Instead of being an ambassador for Christ, I would have been the woman's advocate, her mouthpiece. I realized I was not the right one to counsel that family."

Other pastors admit the temptation to make an appointment with a woman to discuss a problem her husband had mentioned, motivated largely by the pleasure of being with her. In that case, too, the motive is probably sufficient to rule out personal involvement.

Another dangerous and ineffective motivation is self-righteousness. "I've found being dogmatic and legalistic does not lead a person to want help. It turns him against it," said a pastoral counselor. "But if he feels he'll get a fair hearing, he's much more apt to let someone step in. It's crucial to sincerely want to understand that person's point of view. Even if I wind up disagreeing with the decisions he makes, I want to know the factors that went into making those decisions."

Anger is yet another motivation that must be brought under control before attempting intervention. As Laurence J. Peter once said, "Speak when you're angry—and you'll make the best speech you'll ever regret."

Even when the individual has acted so badly as to deserve punishment, "you need to deal with your own feelings before you can deal effectively with the situation," says psychiatrist Louis McBurney. "It's natural to see a child abuser or workaholic as a real villain. But simply being judgmental will not help anyone. The only way I've found to get feelings under control so you can work with the person is to start asking, *What has caused this person to act this way?* Everyone is part victim as well as part villain; every story has two sides. Obviously, we've got to get the individual to stop the destructive behavior, but to do that we must understand what factors led him or her to act that way."

By checking emotions of anger and judgment, we can begin to truly listen and ask the right questions. McBurney observes, "At this point, you can form an alliance with that person so he doesn't see you as being *against* him but *with* him, and often the person can say, 'I hate this about myself, too. I really do need help.' "

A final motivation pastors find they must guard against is seeing themselves as saviors.

"I have a standard speech for my staff I call 'Messiah Complex 101,' " says a pastor in the Southwest. "Everybody gets it several times because all of us in the helping professions have a little touch of the Messiah complex. We tend to believe that given enough time and money, we can love people enough and pray hard enough and work hard enough to help anybody. Not so. There are some people you cannot help no matter how hard you try. Everybody has to learn that, and if you don't, you can create more problems than you solve. Part of learning to be a minister is recognizing there are some people for whom you have nothing to offer—at least at this point in time."

How can you identify the people you *can* help? Do you have to try and see if you get rebuffed? Or can indications tip you off right from the beginning?

When to Intervene

How do you discern the leading of the Spirit from a human compulsion to correct someone? Here are some of the factors pastors point to when deciding whether to help a person who doesn't want help.

God's persistent call. Opportunity does not equal a mandate to act. Just because you become aware of a need does not mean God is calling you to meet that need.

"I do not think God has called me to straighten out everyone," says one long-time pastor. "Unless it's an obvious emergency, I consider a concern God-given only if it stays with me over time. If it's a passing thing, I doubt if it's the call of God. But when the Lord lays it on your heart to help someone, he'll make sure you don't miss it. The story of young Samuel comes to mind. God will call you more than once if it really is of him."

Another pastor said, "In some cases, I've waited three weeks to six months before I knew God wanted me to act. He used that time to show me other facts I needed to know. I became more observant. I gained wisdom and necessary evidence."

When, before God, motives are right. If we are tempted to "straighten someone out," it is doubly important to check our motivations. What *should* the motivation be? Because I love God. It sounds simple, and it is. But in essence, that has to be the primary motive: loving God and wanting to help others love God, too.

"One motivation I have to guard against is feeling pious and smug before God," said one pastor. "It's easy for me to point out misbehavior or sin because it makes me feel righteous. It's even sweeter when something bad happens to the person and I can say, 'Don't you remember when we talked about that? I warned you.' But that doesn't do the person any good, and it certainly doesn't help my spiritual life. It's pride, which leads to the Elijah syndrome: 'It's just you and me, Lord, and sometimes I wonder about you.' "

A check on that motivation is to ask, *Do I care deeply for that person, and not simply for the other people in the situation?* The guidance in Galatians 6, the passage that commands those who are spiritual to restore those who are "overtaken in a trespass," is all couched in language emphasizing the importance of eliminating any self-righteous tendencies. We are to "bear one another's burdens" (v. 2), "watch yourself, or you also may be tempted" (v. 1), not think too highly of ourselves (v. 3), and test our own actions (v. 4).

As counselor Everett Worthington Jr. writes in his book *How to Help the Hurting*, "Only after careful self-examination—more than a cursory overview—praying in the presence of the Holy Spirit, can we see well enough to even attempt to remove the painful splinter from the eye of a friend. It is never hasty."

Before attempting to correct anyone, he asks himself these questions to check his motivation:

- Do I really care for this person?
- Am I a close enough friend that I am willing to bear his or her burdens?
- Is the timing right for a confrontation?
- Is the Holy Spirit directing?

If the answer to all these is yes, then intervention *may* be appropriate, and it is then a question of *how* and *when*.

Sorting Out the Options

Most pastors, as they mature, begin to seek counsel before riding off on any rescue missions. As one pastor described it: "Early in my ministry, I took a solve-them-as-they-come approach. My assumption was, *We shouldn't have problems in this church*, so anything I became aware of I tried to solve. Even though my motive was good, my assumption was not well thought out. I never asked, *How does this problem compare to this other problem, and which of the two should I be spending time on?* I didn't have any plan of action. As the bullets were fired, I tried to bite them. I almost lost my sanity.

"In my second church, I began to trust the advice of my two part-time staff members. Before I acted, I'd sit down with them and discuss the situation. We would decide whether any action was necessary. If not, we'd pray about it and leave it. If we decided action was necessary, then we'd decide who and how, or if anyone else (such as the board) should be in on it."

Before taking the initiative in a ticklish ministry situation, this pastor and his associate asked themselves these questions:

1. Do we have all the facts? Do we have something more than hearsay? What can we do to get a fuller picture?

2. Once we have a better understanding of the situation, is it as bad as we thought? Whom does it really impact? Is it a church-wide problem? Is it going to affect one family, four families, or forty families?

3. Can we afford to wait? If we don't respond, what's the worst thing that could happen in a week? In a month? In a year?

"That's not passing the buck," said the pastor. "That's gaining the wisdom of time. You don't ignore it forever, but instead of rushing to the fire immediately, take some time to gain perspective. If we felt the problem could wait a month, we would let it go. My tendency was to exaggerate the urgency. I was surprised how many 'emergencies' took care of themselves in a month."

Other times, however, the pastor must step in, and a sense of timing is crucial.

Recognizing the Right Moment

Farmers know crops go through three stages: green, ripe, rotten. Harvest is effective only at one of the three stages. Pastors, too, have learned that intervention is not always the appropriate action, but at the right time it can produce a rich spiritual harvest.

When people finally become willing to work on an area of their life, pastors must recognize that moment and not jump the gun. What are some of the signs to look for?

Perhaps the most apparent is a time of personal crisis. With resistant people, the breakthrough often comes as a result of tragedy or failure.

Ike, for instance, was a farmer and a father of the old school—strict with his children and never showing emotion. He would make his children line up when he entered the house, and he expected them to sit without speaking at the dinner table.

His pastor, Eb O'Malley, claimed he could never talk to Ike about anything personal. Ike was always polite but reserved; conversations were kept on a surface level . . . until Eb was called to perform the funeral of Ike's brother.

A few days later, Ike told Eb, "You know, my brother and I were very close. One reason was because we endured a lot together as kids. My father was a harsh man. When I was twelve, my mother died, and the day of her funeral my dad got us up early and forced us all to work in the field from 6:30 to 10:15. Then he called us in, and we had fifteen minutes to get dressed for the funeral. We went to the funeral home, and immediately after the service, he loaded us back in the car, brought us home, and sent us back out to the field. We couldn't even go to the dinner that was served after the funeral. I remember thinking, *Aren't you supposed to cry when your mom dies?* But Dad never gave us a chance. He wanted to keep us busy."

Ike looked at his pastor, "Now, after my brother's funeral, I got to thinking. Maybe I'm more like my father than I'd like to admit."

Eb said later, "From then on, he was much more willing to talk with me about his relationship with God, his wife, and his children. His brother's funeral seemed to be the turning point."

What about situations where there is no personal crisis? What are the signs that intervention might be effective?

One is *increased nervousness*, as evidenced by blushing or inability to sit still. Body language reveals much about a person's internal condition.

A second sign is *a lapse in the defensive posture*. Before a person is ready to deal with an issue, he usually will be defensive about it. "Initially, if someone is defensive, I'll overlook it and show acceptance," says Louis McBurney. "But after I've worked with him awhile and feel we have more of a relationship, if he's still defensive, I might challenge him a bit—'It sounds like you feel a little defensive about that subject.' I may still have to wait, but before long he'll usually say something like, 'You asked me about that before. What do you think about that issue?' Or something will indicate he's not reacting with the same degree of defensiveness, that he's feeling more secure. At that point, I can raise the issue directly."

Both of these principles were put into play by Pastor Daniel Frantz.

Daniel had been approached by Eddie Wiebe, a young man in the congregation: "Pastor, Sherry and I have been married only a year and a half, but we've got problems. She's still seeing an old boyfriend who works with her. They eat lunch together—just the two of them—twice a week."

"Have you talked with her about the problem?"

"Yes, but she says she's not doing anything wrong. I say it may not be wrong, but it sure tears me up inside. When she won't end the contacts for me—for *us*—I wonder if she loves him more than me. Would you talk to her?"

"Does she know you're talking to me about this?"

"I told her we should consider counseling, but she says we shouldn't need counseling after only a year of marriage."

Daniel agreed to talk to Sherry, and as was his custom, he asked Eddie to perform a "familyectomy"—to take himself and their son out of the house so Daniel and his wife, Ruth, could talk to Sherry alone. He didn't want her to feel humiliated or emotion-

ally pressured by any other family members. Eddie agreed that the
next Tuesday night he would tell Sherry about 7:00 P.M. that he
needed to pick up something at the hardware store. "Come back
around eight," Daniel suggested.

The next Tuesday evening, with his wife along, Pastor Frantz
rang the doorbell about 7:10. Sherry answered.

"Hello, Sherry. How are you?"

"Fine, Pastor. Hi, Ruth. Come in."

"First, let me tell you why we came," he said, planted on the
porch. "We don't want to come in unless you really want us. Eddie
told me you two have been struggling with some things. I'd like
to talk about them, but I am not going to push myself in. I realize
you didn't invite us to come here. I've come because as your friend
and pastor, I felt I should. But we won't come in unless you invite
us. If you say no we'll still be friends. We won't say anything
more."

He paused and watched Sherry swallow hard. (He calls this his
"Revelation 3:20 approach" because it makes sure the person
knows her freedom is not being violated. But it also forces a decision.)

As is the case in most of Daniel's experiences, Sherry said,
"Come in." They sat at the kitchen table.

"Eddie tells me he feels he's got some competition for you. I
wanted to hear your side of things."

Sherry reassured Daniel that she wasn't doing anything wrong,
that she and Roger were "just friends," that she had no guilt feelings, and that she was unafraid to be seen with Roger. As she continued to talk, however, Daniel noticed that while her mouth was
saying one thing, her hands were telling a different story.

A box of Kleenex sat on the table, and Sherry unconsciously
took one after another out of the box and shredded it. Before long
the pile resembled a sizable bird's nest.

Finally Daniel remarked, "You keep saying you don't feel
guilty about this relationship, but I'm not sure I dare believe it. You
know why? Because your hands betray you." He pointed to the
nest of shredded Kleenex. "I wonder if your sense of guilt isn't
about as high as that pile of Kleenex."

She was speechless.

"You know," he continued, "when Jesus came into Jerusalem and people were cheering, the Pharisees said, 'Hey! Make them shut up!' And Jesus said, 'If I make them shut up, the stones will cry out.' Sometimes I talk to people who shut up part of themselves, but their gallstones—or ulcers or blood pressure—cry out. Sherry, I think you are crying out through this pile of Kleenex."

Sherry lowered her head and admitted there were things about herself that she hated. "She never admitted guilt, but she did talk about her loss of self-respect," Daniel recalled. "Her bravado was really a cover-up for her self-hate. We talked honestly, and she and Eddie have begun to make progress on their relationship."

Not every case of pastoral intervention ends with such positive results. There are times to intervene and times not to intervene. In this case, the key to effective ministry was timing—noticing the subtle clues that God was already at work in her life, and then moving gently but firmly when the defenses began to come down.

19

Shepherding in the Shadow of Death

*Pastors wield the shepherd's staff in full view of
the grim reaper's blade.*

—Greg Asimakoupoulos

In many ways our local hospital resembles my church. In both, people are in various stages of recovery. And in both, people are in various stages of dying.

I thought about this as I watched a PBS documentary about Mother Teresa's ministry. Her call to Calcutta and my call to Concord have a common focus. We both work with those who won't get well. Clergy of all colors and collars have the privilege of shepherding people through the valley of death's shadow.

Such ministry is awesome—in both senses of the word. It is serious and intimidating business. How do we wield the shepherd's staff in full view of the grim reaper's blade? What are the most meaningful things we can do for the dying? How can we sincerely say, "I care"? How can we make our visits more personal? What do we say if we are unsure of a person's relationship with God?

Little Things That Say I Care

In my first year out of seminary, six people died in the Seattle church I served. A veteran pastor invited me to coffee to share how he ministered to families in grief. As we watched the boats in the harbor and sipped forty-weight French Roast, he encouraged me. Within three months, he himself was diagnosed with inoperable cancer. Two months later, Jon was dead.

Before he died, I heard him say, "When life is threatened, little things mean more than before." That stuck with me. Ever since then I have looked for small ways to say to those approaching death, "I care."

Just this week I stopped to see a man who lives near our church. Doctors told Willie he has less than a year to live. On one of my visits, Willie said he used to play saxophone with a jazz quintet. I located an album in my tape library of saxophone jazz renditions of contemporary Christian music. I gave it to Willie. I wanted to say I cared.

When one man in our church was dying, I learned he had been raised in Wisconsin. I called a friend involved with the Green Bay Packers and asked if he could send an autographed photo. When I delivered the photo, Arvid was thrilled.

Often I'll photocopy a graphic torn from a magazine or the Yellow Pages to create a piece of unique stationary that calls to mind an individual's hobby or interest. On that customized letterhead, I'll scratch a personal note.

I've found that personal notes are one of the most meaningful small ways I can show the dying that I care. Such notes allow me regular and essential contact with the terminally ill, while also preventing me from causing them undue stress. A felt-tip greeting is less jarring than a ringing telephone. Many lack the strength to hold the receiver.

A handwritten note need not be long, but its shelf life certainly is. People can tuck it in a book or drawer and read it over and over again.

One man I recently buried used to chide me for dropping him thank-you notes when, prior to his illness, he helped around the church. But after cancer unpacked for a two-year stay at his house, his response was quite the opposite.

Over the years, I have compiled devotional thoughts, lyrics, and prayers from Leslie Brandt's *Psalms Now*, Dietrich Bonhoeffer, and others. I enclose these in my correspondence, choosing material that will give words to the emotions and voice the prayers of one who is dying.

Making Personal Visits Personal

Written reminders of our prayer and concern, though important, are not sufficient. A person near death longs for companionship and looks forward to visits from the pastor.

Madeleine L'Engle in her book *The Summer of the Great Grandmother* reflects on her mother's death. She insists that dying, by definition, must be experienced in community. "Death is not a do-it-yourself activity."

I attempt to pay a personal call once a week during a terminally ill patient's plateau period. Others from within the congregation also drop by. As death creeps closer, my visits increase.

For home visits I stay less than a half hour. In the hospital, I stay ten minutes or less. More important to the dying than the time we stay is what we do while we're there. Physical touch is powerful and sacramental. It is an outward sign that you, as caregiver, are entering into their pain.

Diane had just lost her cancerous leg to amputation, but the malignant cells had spread to her lungs. I held her hand as we prayed together. That point of contact underscored for her that even in pain, together we were touching God with our prayer.

Holding a person's hand, patting their cheek, or gently placing your hand on their fevered brow conveys much.

When I read Scripture, I have found it means a great deal to the sick person if I read a favorite passage of his or hers. Discovering those treasured portions is as simple as asking. For a Christian aware of approaching death, nothing penetrates the heart like Scripture. I note these favorite Scriptures for use in the person's funeral service.

Sometimes my visits are musical. Although I am not a great singer, I can carry a tune and like to sing. Having grown up in the church, I have committed scores of hymn texts to memory. Singing them, I've found, can be a means of distilling faith. The ailing appreciate hymns of assurance. At times they sing along. Often they close their eyes in private worship. A familiar tune and cherished words can enlarge the faith housed within a weakened frame.

Don, a strong Christian who had served his church for more years than I had lived, lay motionless, near death. I leaned over his bed and softly sang Horatio Spafford's "It Is Well With My Soul." A teardrop scurried down Don's cheek, and he smiled a thank-you.

When I pray, along with asking God to minimize physical discomfort and envelop the patient with a tangible sense of his presence, I try to help the person turn their eyes and hopes on the glory that awaits them. Using Revelation 7 as a backdrop, I sometimes invite a person to visualize the throne room of heaven and hear the voices of worship.

In prayer with Ralph, I talked about his future with Christ. I painted verbal pictures of heaven and thanked the Lord that in a brief time Ralph would realize the purpose for which he had been born. Prayer can celebrate the patient's acceptance of death.

Some shy away from the Lord's Prayer as a mechanical ritual, but I often incorporate it into my prayers with the dying. Familiar words are especially meaningful near death. I have watched parched, lifeless lips begin to move to the cadence of my voice as I recite, "Our Father who art in heaven. . . ."

A prayer repeated since childhood can engage the mind of someone decreasingly aware of the present.

The Soul of the Visit

An essential part of my pastoral care to those who hear death knocking is to prepare them not only for death but for eternity. Many who face death, however, are afraid to acknowledge the topic. When they seem uneasy about discussing such things, we also may feel awkward talking about eternity.

I have found it helpful simply to ask:

"Are you afraid of what's ahead?"

"How are you feeling about leaving your family?"

"Do you feel ready to meet the Lord?"

These opening questions give a dying person opportunity to express a desire for assurance.

I can't assume a person who attends my church has a strong sense of peace and assurance about life after death. I've made it my policy to quote familiar Scriptures of assurance such as Psalm 23, John 14, Romans 8, and 1 Corinthians 15. Such passages indicate God's companionship is available on the other side of the border. Reading these Scriptures can water parched faith.

I stood over Leslie's bed. Cancer had robbed him of his muscular physique. Yet as I stood beside his shriveled body, using familiar promises from the Bible as well as poems to remind him that "Christians don't simply die; they enter into the presence of the Lord," I saw a smile cross his face.

I will read the same verses when I am not sure where a person stands with God. This enables them to see the benefits to which a believer is entitled. I don't want to give them false assurance if they have not received Christ as Savior, but asking about their fears and hopes allows me to probe their spiritual status. Such probing requires creativity, sensitivity to the circumstances, a sense of timing, and courage to "just do it." Every person is different.

I met a man on the golf course whom I later learned was dying. I sent a number of get-well cards. At times I included a devotional article. The last time I saw Jerry before he died I asked if I could pray with him. In my prayer I talked about God's plan of salvation, admitting my own tendency not to take God seriously enough.

"I think Jerry is just like me," I added as I thanked God for his love in sending a Savior to the cross and bringing him out of the grave to prepare us a place in heaven. I concluded in such a way that Jerry could receive Jesus into his life by agreeing with my prayer. He did.

Coached Grieving

"There's no place like home," it is said. Home may be the place we reminisce about—where we grew up, or the place to which we retreat after a harried day at the office. Many are now finding, when it's time to die, there is no place like home.

Certain illnesses and circumstances require a patient to be hospitalized until their death. But when they can, more and more are opting to die in familiar, loving surroundings at home.

In many communities, hospice programs offer in-home nursing care for the terminally ill and their families. Besides medications and medical equipment, a hospice provides professional workers who can talk about what is happening and what to expect. Many

I've met are Christians. I view hospice nurses and social workers as members of my pastoral care team.

Many terminally ill people are helped by having not only a place to die but also permission to die. Sometimes the family, especially a spouse, has difficulty adjusting to what lies ahead. That's when I need to help the family give the dying member permission to die.

Mary knew her husband had only weeks to live. She had accepted it cognitively but had not been able emotionally to embrace her husband's departure. Whenever I'd stop by the house, she'd greet me cordially and then excuse herself while I visited with Hap. Before leaving, I'd stick my head in Mary's office (where she buried herself in her work) and inquire of her feelings. I always encouraged her to call. She never did.

When hospice nurses increased their visitations, however, I watched as Mary gradually accepted what was happening. When I visited, she stayed in the room with Hap and me. She lingered at the door as I began to leave. We'd chat. She'd express her fear.

At one of our doorside chats, I encouraged Mary to give her husband permission to let go. Initially she balked at the suggestion. After fifty-two years together, she couldn't imagine life without him and couldn't bring herself to hasten his death. She wanted him to hang on at all costs. But such permission is essential to the healthy passing of the terminally ill. Mary finally recognized the value of this gift and gave her husband permission to wait for her in heaven.

One of the last ways we help someone die is to assure them we will comfort and care for their loved ones after they are gone. We can express some of the love they no longer can.

Dr. David Gardner shocked his colleagues several years ago when he resigned his position as president of the University of California. Citing the inexpressible and crippling sorrow that accompanied his wife's death nine months earlier, Gardner confessed to being unable to perform the tasks his job required. Gardner was praised for his candor. Psychologists validated his reasons. He is not alone.

I have a friend who is a funeral director. Scott routinely concludes his remarks at the committal service with a challenge to friends and extended family of the grieving. He invites them to remember the spouse and family members with a call, a card, or a visit a month down the road, at six-month intervals, and especially on the anniversary of the loved one's death. Pastors can coach their congregations in the same manner.

Making Last Words Count

The phone rang in my study. "I think we should do it soon," Bill said. I knew what my middle-aged friend was signaling. His inner clock said it was time to plan his funeral. We did it the next day. Within two weeks Bill was dead. At his funeral the words and music he chose to celebrate the resurrection were a powerful witness of his faith.

Most people don't plan ahead as Bill did. When their doctor tells them to put things in order, they don't think that includes outlining their final visit to church. It is up to me to encourage the dying to think of such things. Once the person accepts his or her condition, most are receptive to the idea. Planning their own funeral gives the dying a sense of purpose in an otherwise purposeless period of life.

I ask them to choose the funeral participants. I encourage them to think of musical selections, Scriptures or readings, hymns or praise songs for the choir or congregation—even sermon themes. When Hap planned his service with me, he gave me a message he wanted his fellow employees to hear. Because he was willing to anticipate the inevitable, his co-workers heard their friend's values and final goodbyes with unmistakable clarity. Though dead, he still spoke.

The Sunday after Bill asked me to help plan his funeral, I mentioned it in church. I wanted to model for the congregation what it means to trust God.

"Bill and I talked about heaven this week," I said from the pulpit. "And it appears he will be moving there soon." I was verbalizing as much faith as if I had asked God to heal his worn-out heart.

When Hap was dying, I referred to him in the pastoral prayer on Sunday and said, "Please come quickly for our friend, Happy. He's ready to meet you, Father."

Our people need to know that in God's health-care plan, healing doesn't always mean getting better. Sometimes it means resurrection.

I reached my friend Hap less than half an hour after he died. I gripped his fragile, still warm hand beneath the sheet. Tears crawled down my face as I realized that his hand, with that familiar severed half-thumb, would not grip back this time.

I kissed him on the forehead and thanked the Lord for his life. Hap had not only taught me how to serve God and his church, he had taught me how to serve a tennis ball. He showed me how to live. He taught me how to die. He taught me how to escort others to the edge of eternity.

I left his bedroom and headed for the den to comfort the members of his family. As I walked down the hallway, I felt a warmth of contentment surge through me. Despite the sorrow, I had no regrets. For the past six months I had invested my gifts and concern in Hap's life.

Helping a person die with grace is one of ministry's most significant privileges.

20

After a Suicide

The awkwardness of grief tempts all of us to hide from the truth, but doing so only makes it harder to recover from the grief.

—Randy Christian

It's 10:55 on a Thursday night. Your meeting with the board is running late. Just as you're about to vote on rules for keeping the multipurpose room clean, the church secretary returns from answering the phone. There is something about her face—the tightness or the worry in her eyes—that makes you uneasy.

She hands you a note. *Emergency*, it says. *Call your wife.*

Your throat is dry as you punch the buttons on the phone in your office. When your wife answers after a single ring, her hello seems scared, forlorn, raw from crying.

Two minutes later you hang up the phone. Your hand is trembling. Your throat feels swollen. All you can do is stare at the darkened wall, swallowing again and again. You've just learned that your son, age seventeen, has been killed tonight in a car accident.

A mistake, you think at first. *I saw him just a few hours ago. He can't be dead.*

You feel dizzy as you tell the others that you have to leave. You offer no explanations, and quizzical looks from board members follow you as you hurry out. It is all you can do to get into your car, turn the key, and drive home.

Somewhere in your numbness, guilt and anger flash. *I shouldn't have let him go out tonight. His friends shouldn't have asked him to come. He shouldn't have gone. God shouldn't have let it happen!*

By the time you and your wife reach the hospital, you have felt more emotions than you ever thought possible—from guilt to helplessness to rage to grief. And there is a numbness, a feeling that makes you feel dead yourself—but does not stop the pain.

In the hospital chapel you ask questions of a doctor and a policeman: "Was . . . was it quick? How did it happen?"

Though you didn't think it possible, you're thrown into deeper darkness by their answers. The police officer says quietly, "Your son drove his car into a concrete abutment. He left a note with a friend. It was suicide."

You sit, disbelieving, as it slowly sinks in. Your son didn't just die; he *decided* to die. It is the ultimate rejection: for some reason he felt it was better not to live than to live with you.

Finally the tears come. You sob with guilt for allowing your son's death to happen, even though you don't know how you could have prevented it. You feel guilty on his behalf, somehow, for this self-murder.

During the sleepless night that follows, your sense of rejection sours into bitterness. *How could he have done this to me?* Your grief turns to shame as you think of explaining this to relatives, friends, the congregation, the board. As this shame takes hold of you, you begin to feel a loneliness so intense that you doubt anyone—even your wife—could ever penetrate it.

This exercise in imagination only hints at the emotional whirlpool that traps those bereaved by suicide.

It's impossible to predict precisely how any of us would react to such a tragedy, because grief is not a tame emotion. But it is usually true that the grief felt by someone who has lost a loved one to suicide is more terrible than most of us can imagine.

When suicide strikes, the survivors often find that few of their friends are able or willing to help. Often a pastor or other spiritual leader is called to the suicide scene, home, or hospital to comfort the survivors—whether or not he or she knows what to do.

That was my predicament when I first faced suicide bereavement. I was a police chaplain, called to assist a family whose son had shot himself in the head with a shotgun. I had no idea what to do, what to say, or what in the long run would be healthy for the family.

Since then I've had opportunities to serve many families who were bereaved by suicide. Those experiences, along with the insights of others I've worked with in this ministry, have helped me train pastors, police officers, police chaplains, and counselors. I've found that we can have a tremendous ministry to those left behind by suicide, even in the midst of their shock and sorrow.

Be Honest

The first and perhaps most important insight I've gained is the need to be honest. This starts with our choice of words, speaking plainly to the survivors, using "suicide" instead of euphemisms like "the unfortunate incident."

This isn't easy. The awkwardness of grief tempts all of us to hide from the truth. This is especially true of those bereaved by suicide, who are tempted to avoid the painful fact that a loved one took his or her own life. But hiding from the fact only makes it harder to recover from the grief.

Clara tried to hide. When she was a young woman, her husband died in a tragic "accident." She lived in a small town, where everyone knew she and Jim had been having marital problems and that Jim had been deeply depressed.

Clara suspected Jim's death was suicide when the police explained the "accidental" circumstances. She heard the cruel gossip of those who had picked up rumors concerning the coroner's findings. She knew that many in town were saying Jim had killed himself—and that the coroner, an old family friend, was trying to ease Clara's pain by ruling it an accidental death. In fact, the rumors were true. But Clara didn't dare confront the truth, and friends shielded her from having to do so.

Years later, when her son was old enough to question his father's death, Clara was forced to face the reality: Jim had committed suicide. The shock and shame were too much for her; admitting years of deception and accepting the suicide of her husband nearly crippled her emotionally. Clara's friends had done her no favor by helping her hide from the truth.

No one is comfortable with the reality of suicide. No one should expect to be comfortable talking about it or even thinking about it. But I've found that grieving can't be completed, and healing can't come about, if dishonesty takes over.

Honesty, of course, doesn't mean emotional brutality or insensitivity. The facts can be faced gently and lovingly. It's understandable if we try to mask our own fear and sadness by being brusque or superficial with survivors, but it's dishonest. We don't have to pretend that we aren't afraid, awkward, or hurting. In fact, when we show these feelings, we assure the bereaved that it's all right for them to feel and express these emotions.

Accept "Outrageous" Feelings

Being honest doesn't mean short-circuiting survivors' feelings, either, no matter how objectionable their emotions may seem. Hearing and accepting feelings is an important part of this ministry, but it can be tough—as it was when I went to see Mark's family.

Mark had shot himself. Now his family was so intensely angry at him that some members actually expressed the wish that he were alive again—just so they could kill him!

My first reaction was to try to calm them down. "You don't really mean that, do you?" I asked.

The answer from Mark's sister was cold and clear. "You bet I do!" As I looked into the eyes of that suffering woman, I knew she was serious. But somehow when she voiced these feelings, she disarmed them. Slowly she was released from their power. Eventually she was able to let go of her hate and to deal with the loss she felt. Had I successfully stifled her comment, this might not have happened.

I learned a valuable lesson from this. Everyone has the right— maybe a need—to feel and express such feelings. Mark's sister could no more stop her rage than I could stop a cloud from passing over my head. She needed to face that rage, and when she did, she eventually was able to control it.

We need to be ready to hear and accept a wide range of emotions. Some survivors feel intense anger and hatred; others experience remorse or guilt. Still others may feel a sense of relief or even

peace and happiness. The question is not whether people should
have these feelings. The feelings are there, and they won't leave
just because a would-be counselor gets indignant. Nor is a question whether or not these feelings are healthy, though this may
become an important issue later in the person's life. The question
is this: What feelings are there, and what is the healthiest way to
express and deal with them?

When I feel survivors' emotions are too extreme or not deep
enough, I force myself to listen, to hear them out without cutting
short their need to express these things. This frees them to experience grief in their own way and sets an example for other family
members to follow. It is a way of saying, "I'm open to listening to
any feelings you might have, and you need to do the same for each
other."

Leave Judgment to a Higher Court

I remember John, who seemed to be handling his mother's suicide as well as could be expected. But every night he would wake
up, tormented by the thought that his mother was in hell because
of what she had done.

Had God condemned her for killing herself? I knew theologians had long debated the question of a suicidal person's eternal
destination, but I could find no justification for John's fear in Scripture. I encouraged him to trust God, the only One who could judge
his mother.

John began to do so. As he did, his focus changed from what
his mother had done to what God had done for both of them.

Leaving judgment to God is especially important for church
leaders, who are often seen by the bereaved as God's bodily representatives. By refusing to pass judgment on the one who committed suicide—even when the bereaved want such a judgment—
we encourage the survivors to leave judgment in God's hands.

This does *not* mean offering false judgment. Many grieving rel-
atives have approached me, asking of a loved one, "Is she with
God?" Hard as it is, the only right answer for me is, "I don't know."
Judgment is no more my right when I want to pardon than when
I want to condemn. My role is to remind the bereaved that God is

the only rightful Judge, and that the basis of his judgment is our relationship with Christ.

Replace Rejection With Acceptance

Life may be filled with rejections—an unkind word, a failure to listen, walking out in the middle of a conversation—but none of these begins to compare with the total rejection felt by many survivors. To them the suicidal person has said, "I don't want to be around you anymore—ever."

A friend of mine, a police chaplain, was able to help in such a case. He met with a young woman whose husband had killed himself while arguing with her. Just before the husband had pulled the trigger of his revolver, he had shouted, "I'll show you!"

The young wife was devastated. She felt that her husband, who a few years earlier had committed himself to spending his life with her, had chosen to end his life to get out of that commitment. She had been rejected in such a final and horrible way that she believed she was the most worthless person alive.

My friend sat with her for hours. He called her the next day. He stopped in to see her occasionally after that. By his words *and* actions he was saying, "God accepts you." Had he not been there, she might not have believed this message.

Offering this type of acceptance can be time-consuming, and the bereaved can become too dependent on the helping person's presence. To avoid these problems, the primary helper can, without breaking contact with the person, introduce others who also will care. This tends to show the bereaved that others also accept them.

Remember the Power of Presence

The temptation for some pastors, thinking they must have exactly the right words for the bereaved, is to avoid this ministry for fear of saying the wrong thing. It helps to realize the value of simply being there.

On one of the first suicide calls I received, I was asked to sit with family members in their dining room while the police and coroner worked on the other side of the house to examine the scene and remove the body. It was a small house; we could hear virtually every word, every sound.

I asked family members whether they would prefer to leave the house while the coroner finished his work. They declined and sat silently. For ten minutes I tried to start conversations that might have some meaning to the survivors, but in vain. So I asked whether it would be all right if I simply sat with them. They agreed.

For more than an hour and a half we sat. Occasionally someone would shift his or her weight, and our eyes would meet as if we were all having some kind of visual conference. I have never been more uncomfortable than I was in that dining room, but I felt the family needed someone.

When the coroner and police had gone, I stayed for another hour. By the time I left, I doubted whether we had spoken even for fifteen minutes.

The next day I was asked to conduct the funeral because the family had no church home. During the months that followed, I had sporadic contact with them. All that time I felt defeated. *I don't have what they need*, I thought. *If only someone else had been available to them.*

Nearly a year after the suicide, a mutual friend mentioned seeing one of the family members. "I don't know what you did," my friend told me, "but they sure are grateful to you."

All I had done was commit myself to being with them. Had I attempted a monologue or continued my drive toward conversation that day, I don't believe the result would have been so positive. Those family members needed someone who would simply be with them and hurt with them. Now I purposely allow a period of silence at such times; it is one of the few things the survivors comment on when they talk to me later.

The amount of time spent "being there" depends on the helper's schedule, of course. I've found that one to three hours in the beginning is usually sufficient—and very much needed—to show the family that I care. During that time I don't leave family members alone unless they ask me to. I know they don't want me there forever, but they want to sense that I'm committed to them.

Point to Forgiveness

Do I remain silent whenever I spend time with survivors? Not at all. Sometimes my willingness to be there earns me the right to share personal thoughts and feelings. When this is the case, I can begin to lead them toward forgiveness.

Two kinds of forgiveness may be needed. The first involves the survivor who hungers to be forgiven, who feels somehow responsible for the suicide. "If only I had watched him more closely," this person mourns. "If only I had been more loving, or had let her see her boyfriend, or . . ."

While no one can take full responsibility for another's decisions or actions, sometimes the "if onlys" have enough legitimacy to cause great pain. This was true of one family I encountered.

Janet's family knew she was considering suicide. They were determined to stop her if they could. They kept watch, driving past her home every fifteen minutes or so to check on her. On one of those "drive-bys," they saw her car running in the driveway and investigated. There was Janet, sitting in the car with the windows rolled up—except where a vacuum hose from the exhaust pipe was pouring deadly fumes through a back window.

They had arrived early enough; Janet was not injured. Removing the hose, they moved the young woman into her house and discussed what to do. Should they call the police or take Janet to the emergency room? Janet assured them that she would not try anything else that night; she only wanted to get some sleep. Finally, the family took Janet's car keys and the vacuum hose and left.

But Janet had a duplicate set of keys and another hose. The next morning, neighbors found her in the car. Dead.

The members of Janet's family knew they had made a bad decision. They kept bringing this up when I met with them, and it would have been dishonest of me to deny it. But I could show them that they could be forgiven for their error.

My first step was to show that *I* could forgive them. They needed to see in my actions that Christ was willing to forgive them, too. Then they needed to understand how to forgive themselves. Over the next several months I kept reassuring them that forgiveness was available; in time they accepted it.

Theological discourses are not the cure for people like those in Janet's family. But a simple sharing of Christ's love for us and his willingness to forgive our sins is always appropriate. I would explain the concrete, practical side of forgiveness.

"I know you don't *feel* forgiven right now," I might say, "and you probably shouldn't expect to. Forgiveness is more of an action than a feeling. It's deciding not to make a person pay for what he or she has done. That's what God does for us in Christ—not making us pay for our sin. If God forgives you, then you can forgive yourself, too."

When a survivor feels forgiven, it may help to explain that he feels angry with himself for not preventing the suicide. The anger is rooted in hurt, and he will probably feel angry with himself as long as he feels the hurt. But he doesn't have to act on the anger by refusing to accept forgiveness.

"Think about what you're doing to yourself," I might say. "You're trying to 'pay yourself back.' But you don't have to pay. You don't have to keep punishing yourself, constantly reminding yourself of what you did, depriving yourself of the help you could be getting from others. You can decide, step by step, to accept God's forgiveness, forgive yourself, learn from your mistake, and maybe help someone else." Once this is accomplished, the survivor is free to move ahead in the grieving process.

Some, like Janet's family, need forgiveness themselves. Others need help with a second kind of forgiveness: the ability to forgive the person who committed suicide.

This was the case with a boy named Jack. Only thirteen years old, he had experienced the ultimate rejection from his father, who had killed himself. Jack had loved his dad but now felt abandoned. He needed help to forgive the father who had left him.

No matter how many explanations Jack heard about his father's mental state, no matter how many times he was told about the pressures his father had felt, it didn't help. Jack couldn't change his anger and resentment.

The first step in helping Jack was to let him see others forgiving his father—not condoning the man's action, but showing a willingness to forgive. Then it was important to help Jack see that refusing to forgive was not hurting his father; it was hurting Jack.

It took a long time for Jack to accept his father's imperfection, but eventually the boy was able to forgive and proceed with his grief.

When the Next Call Comes

There are no surefire formulas for helping those left behind by suicide. And there may be times when, in counseling the bereaved, we will feel out of our league and will need to refer. But that need not keep us from answering the next call from a stunned, devastated survivor.

Standing with those who have experienced the pain of suicide is a special opportunity to serve. As helpers, we become special to the survivors because we are there. To them we represent God, and they will usually take our ambassadorship seriously.

That does not require perfect performance on our part; it gives us a unique chance to model the compassion and forgiveness offered by the One who sent us.

21

Rebuilding Marriages in Crisis

*Our very entrance into a marriage crisis is often strewn
with ambiguity: they want a pastor, but they don't.*

—James D. Berkeley

E very once in a while I hear of a couple married dozens of years
who "never quarreled once." I always wonder whether they're
amnesiacs or liars.

Place two sentient people together in marriage, and conflict is
bound to occur. In measured doses, conflict can be productive; it
forces growth and change, compromise and resolution. It releases
tensions constructively, rather than letting them build to dangerous levels.

But when does the normal jostling of any marriage relationship
become a crisis? It depends on the individuals involved.

"Just as some people can handle more physical pain than others, some couples tolerate more marital discord. But a body can
stand only so much pounding, and a couple can take only so much
anger and quarreling," says Ed Smelser, a counselor at Fairhaven
Ministries in Roan Mountain, Tennessee. "Tension is inevitable.
Arguments are common. But when the situation becomes so painful that a couple can't see the marriage continuing—that's a crisis."

What is the pastor's response when a shaken marriage totters
in near collapse—and when some do eventually topple? Here are
engineering plans to shore up the tottering and rebuild the devastated.

Outsider In

While our presence in some crises will be welcomed, our very entrance into a marriage crisis is often strewn with ambiguity: they want a pastor, but they don't. Or *one* does, but the other resents it. It's difficult for the pastor, an outsider, to know the expected role when summoned, sometimes ever so faintly, into a marital crisis.

A marriage crisis rarely grows in complete obscurity. Signs of disintegration begin to appear around the edges of the relationship: an increase in separate activities, coldness toward one another in social situations, marital "humor" with barbs, public bickering, rumors of family fights, children who suddenly become behavior problems or allow their grades to plummet at school, a drop-off in church involvement. Pastors notice these signs and wonder what to do.

Sometimes unwelcome messages reach the pastor: "Do you know the Schulzes are having trouble?" When the rumors prove accurate, the pastor has a decision to make: to initiate or to wait until they make the first move. Both tactics have pros and cons.

Initiating can make you an unwanted intruder. Therefore, many pastors wait, prayerfully, to be contacted by one of the spouses. "Unless someone is willing to reach out for help, willing to change," I heard over and over as I talked to pastors, "the chances of helping that couple are nil. Somebody has to want help enough to be willing to involve you. Otherwise they may listen politely (or not so politely) to what you say, but they'll go out and do what they'd planned to do all along."

Thus it appears wise to wait until invited.

But waiting for the drowning to call for help is a wrenching job for lifesavers. Aren't pastors supposed to care for their people, even when parishioners don't know enough to request it? Should pastors helplessly sit on their hands while marriages go under?

These difficult questions have led many pastors to adopt this philosophy: Under normal circumstances, I'll allow couples the dignity to ask for help. But I won't knowingly allow a marriage to disintegrate solely because no one invited me in.

Charles Shepson, founder of Fairhaven Ministries, says, "Sometimes when I hear a former student or acquaintance is having marital troubles, I'll write to tell him I care and to offer help. The vast majority of the time I get no response. Or when I do hear back, it's usually months later, *after* things have really fallen apart or when things are safely back together. In the midst of a crisis, they often seem unable or unwilling to let me help. But when they reach out to me, it's another story altogether. Then I've seen a lot of good things happen."

Care's Beginnings

Of all people, one's spouse has the greatest opportunity to cause pain and frustration, just as that same person is most capable of giving pleasure and fulfillment. Thus, marriage difficulties cut deeply.

When initiating pastoral contact, one of the biggest jobs is to control and channel a range of emotions. The crisis often unfolds with one spouse unable to cope with the pain of a rocky marriage and thus seeking the pastor's help. A woman whose wedding I had performed about a year earlier called to ask if she could see me in my office. While settling into our chairs, she got to the point: "Jim, Keith and I aren't doing well."

"I'm sorry to hear that, Jeanne. What seems to be the matter?"

"It's probably not fair to put it this way, but it's his family. I don't think I'll ever be a part of them."

"What about them is hurting you?" I asked.

"Keith and his parents and brothers are in the trucking business together. Don't get me wrong. It's going well—maybe too well. That damn business is all any of them ever think about!"

It was the first time I'd heard her use that kind of language. "You sound put off by the Kalahars! But every new couple has to learn how to fit into each other's family. Is there anything else?"

"It probably wouldn't be that bad for anybody else, but do you know how clannish the Kalahars are? I mean, we all live together on property right near the shop—my mother-in-law is right out my kitchen window! They're always having birthday parties and anniversaries and business celebrations. But if the party's for my side of the family, forget it! They expect Keith and me to *live* for the business, and Keith does whatever the rest of his family wants. Well, I don't want to be a Kalahar—at least not that much. I want at least a little piece of Keith for myself, and to do things our way."

"I can understand. Have you and Keith been upset with each other?"

"*Upset* is hardly the word for it. I didn't feel good on Tuesday, so I told Keith I didn't want to go to a party for his cousin. We had a big blowup. He accused me of trying to turn him against his family, and I was so mad by then, I told him I hated his stupid family. Then I split for Carol's place. I ended up going back home that night, but Keith and I have hardly been speaking. Keith's been out of the house most of the time. But what's new about that? He cares more for his trucks than he ever did for me!"

Jeanne had a crisis: she still loved Keith, but they had a lot of things to work out. Jeanne came looking for help, and I wanted to see that the marriage God had joined together no one would put asunder. How should I best proceed?

Ed Smelser offers sound advice: "When people first come to you, they tend to describe situations to best fit their needs. Out of frustration, anger, bitterness, and hurt, they tell you everything that's wrong with the other person. I like to meet with a couple together to have them both tell their side."

Jeanne was probably telling me the truth as she knew it, but it was edited truth, a piece of the story. I was sure Keith had plenty to fill in from his viewpoint. I had to be careful not to jump to conclusions. I needed Keith's insights and attention to do all I could for them.

"It's important to get them together," Smelser continues, "because even sitting in front of you, they have to practice good marriage communication: letting the other person speak, letting him or her finish, not controlling the conversation. I like to observe how they relate to each other, so I 'let them go at it' to a degree. I learn a lot about them and their relationship in that initial interchange."

After an initial meeting with both parties, many counselors find it wise to meet with each person separately. Charles Shepson usually follows this routine. "The second time I meet with a couple, I try to talk with each of them alone for thirty to sixty minutes.

That's a time when each can talk openly without any regard for how the other is taking what's being said. For instance, the husband may say, 'I feel almost nothing for my wife anymore.' He couldn't say that in front of his wife without hurting her, so probably it wouldn't be said.

"The wife may say, 'I've told Bill about one lover, but actually I've had three. He'd never be able to take it if he knew how many, and especially who they were.' That's valuable information that eventually Bill needs to hear and handle, but it never would have come out had I not talked with Bill's wife in private. I can ask questions and get answers unimpeded by the effect those answers would have on a spouse."

"I tell them they may say anything they want about our individual session," Smelser says, "but I make a case for not talking about it outside our sessions together." Why? Because when they tell each other about their time with the counselor, they often "forget" parts embarrassing to them, misquote the counselor for their benefit, or give some misreading of what was said or done.

After he meets with them separately, Shepson gathers them briefly to plot their next steps. This helps discourage excessive curiosity about "What did you say about me in there?"

If a counselee doesn't talk, says Smelser, "I try to draw out that person by saying something like, 'You must have your reasons for being quiet.' Suppression of anger, or passive aggression, can be just as injurious to a marriage as active hostility."

The idea to keep in mind here is that emotions *are*. They may be acted out or stuffed deep inside, they may frighten or bewilder or dominate, but they need to be acknowledged. *Then* they may be faced and worked on.

Shepson says, "One of my jobs is to get feelings out into a setting where they are neither judged nor discounted. I want the person to know his or her emotions have a right to exist. Later we may talk about the right and wrong actions springing from these emotions, but at the moment, I need to give permission for these emotions to be expressed."

Care Objectives

Once the couple has expressed their emotions and described
the basic issues, the counselor can work on some basic objectives.
Ed Smelser has five objectives for the next few sessions. These provide a marriage counseling routine in outline.

Controlled release of tension. Smelser's initial goal is to gather
data in a "safe" setting. He lets the couple get things off their
chests, but disallows verbal abuse and hateful statements that will
later be regretted. A couple has built pressure in their relationship
for a number of months or years. When they finally reach a crisis,
that pressure is ready to burst out in destructive ways. Merely allowing them the dignity of being heard releases pressure.

Increased understanding of issues. Emotions cloud reasoning,
and both parties likely come with a limited or distorted view of
their marriage. Whether overly pessimistic, unnecessarily blame-
ful, or excessively naïve, their understanding often needs massive
doses of unbiased observation.

"Have you considered . . . ?" questions help couples view their
problems from a new perspective. With Jeanne, I mused, "Keith
has had thirty-some years in close association with his family. I'd
probably have a hard time including new ways into old habits, too.
I'll bet he isn't even aware of how much his family continues to
influence him." Jeanne, in her hurt, may not have had the charity
or clarity to even consider that.

Communication with, rather than at, each other. The prior
need, of course, is to get them talking *to* each other. It's not uncommon for a counselor to hear a spouse talking as if the other
weren't there: "I wish she'd just once—only once!—be on time for
church!"

The natural response to that is, "Jill's here. Maybe you could
say it to her."

"Oh, yeah. Uh, Jill, do you think you could try to be on time
more often? I hate being late for meetings."

Since communication problems are at the heart of so many
marital crises, simply getting the two parties talking *together* can
be a major step toward health. But the quality of that talk is im-

portant. According to Smelser, "Many of the things one person says make the other erect defenses."

The wife says, "You never think about all the things I do for you." The natural response from the husband is, "I do too! Just yesterday I thanked you for packing my lunch."

To the wife, Smelser might say, "The way you talk seems to be triggering defensiveness in your husband. If he feels you're attacking, he's going to want to defend himself. How about saying something like, 'I sure like it when you notice the things I do to keep this family going'?"

Smelser continues: "Most wives, when they say, 'Don't read the newspaper,' don't really have anything against newspaper reading. What they intend to say is, 'Talk to me!' If the husband would only talk a few minutes with his wife, he could read the paper unmolested for hours. So we have to get people to say what they *want*, not what they don't like."

Refocusing on one's own responsibilities. By the time marital problems get out of hand, both parties have likely done a lot of brooding on what the *other's* failures are. The wife is full of "He doesn'ts," and the husband is loaded with "She won'ts."

"The focus must be taken from 'faults I think my partner ought to work on,' " Smelser says. "I may say, 'I'm really not interested in who has the majority of problems. The issue is for each of you to say, "What am *I* doing to contribute to our problems? What can *I* work on to make things better?" I try to help them refocus on their own choices, on their individual responsibilities, on what they themselves need to know or do or say. It's in the present *doing* that the marriage is going to be saved."

Genuine appreciation for the other's feelings. "People don't have to agree," Smelser assures us, "if only they *understand* the other person's position. I want to work with a couple until each develops a genuine appreciation for the other person's position— regardless of whether he or she agrees with it. One woman said to me about her husband, 'We still don't agree, but I feel so much better simply knowing he fully understands my opinion and is taking it into consideration.' "

This understanding applies not only to husband and wife but to couple and counselor. Smelser believes that "people seem to know, at some level, where their problems are and what needs to be done. But they're in crisis and feel incapable of doing anything. I've found that simply agreeing with their intuitive analysis actually helps them do what their intuition has told them is right. Also, when they get my confirmation—'He agrees with me!'—they're accountable because I've said, 'I see what you see.' It's a lot harder for them to rationalize after that."

Separation and Divorce

Questions of separation and divorce arise with more regularity than any pastor would want. However we may feel about divorce, people come to us bleeding from its beating and in need of crisis care.

"Before students leave this seminary," says David Seamands of Asbury Theological Seminary in Wilmore, Kentucky, "I tell them they must have their theology of marriage, divorce, and remarriage worked out. If they don't, they'll find out within the first few months in the parish why it's so important."

One of the early concerns is when to advise separation. In cases of abuse, nearly everybody urges separation. No one should be required to live with fear of injury. Other situations also point toward separation. Some spouses participate in illegal activities, and remaining in the same household could subject a mate to legal implications or criminal dangers. Sometimes a dominant spouse insists the other participate in immoral actions. When it comes to obeying man or God, that person has to obey God—away from the control of a tyrannizing spouse.

Other situations are less clear-cut. What does one advise when two people seem to be tearing each other apart, when all that's resulting from their crumbling union is destruction and pain and anger? Many suggest a trial separation to allow tempers to cool, emotions to change, and clearer heads to prevail.

Separation is not intended to be a prelude to divorce, but rather a means toward eventual reconciliation. Crisis counselors need to make clear with the couple their intentions. "I come right out and ask them 'Why are you separating? What do you expect to gain from this move?' " says one pastor. "If they hem and haw and come up with vague answers about 'needing space' and 'wanting more freedom,' then I try to get them to be more specific. I may point out the costs of living apart, and they're substantial. I draw a mournful picture of the effect on the kids, if there are any. I don't want separation to look like a simple answer. It can so easily be a regression to immature coping mechanisms, like running away from the problem.

"But if the couple has thought through the implications, and if they're able to set up a way to continue working on their relationship while separated, separation can break a hurtful pattern. I've seen couples return to marriage gladly; they don't find being apart much fun."

The separated need help coping with their new arrangements, and direction and impetus to keep working on their tottering relationship. The counseling concerns expressed earlier still apply, but with greater urgency.

Divorce sparks many wildfires in a person's life. Questions of finances, identity, sexuality, "success" as a man or woman, child raising, and living accommodations smolder beside the smoky issues of sin and guilt. Because divorce involves brokenness and sin, confession and forgiveness are in order. Divorce is not the unforgivable sin. By clarifying a person's responsibility for the sin of divorce and by "absolving" the truly repentant through prayer and pronouncements of forgiveness, many pastors have helped the divorced work through their sense of guilt.

Fortunately, the pastoral counselor is not alone. The body of Christ can help people cope with the many transitions of divorce. For some, the crisis may be as prosaic as a lawn mower that won't start when the lawn is a foot high and growing by the hour. Single parenthood, job reentry, household maintenance, cooking, loneliness—the newly single may have a tough time handling such experiences.

That's where a church fellowship can shine. In one church, for instance, several men who are proficient in car maintenance regularly provide safety checks, oil changes, and simple repairs on the cars of single parents in their church. In other communities, men take the sons of divorced mothers fishing, and women help the daughters of divorced fathers with shopping or hair care. In other places, self-help groups like Parents without Partners meet in churches. Pastors may provide individual counsel, but church families have the ability and availability to care deeply for the divorced in their midst.

Personal Considerations

It's remarkably easy to get caught up in someone's marriage crisis. What's not easy is maintaining that delicate balance between professional distance and pastoral warmth. Many pastors say the most volatile counseling situation involves a male pastor and a woman with a troubled marriage. The "thoughtful, caring pastor" can easily be seen as the "answer" for a woman with a "thoughtless, brutish lout" of a husband. The warm affirmation can readily translate into sexual attraction. The flesh is weak.

It's also vulnerable. It's not unknown for pastors to be intimidated by passion-torn spouses. One pastor tells the story:

> One day a woman from my church asked to talk with me. She said she felt in danger from her husband. When I asked why, she said, "He wants to get rid of me."
>
> I didn't know her husband, and from the way she described him, I was glad I didn't. Apparently he'd grown fed up with her and wanted her out of his life, so he was doing incredibly mean things to her. He probably figured if he intimidated her enough, she'd leave.
>
> He especially wanted her to sign over the house to him, but that would mean she'd leave without a penny of assets. I told her she didn't have to be bullied into signing anything and encouraged her to stick up for her rights. I also warned her to leave the house if he started acting dangerous.
>
> Not long after that her husband came to see me. He wasn't at all pleased with what I'd told his wife, and he seemed intent on changing my mind. When his six-foot-four frame came through my door, I knew I was in trouble. Pointing accusingly at my sternum, he raged, "If you hadn't talked to my wife, she would've signed the papers and let me have my house!"

I don't know what came over me, because I was scared, but I said, "You may be over six feet tall, but you're only half a man if you're trying to take that house away from your wife." Somehow that worked. They did divorce, but she got the house, and she lived in it for years in retirement. Although he swore there was no other woman involved, the husband married two weeks after the divorce.

Another danger: being linked too closely to one party. Ed Smelser says, "It's easy to feel closer to one person in the couple. Maybe you feel that person has a better handle on what needs to be done and is more willing to do it, or maybe the person seems to be more the victim. That can be a problem, because both persons ought to be able to expect your impartiality.

"Often the woman seems to garner special favor. Maybe it's because women are generally more sensitive to relationships. Perhaps it's a protective instinct. Whatever the cause, though, I need to remain impartial to be effective."

One cost of marriage crisis intervention caught me by surprise. Soon after I had met with Jeanne, she seemed to turn on me. She'd taken some turns for the good in her marriage, but suddenly in church matters, whatever I was for, she was against. After several months of locking horns with me, she finally announced her decision to leave the church.

I hadn't failed her as a counselor; she had been appreciative of my concern, and she appeared helped by my advice. Nor had my opinions and pastoral style changed. So why the clash?

Probably because I knew too much. She had revealed their difficulties, and my being privy to their problems was hard for her to live with. In her awkwardness, she left the church, ostensibly over our disagreements. That is sometimes a price to be paid for crisis intervention.

Marriage crisis intervention also can be highly frustrating. I worked with one couple for nearly two years. To the husband, his wife was a cold fish, with unreasonable expectations that she never allowed him to attempt to meet. To the wife, the husband was a troubled and selfish mother's boy who was unable to show he really loved her.

I could see why both felt as they did. From outside the labyrinth, I watched them bumping their way through the marriage trying to find each other. But they could see only an endless array of walls. Although I could visualize what it would take for them to succeed, they were either unwilling or unable to make it happen.

In frustration and dismay, I watched them wend their way out opposite exits of the maze, unable to find and hold on to each other. Pastors who care about people and see the awful destruction of divorce, feel the sorrow of a home divided, of children uprooted, of love turned into bitterness and self-reproach. Sometimes it hurts to be called into crisis.

It Isn't All Ache

But what keeps us going are the occasions when our intervention has impact. One missionary wife sent this testimony to Charles Shepson following a visit to Fairhaven:

> I felt trapped between my feelings and my Christian convictions. I hated my husband and wanted to leave him. I honestly did not know how I could go on living with him, feeling the way I did. I knew that to leave him was wrong and would have far-reaching consequences for my family. *And we were missionaries!*
>
> I knew what was right. I could quote all the verses, yet I had myself convinced at times that it was more cowardly to stay in the marriage than it would be to leave it. My whole life was misery. I was rejecting everything I believed in.
>
> My husband and I were given an opportunity to go to your retreat center for counsel, and in agreeing to go I made my first tentative choice to work on our marriage. My first day there, I made a deliberate choice to commit myself to my husband and to our marriage. It was a decision based upon what I knew to be right, but it in no way reflected my feelings at the time. I still felt rebellious and bitter. I felt no love, and these feelings stayed with me. Each positive step I took was a response to my choice as I ignored my feelings.

We started to rebuild our marriage. Our first aim was friendship, since we felt this was a measurable, reachable goal. I had no expectations, but I stuck with it, knowing only that I was doing the right thing. My miracle happened—slowly, very slowly. As I acted on my choice and built on it, my feelings began to change. Over the months I began to feel respect, then tenderness, and finally love for my husband. I saw his weakness, and I saw his strength. I saw him through entirely different eyes, and I loved him.

Success!

PART 5

Specific Care

22

What Do You Say to Job?

There is nothing like severe nausea to increase our humility and remind us that we too are only human.

—Kathryn Lindskoog

M ost illnesses, especially the major ones, are blind accidents we have no idea how to prevent. I have had multiple sclerosis for more than twenty years. I was an extremely active young adult in love with life when the disease hit me. No bad habits brought it on. None of my friends or relatives got it. It just happened.

It is an unpredictable disease that acts like polio in slow motion, weakening and paralyzing the whole body. The fatigue is indescribable. There is nothing to do for it but rest.

Other major illnesses we don't know how to avoid include intractable heart disease, rheumatoid arthritis, the majority of cancers, nephritis, stroke, schizophrenia, and several other things you wouldn't want to have. By now you have probably already thought of someone in your church with one of the above.

Thank goodness, some of our old enemies are now vanquished. Tuberculosis was a major scourge that was fought in vain with a kind of early holistic medicine. George Orwell, author of *1984*, was one of the last of a huge number of great authors who died young (in 1950) of TB. People thought the disease was caused by a combination of factors such as night air, lack of sunshine, poor food, and overwork. They treated it accordingly in sanitariums, and the patients usually died. But when we learned how to get rid of the tubercle bacillus, we conquered the disease.

Whose Fault Is It?

I mention Orwell in order to show the problem with holistic assumptions about major illness, which are so popular today. Holistic medicine is a current fad.

Perhaps it should be called *hope-istic* medicine. Lewis Thomas writes in his essay "On Magic in Medicine" that the (still useful) idea of single causes for complicated diseases is out of fashion today. We somehow prefer to think that everything (except currently identified infections) is caused by wrong personal lifestyle and wrong environment. (I have a book that claims Parkinson's disease is caused by a lust for power.) People want to believe that if they live right, they won't be hit by serious disease. At best, this idea can lead them to take better care of themselves; as a result, they are apt to feel better and look better—but they may or may not escape serious disease.

Much of the insight of holistic medicine rings true because we always knew it. Is it news that we are what we eat, and we are what we think, and worry wears us out? Is it news that people die of broken hearts, that no man is an island, that the whole is more than its parts? Is it news that we are more than machines, that our bodies are the temple of the Holy Spirit, that a merry heart doeth good like a medicine? Eternal news, maybe.

The sick side of holistic medicine is that it promotes a blame-the-victim attitude toward people hit by serious disease. Let me illustrate not from a church context (although examples abound) but from a medical setting to clearly make the point. I spent a bizarre month in a local hospital three years ago trying to withdraw from physical addiction to prescription Valium. All I wanted was basic physical care; I needed someone to give me dry bedding during the night. Instead, I was forced to sit through nine hours of daily lectures in hot, smoky rooms no matter how ill I was. The lectures were poorly prepared, but that was supposed to be part of the cure. The creed at that hospital (part of a successful chain that advertises on television) was that everyone who becomes addicted to anything is selfish and irresponsible and manipulative.

So they did not provide dry bedding, much less change the bed. Instead, they tried to get me to break down and admit that my life had been useless and unproductive to this point. They urged all the patients to become a bit religious (they brought in a preacher who recommended the *Judeo*-Christian religion), and they pressured us constantly to admit how we craved alcohol or drugs.

"But I have no interest in alcohol or drugs," I exclaimed in dismay.

"Your denial proves your dishonesty," they answered. "It's that dishonesty that got you addicted to your medication. You won't get well until you admit that you brought all your troubles on yourself. You are responsible."

That was poppycock. When my doctor prescribed Valium for multiple sclerosis symptoms, he had mistakenly assured me it was nonaddictive.

According to Lewis Thomas and many other thoughtful observers, an ideological (and financial) purpose underlies the increasingly popular notion that every American is responsible for his own health. It gives conservative reassurance that sick people have brought their troubles on themselves and therefore they should pay for it and endure it without help. On the other hand, it also gives political radicals reassurance that the only answer to disease and death is some kind of social upheaval they happen to favor, since our old system hasn't enabled Americans to achieve good health for themselves.

I'm the last person to think we should live carelessly in these fragile (yet wonderfully strong) bodies and then expect doctors to fix whatever goes wrong. I've always been a bit of a health nut. I expressed myself on the clean-air issue as soon as I was born, straining to escape the smoke of my parents' cigarettes. I still feel bad that I trusted the baby food companies and fed my children countless jars of stuff that was low on nutrients and high on sugar and salt. I don't want sawdust in my bread or aluminum in my cheese or wax on my cucumbers and apples. I think we live in a smog of radiowaves and that it can't be good for us. Every breakthrough toward health cheers my heart.

But the present cult of physical fitness, both inside and outside the church . . . what does it all mean? Does it possibly express selfishness or fear? As Melvin Maddocks, my favorite columnist, writes, "Someday, with all the manic force he likes to muster, Richard Simmons should warn us that history won't much care how flat our stomachs are if that becomes our only ideal of fitness."

Our Real Fear

Perhaps, in the words of Hugh Drummond, M.D., "the issue is not death. It may be that death is a kind of refuge from a less dramatic but more real source of anxiety: chronic illness. . . . Mahler composed symphonies to death, not to diabetes. There are no odes to cancer. Chronic disease is an unsung presence, which hovers, fluttering, like an uncertain bird of prey."

Drummond made me think. I know of no poetry about chronic disease, but three of my favorite selections in world literature are about it: "The Metamorphosis" by Franz Kafka; "The Death of Ivan Ilyich" by Leo Tolstoy; and the book of Job in the Bible. They terrify people. They are incredibly honest about what it is like to have a serious, unavoidable disease.

Kafka's story is a kind of allegorical fantasy about the tuberculosis that was slowly killing him. In his extremely calm, matter-of-fact way, he tells how mild-mannered Gregor Samsa awakened one morning to find he had somehow become a huge cockroach. "He slid down again into his former position. This getting up early, he thought, makes one quite stupid. A man needs his sleep."

Gregor's parents, whom he supported, became upset because he wouldn't open his locked door and come out and go to work. His boss came from the office to find out why he was late. Everyone kept insisting that Gregor come out and perform as usual.

His boss called through the door, "You amaze me, you amaze me. I thought you were a quiet, dependable person, and now all at once you seem bent on making a disgraceful exhibition of yourself." Gregor couldn't make himself understood, and he didn't know what to say anyway.

After a while, Gregor became eager for the others to see his condition. If they were horrified, he would know he couldn't go to work. If they took his transformation calmly, he would somehow catch the train and get to work, knowing this disorder was nothing too serious.

When the family called for a locksmith and a doctor, Gregor felt much better. Now people believed there was something wrong with him and were ready to help. "He felt himself drawn once more into the human circle and hoped for great and remarkable results from both the doctor and the locksmith, without really distinguishing precisely between them."

Alas, when his family and his boss saw what had happened to him, their revulsion and terror sealed his doom. Gregor tried to put a good face on it by saying, "One can be temporarily incapacitated, but that's just the moment for remembering former services and bearing in mind that later on, when the incapacity has been got over, one will certainly work with all the more industry and concentration. . . . I'm in great difficulties, but I'll get out of them again. Don't make things any worse for me than they are."

His boss's only response was to scream "Ugh!" and flee hysterically. His mother collapsed on the floor in self-pity, and his father attacked him. They scared him back into his room, slammed the door, and left him there.

The rest of this story is a gripping and wryly humorous account of Gregor's life with this disease, cut off from work, affection, and company. At the end of his life, "He thought of his family with tenderness and love. The decision that he must disappear was one that he held to even more strongly than his sister, if that were possible." The reader sighs· with relief, along with Gregor's family, when his dried-up body is tossed out with the trash by a malicious old charwoman who had liked to poke at him with a stick.

The power of this story is in the fact that all of us who are still in the prime years of our lives may wake up some day and find that we, like Gregor, have lost our acceptable form in the night and become monstrosities. "Now all at once you seem bent on making a disgraceful exhibition of yourself," many friends, relatives, and colleagues tend to respond along with Gregor's boss. The attitude is not uncommon.

"Don't make things any worse for me than they are," all the ill wish along with Gregor. But it is the nature of chronic illness—and the nature of people—to often make things worse. Kindhearted humans can rally magnanimously at a deathbed, but they are not prone to rally to a person who can't manage either to get better or else to die. Like Gregor's beloved sister, some make warm commitments at first; but time and other concerns draw them away.

Kafka has portrayed for us the isolation and rejection felt by victims of nightmare disease. This Gregor was the kind of person who had spent his life serving and supporting others; when he lost his usefulness, he lost everything.

Remarks to Forget

Like "The Metamorphosis," Leo Tolstoy's story "The Death of Ivan Ilyich" tells of an incurable illness, in this case kidney disease. Ivan gradually realized that his health was gone forever; his life had ground to a halt. Ivan's family kept up the superficial appearance of caring, as most families do. But, in fact, they felt martyred by inconvenience and were intensely resentful.

Ivan was isolated.

Ivan was an entirely worldly man caught up in his flourishing career. His suffering finally brought him to the point where he became aware of what God was trying to tell him. Furthermore, he had a kind young Christian servant named Gerasim who sat with him and tried to ease his pain and accepted him as he was. They didn't talk much, but there was human warmth and touch. The good young servant wasn't horrified by Ivan's illness; he knew that such things happen.

Like "The Death of Ivan Ilyich," the book of Job tells of disaster striking a successful family man at the height of his career. Chronic illness was only one of his misfortunes, but it was central. An additional misfortune for Job was the discomfort he got from his friends who came to comfort him. Unlike most sick people, he lashed out at his fair-weather friends and told them what he thought of their pious, self-serving platitudes. In turn, they castigated him for putting God in a bad light.

The story is full of poetry, eloquence, wit, and even sarcasm. It isn't the kind of thing one expects in the Bible. Many readers are apt to side with Job's friends until they come to the end and hear God's judgment against them. The forty-two chapters, besides being sacred Scripture, comprise one of the best books ever written. Kafka and Tolstoy knew it well. The world has always had people like Job and his friends. Some things never change.

I've had my share of Job's comforters, and so have most other people with MS and similar diseases. It seems as if we scare other people so much that at times they can't think straight. Their defenses can pack a wallop. Here are a few typical examples from my own experience, remarks I would rather forget:

"You must really like to be sick; you bring so much of it on yourself." That from a nearby relative who never so much as sent a get-well card.

"The reason I have perfect health is that I think right; nobody gets sick unless he thinks wrong." That from a relative who seems to feel insecure about all his good luck in life.

"Have you heard about the woman whose MS was cured by Shaklee products?" That from a Shaklee dealer who very much wanted the story to be true.

"Dear, if your faith is sincere, tell everyone right now that God has healed you completely." That from a friend who couldn't wait to report such a claim to her Bible study.

"I know just how you feel about being crippled; I had a bad case of tennis elbow last month." That was from one of the local country club crowd.

"If you'll take a long, fast walk every day and soak in hot water, the pain will go away." That from my doctor who didn't want to admit that I could no longer take a long fast walk at all, and that hot water doesn't help nerve pain.

"You never should have adopted your children." That from a friend who knew I needed help but who can't stand housework.

"If you don't make the effort to get out and mix, it's no wonder you get lonely." That from an old friend who can't make time to see me.

"I admire you so much for your bravery." That from many people who seem unaware that I'm scared. (I think they are afraid that I'm afraid.)

"God must cherish you to trust you with this burden." That from people who would rather die than to be cherished by such a God.

"Your present improvement is just wishful thinking." That from people who are very rigid about sticking to current medical orthodoxy.

"I know you fake your limp to try to get attention." An entirely serious remark from my pastor after a dozen years of seeing me hobble around our large church complex. That's the one I haven't gotten over yet.

If people think I invented some of these, I don't blame them. I can hardly believe some of them myself—and I was *there*. They don't ring true in the world of Mother's Day teas and Hallmark cards, but when I stop and think about it, they ring true according to the Bible. It's not the Bible that says things are going to be easy.

In our polite society, we tend to gloss over hurtful remarks and forget them. It's bad style to complain. And goodness knows one of the trials of chronic disease is that it spoils your style. Gone are the smashing backhand, the dainty shoes, the fantastic cooking, the light step, the perfect grooming, the coordinated wardrobe, the skill of circulating at a reception, the memory for names. If you weren't a klutz to start with, you'll soon become one when disease takes its toll. So while still trying to pass as a normal person and win acceptance, you don't dare offend people by exposing sensitive feelings.

Job, of course, wasn't even trying to pass as normal or to win acceptance. So he fought like a tiger. He not only exposed his sensitive feelings but filled one of the greatest books of the Bible with them.

Job's friends assumed they were wiser than he, knew more about God, and were spiritually superior. That's a common pose for healthy people to take when dealing with a sick person in despair. I challenge anybody to check how spiritually victorious he feels in the midst of violent seasickness or a bad case of intestinal flu. There is nothing like severe nausea, I think, to increase our humility and remind us that we too are only human.

Fear of blundering or not knowing what to say keeps some people away from those who suffer. But willingness to be with a sick person as a warm human friend means more than a talent for talk. An occasional awkward or ill-chosen remark is the least of the problems a sick person faces. It is really rather foolish to so often feel we have to say something brilliant and enlightening to someone who is suffering. He doesn't expect that. Why should we? Kafka and Tolstoy and the author of Job make it clear that simple companionship (a form of love) is what suffering people often crave—not a course in philosophy.

The Greatest Need

On the positive side, here are ten suggestions for those who want to help people with chronic disease:

1. *Object to propaganda that blames the victims.* Get into the habit, even if you object only in your own mind. Blaming the victim is an everlasting temptation; remind yourself that it is arrogant stupidity.

2. *Keep in touch.* I have had old friends drop me off their Christmas letter list (I learned later) because they didn't want to have to hear bad news about my MS, and they figured the time had come when my prospects looked bad. They didn't want to risk their feelings.

3. *Be accepting.* Allow the person to feel sick and scared and frustrated part of the time if need be. If he ever lets down his happy façade with you, it's not a social atrocity. Take it in stride. Likewise, allow him the luxury of seeming wildly optimistic. Stay calm.

4. *Don't trivialize his or her problems* by equating them with petty irritations of everyday life. I went to hear a Christian teach on "How to Respond When Tragedy Strikes," and his whole talk was about how he kept his serenity when he had a flat tire. I thought *he* was a flat tire.

5. *If you have an item of health news, pass it along*—but acknowledge that it may not be accurate or relevant or that it may be old information recycled. One of those is usually the case, and your statement eases the disappointment. Your thoughtfulness will usually be appreciated. But don't pass on items that are depressing. Stick to the positive.

6. *Take time to learn the facts about this person's condition.* Read up on it if possible, or question someone who is reliable and informed. Realize that the person may (or may not) be sick of describing it. Caring enough to understand what's wrong is a rare

gift. I have seen a dying woman flinch with pain when her friends at church carelessly congratulated her for managing to get her face to fill out so nicely. I could see at a glance that her face was bloated from cortisone and that she was going downhill and frightened. Her old friends refused to look or listen.

7. *Form a pool of practical helpers in your church*, or use the deacons' fund to hire professionals to do chores for the chronically ill. Most churches have casserole brigades to help people with short-term ailments, but no casserole brigade wants to touch the tar baby of chronic illness. The chronically ill are least apt to have money for hiring help, and they need it most.

8. *Be tolerant of the person's views about prayer and healing.* Perhaps he believes in divine healing today and you don't, or vice versa. Respect his belief. You can pray for him even if he thinks healing is impossible (or even if *you* do). After all, some chronically ill people *do* recover, even when doctors have little hope. Job did. So share your ideas if they are uplifting and the sick person wants to hear, but if he doesn't buy in, don't go off in a huff like a disappointed vacuum cleaner salesman.

9. *Follow your urge to touch often.* It is said that sick people need human touch most of all and get it least. If you're glad he's alive, let him know it. You may counteract other recent input that has made him feel physically rejected and useless.

10. *Be brave.* Be brave enough to read Kafka, Tolstoy, and Job very slowly and thoughtfully. Then be brave enough to be kind.

23

Care for the Chronically Wounded

Pastoring the deeply wounded is actually a gift.
It exposes my impatience.

—Matthew Woodley

F or the third time in a week, Ed Hastings burst into my office
with a health crisis—only this time, it was really serious. He
threw his arms around me and began to weep. "Pastor Matt," he
choked, "you better start planning my funeral. I think I have
AIDS."

As it turned out, Ed had never engaged in high-risk behavior
nor had he been tested for AIDS. It was simply Ed's way to up the
ante on his personal problems.

So as he clung to me sobbing and shaking, I began to mentally
list his other ailments. Over the past seven years, Ed had called the
Mercy Ambulance crew for half a dozen alleged heart attacks (one
during a worship service), two cases of dehydration (he forgot to
drink), an ulcer, and a possible hernia (it was just a pulled groin
muscle). I also recalled my tri-weekly sessions to deal with Ed's
depression, addictions (including pot, sex, alcohol, prescription
drugs—to date), suicidal thoughts, relational crises, employment
struggles, family problems.

For six years I had pastored Ed through every crisis, praying
with him in countless hospitals and emergency rooms. But his
"AIDS crisis" was the last straw. I finally realized that Ed's soul
functioned like a sieve: the more I poured in, the more he leaked
out. After dozens of crisis counseling sessions, Ed was still looking
to me to fill him up, and my arm was weary from pouring.

Whether we like it or not, Ed represents a growing subgroup in our increasingly dysfunctional society. Carl George calls them EGRs—the Extra-Grace-Required parishioners. Gordon MacDonald prefers VDPs—Very Draining People. I like CWN—the Chronically Wounded and Needy parishioner.

Who Are CWNs?

Like Ed, every CWN is deeply wounded. Often traumatized by abuse, abandonment, or family dysfunction, CWNs limp through life. Their wounds are real, though they develop self-defeating methods to seek healing.

CWN parishioners exude neediness. And they are often clear about who can cure their neediness: the pastor, who is friend, guru, and handy therapist. So they hang around the church. They cling. If ignored, they may pout or create a new crisis—anything to get the focus back on their needs.

Third, this is usually a chronic condition. There is no quick fix—a fact I have often failed to appreciate. Instead, I have thrown myself into fixing a schizophrenic young mother, a transvestite father of three, a teenager with fetal alcohol syndrome, a young woman with borderline personality disorder, and, of course, Ed, the hypochondriac. But after exhausting my bag of pastoral tools, most of these people were still wounded and broken.

By demanding so much and giving so little, people like Ed Hastings leave their pastors—and sometimes the entire church—feeling confused, tired, and frustrated. How can we minister to the chronically wounded and needy without feeling chronically tired and used up?

I try to remember a few practical steps that help me while I'm helping people like Ed.

Practice Christlike Acceptance

CWNs burn up pastoral fuel and then press harder on the accelerator. It's easy to resent their presence. Healthier church members often gossip or gripe about CWNs. "Remember, Pastor," a pillar of the church sternly warned me, "that element (referring to

CWNs) doesn't pay the bills around here."

Personally, though, I can't imagine Jesus gossiping about those chronically wounded lepers or griping about that incredibly needy Gerasene demoniac. Christ accepted them. He touched them. He healed them. True, Jesus spent only a minority of his time with the chronically needy, but there was space in his schedule for some powerful ministry encounters with CWNs. Jesus never anesthetized his heart to the hurt that surrounded him.

I try to remember that every CWN is bearing a painful soul wound. Consider Mike, who for years struggled with deep-seated transvestitism. Most people couldn't or didn't want to understand Mike's struggles. They never listened long enough to hear the incredible brokenness in Mike's past: two abusive older brothers who ridiculed his masculinity, a needy mother who dressed him in girl's clothing, and a violent father who affirmed only little girls. This doesn't justify Mike's sinful choices (something he freely acknowledges), but it shows that Mike the very draining person is also Mike the very damaged person.

Prayer helps me cultivate an attitude of acceptance for CWNs. As Dietrich Bonhoeffer wrote, "I can no longer condemn or hate a brother for whom I pray, no matter how much trouble he causes me" [or how much he drains me]. "His face, that hitherto may have been strange and intolerable to me, is transformed into the countenance of a brother for whom Christ died, the face of a forgiven sinner."

CWNs are not just a category; they are precious souls for whom Christ died. They may drain me of resources, but Jesus continues to weep and wait for their healing. So I must begin and continue my ministry with the wounded and needy by quietly, humbly, obediently accepting them as Jesus accepts them.

Communicate Clear Boundaries

This may seem a contradiction to acceptance, but only if we confuse that with availability. They are not the same.

Chronically wounded people usually overdose on an unlimited supply of pastoral availability. Like Ed Hastings, they often expect, even demand, my availability—anytime, with any crisis. It was a perfect match: I was chronically available; Ed remained chronically needy. I reinforced his clergy-dependence; Ed reinforced my need to be needed.

The solution was simple but painful: communicate clear boundaries. Lovingly but firmly, I lowered Ed's expectations of my availability. When Ed entered a twenty-one-day treatment program for marijuana addiction (his fourth treatment program), I expressed my concern and promised my prayer support, but I told Ed I would not visit him during this inpatient program: "Ed, you are too dependent on others, and I want to give you the space you need to grow strong in God's love."

This may seem blunt, but Ed never grasped all my previous hints and implied boundaries. Working with people like Ed has led me to three principles regarding boundary-setting:

1. I must take the initiative. If I don't, people like Ed will innocently assume total pastoral availability.

2. Boundaries must be specific, clearly defining when and where I will be available. Vague boundaries won't work.

3. With love and gentleness, I must verbalize boundaries and then lovingly stand my ground.

John, a severely dysfunctional twenty-year-old, had a knack for calling me at home during critical family times—supper, bedtime stories, sibling rivalries, *Home Improvement*. His timing was uncanny. (I think he bugged the house.) Finally, I set the following boundary: "I'd love to talk to you, John, but I can't accept calls at home anymore. If you call me at church, I'll give you my full attention." It may take a few more supper-hour calls, but it's important to stand by my boundary—for my family's sake, and for John's sake.

Boundary setting has felt cold and unpastoral, yet I believe it's necessary for pastoral effectiveness. For the CWN, it can foster spiritual growth. Henri Nouwen calls this a "ministry of absence." Without establishing clear boundaries, Nouwen contends, "We ministers have become so available that there is too much presence and too little leaving . . . too much of us and too little of God and his Spirit."

I have sometimes been so available that needy people used me as a substitute high priest. Unwittingly, I usurped Christ's role in the sanctification process. By prayerfully limiting my availability, I'm encouraging CWNs to stand up straight and receive the healing that only Christ can give.

Pursue Servanthood, Not Only "Success"

For the first six years of my ministry, I assumed I could solve every CWN's problem. Success was my focus.

It never occurred to me that some deeply wounded people might go backward instead of forward. After renewing his commitment to Christ, Mike vanished, most likely rejoining the transvestite subculture of Las Vegas. Darlene, a schizophrenic mother with a young son, started a new "wonder" drug, regained custody of her son, and even joined our church choir. But within four months, everything had unraveled. Darlene left the church, lost her son, and returned to the local psychiatric ward.

Ministering to CWNs involves an openness to failure. I won't help every CWN. I may take all the right steps—sowing the seed, tilling the ground, watering the vulnerable plant—and still see no fruit. Or if a small harvest is reaped, it may take years of toil and sweat.

This reality challenges my notion of pastoring. I prefer—sometimes demand—success. At the least, I want to avoid failure. So I gravitate toward people who will make me look and feel successful about my ministry. The chronically wounded usually don't qualify as success-enhancers.

They do, however, qualify as servanthood-enhancers. People like Ed, Mike, and Darlene have taught me a profound lesson: servanthood, not success, is my calling. Success is about me, my need for approval and control; servanthood is about God, my heart's longing to glorify him. Success craves applause, growth, efficiency. Servanthood is content with the intangible "Well done" of the Master.

So pastoring the deeply wounded is actually a gift. It exposes my impatience and self-centered agendas about ministry. Slowly, painfully, I relinquish my unholy hankering for success. Then, as Jesus calls me into the freedom of servanthood, I can wait quietly for the Holy Spirit to heal in his way and in his timing.

Encourage Spiritual Growth

Unlike the paralytic who picked up his bed and walked home, a CWN parishioner might roll off his mat and crawl a few feet. The spiritual learning curve is abnormally long and flat. That's the bad news. On the bright side, there's always lots of room for growth. And since God can make it happen, I can join with him by faithfully encouraging spiritual growth.

I like to support small steps of spiritual growth by asking two simple questions:

1. What goals would you like to set?
2. What gifts would you like to share?

The first question deals with *spiritual goal setting*. Consider Christ's direct approach to blind Bartimaeus: "What do you want me to do for you?" (Mark 10:51). Recently, as Ed complained about a new crisis in his life, I interrupted and asked a similar question: "Ed, by God's grace working in you, what can you do—just one thing—to make your life better?"

Ed was stunned. For over three decades Ed cruised in spiritual reverse, or in his better moments, spun his tires in the ditch. It never occurred to him that he could move forward in his spiritual life.

Much to my surprise, Ed returned a week later with not one but two goals: he wanted to finish his GED, and he wanted to pray every morning. Obviously, two goals won't place Ed on the expressway of discipleship. But at least Ed now views spiritual growth as an option.

The second question is "What gifts can you share?" Because they're hurting, many CWNs are mired in a taker mode. Ed spent hours every week dwelling on his problems, taking from me, taking from his family, taking from the church. But then again, we let him. We never invited Ed to offer something in return.

I now assume that eventually even the deeply wounded can share gifts with the congregation. I prefer the direct approach: "What gifts can you share to enrich the body of Christ?" Or, more bluntly, "What can you do around here for God?"

One CWN parishioner was thrilled to bake the bread for our Communion service. Recently I asked an emotionally disturbed adolescent boy to serve as my "worship prep specialist." Every Saturday night he prepares the sanctuary for the Sunday service.

All this pastoral encouragement may lead only to little spiritual goals and little gift sharing. But for the CWN, any progress is big.

Connect With Other Resources

I can't do everything for my CWNs. I cannot provide the long-term therapeutic relationship that is sometimes required. I cannot give medical advice. I cannot pay the rent. I cannot fill the role of omnipresent mentor-friend-guide.

This simple fact forces me to collaborate with other resources. Obviously, I need to network with the medical community, good counselors, and social service agencies. But we often neglect one handy and free resource—the body of Christ. Some saints will balk at the idea of helping the emotionally needy. But I've found saints just waiting to be asked, who will volunteer as mentors, friends, or lay counselors.

An experienced grandma in our church walked Darlene through the darkest days of her schizophrenia. I asked Dick, a retired engineer and widower, to mentor some foster boys; last summer he hauled them to weekly softball practices. Everyone benefits from these connections—me, the mentors, and the wounded.

Working with CWNs also requires that I connect with resources for myself. I love my needy parishioners, but they can reduce my spiritual flame to a dim flicker. Then my soul longs for *my* mentor, a godly pastor friend who comes beside me to reignite my passion.

Keep Bringing Them to Jesus

Early in my ministry, I told my seminary adviser about my first encounter with an entire family of CWN parishioners. His advice was simple, direct, and (so it seemed at the time) incredibly shallow: "Just keep bringing them to Jesus." I was disappointed. Actually, the next day I was a bit disgusted. *This guy gets paid to train pastors*, I thought to myself, *he writes articles on ministry, he leads workshops on pastoral care—he even has a doctorate! And that's the best he can do: "Keep bringing them to Jesus"?*

I think I finally know what he was saying: "As a pastor you are just a little channel for Christ's love and grace. You—your wisdom and counseling techniques, even your love—are not the source of healing. Christ is the Source. So never forget your primary calling—to bring needy people into the presence of Jesus."

His unadorned advice constantly points to my greatest resource in ministering to the wounded—prayer. Not just praying *for* people, but praying *with* them, entering the presence of Jesus together. "The ministry of prayer for healing," writes Leanne Payne, a veteran in praying for the deeply wounded, "consists simply of learning to invoke the Presence of the Lord, of coming into that Presence with the needy one, and there listening for the healing word that God is always sending to the wounded and alienated."

Too often I've neglected the incredible resource of healing prayer. For five years I ministered to David, a young CWN struggling with depression, low self-esteem, loneliness, and a constant barrage of dark and fearful dreams. All of these combined to create a deep sense of spiritual oppression and hopelessness.

For five years I helped David. I offered advice. I encouraged him. I listened. I set goals with him. I prayed for him.

God used my efforts, but I always sensed that David needed something more. He needed to encounter *Jesus*, not just me. So after a worship service, I quietly anointed David with oil and prayed with him, bringing him into Christ's healing presence. I simply asked Jesus to reveal his love deep into David's heart, even into the hopelessness and fear. I'll never know the long-term results of those prayers, but I do know that something shifted in David's soul. The dark dreams disappeared. The hopelessness lifted. More important, the focus of David's life was reoriented from his neediness to Christ's love and power. David is still wounded and needy, but he's also trusting Christ to heal and transform him.

Healing prayer (or "bringing people to Jesus") is not a quick fix. It doesn't bypass the process of slow, steady growth. It doesn't remove the need for pastoral acceptance, encouragement, boundaries, even professional counseling or lay mentoring. Sometimes it simply reorients the wounded and needy, directing them to the proper source of healing—Christ. Then, like David, the chronically wounded and needy can become the continually transformed and hopeful.

24

Key Questions in Remarital Counseling

Little attention has been given to the unique needs of those remarrying. Yet the statistics show they are even more in need of premarital preparation.

—Randy Christian

J ack and Lois wanted to get married. They also believed God wanted them married. Jack was divorced five years earlier and had two adolescent children. Lois had never been married but felt certain Jack was "the right man." As they spoke with their pastor about their engagement, they were excited about the future, about the possibilities of being a "real family."

But they also had a number of anxieties. Jack's divorce had made him wary of another marriage, and his children weren't certain they liked Lois. Lois was sure she and Jack should marry, but her family had been cold to the idea. She wanted children, but Jack wasn't sure he could handle "another round of kids."

As a pastor, I see more and more couples like Jack and Lois. People today are as enthusiastic as ever about marriage, and those who have been divorced are even more likely to get married than those who have never been married: 83 percent of divorced men and 76 percent of divorced women remarry. And while many ministers offer premarital preparation, little attention has been given to the unique needs of those remarrying. Yet the statistics show they are even more in need of premarital preparation. While 35 percent of first marriages end in divorce, approximately 65 percent of remarriages end that way, many of them within the first few years.

Some time ago, I recognized that the majority of my premarital counseling was being done with couples for whom this was not the first marriage. Out of my experience with these couples, let me offer some observations as a springboard for you to develop your own approach.

Clarifying Our Position

While not all remarital preparation involves divorce, most does—which means I had to come to a clear personal stance on divorce and remarriage. We may apply the relevant Scripture passages differently. I personally feel the Bible allows for at least some remarriage after divorce. But even pastors who don't accept that position will be confronted by widows and widowers wanting to be wed, and thus remarital counseling is still an important issue.

I also learned the hard way about the need to understand the beliefs of the congregation. Early in my ministry, I made a decision not to marry anyone who had not undergone premarital counseling. My church leaders seemed supportive of this until I applied the rule to a remarital couple. Since the couple was older, the leaders felt they didn't need counseling and they insisted I conduct the wedding ceremony anyway. When I stood firm, they went informally to one of my elders. It was then I learned that my understanding of the leaders' stance was incomplete! This well-meaning elder explained in firm tones that I was a servant of the church and had no right to make the decision not to marry this couple "simply because I wanted to do counseling with them."

Eventually, the elder board upheld my stance, but I learned a valuable lesson about assumptions—don't make them. Find out your church leaders' understanding of divorce and remarriage. If they don't have one, study the Scriptures together. As I discovered, the minister and the layleaders need to agree on a stance. This protects the minister from being seen as arbitrary, and it involves the church much more in the ministry of remarital preparation.

Assuming No Maturity

Rudy and Karen were a likable, seemingly mature couple. Everyone had been speculating on how long it would take them to decide to get married, so when they announced their engagement, no one was surprised. I thought I knew them well, and I had a high opinion of them. Both were older than I, and both had experienced much in their lives. I was tempted to forgo my usual premarital program because I figured they knew it all already.

Fortunately, they were honest enough to reveal some concerns to me, and they encouraged me to guide them through the sessions. As I did, I was amazed at how many difficulties surfaced in their relationship. I had assumed they had learned from their experiences in former marriages. I was wrong. Neither recognized his or her contribution to the failure of the first marriage and both had difficulty looking at their new relationship realistically.

I have observed many couples who married later in life. When either person has been divorced, it has almost always been a handicap to future healthy relationships. People can gain a great deal of experience, but they don't always learn from it. Communication, role expectations, use of leisure time, vacation plans, sexual adjustment and birth control, conflict resolution, family background, personality issues, spiritual priorities, and church participation are some of the more important areas of any marriage, and they're now among the issues I discuss with every new couple, regardless of how experienced they are.

Evaluating Round One

One of the first steps in remarital counseling is to take an honest look at the first marriages. Describing those relationships is often uncomfortable for everyone, but it's necessary. It should be done with both of the engaged parties present. They need to hear each other describe openly the relationship with the former spouse, which will continue to influence the new marriage.

I ask the couple what steps they have taken to resolve the problems that led to the breakup of their first marriages. I look for a mature response. Have they accepted their share of responsibility? Have they sought forgiveness? Have they addressed the personal problems that may have contributed to the marital stress? If they have not, they aren't ready to enter a new relationship.

The goal of this process is to help each person own up to his or her own responsibility for the failure of the first marriage. It also allows the partner to gain a more realistic perspective on the potential problems in the new relationship.

This was the case with Steve, a minister in his late thirties. His wife had left him several years earlier for a close friend. Steve's congregation was shocked, and a ground swell of anger toward his wife began to rise. Steve was hurt and didn't feel particularly positive about his wife's action, but he was able to go before his congregation and admit that he had contributed to her unfaithfulness. He confessed that he, too, had been unfaithful by making his wife compete with the church for his time and attention. For years he had given his best hours to the church. When his wife tried to talk to him about it, he accused her of being unspiritual. "I can't blame her," he said. "I left her years ago without moving out."

Steve had made some significant discoveries and was able to forgive his wife and himself. He also sought help for his unhealthy way of looking for approval through growth in the church. Whether he ever remarried or not, his honesty allowed him to grow.

In addition to exploring past relationships, it's important to look at the current status of things. If one person is still carrying a great deal of bitterness toward a previous spouse, the likelihood of strife in the new relationship is strong. On the other hand, it's also good to be careful about close relationships with former spouses.

Julie had divorced her husband two years ago, but she was never able to handle maintenance tasks on the house by herself. She relied on her ex-husband, Wayne, to fulfill the maintenance role. This was awkward at times, but since they had two children and Wayne wanted them to have a positive environment in their home, he was willing to provide the assistance. The problem came when Wayne became engaged. Carol, his fiancée, understood his feelings about providing a decent home for his children, but she had difficulty accepting his continued contact with his ex-wife. It seemed to Carol the closer they came to their wedding date, the more Julie expected Wayne to help her. Finally, Carol told Wayne she didn't want him going over there anymore. He couldn't understand why she was being so unreasonable; and the subject was a regular source of irritation.

In counseling, I asked Wayne and Carol to explore the dynamics of this problem. What made Carol uncomfortable about this? What didn't Wayne understand about her reaction? How much contact with his first wife was reasonable? How much could his new fiancée accept? What alternatives were there?

It's also important, I've found, to explore the relationships with ex-in-laws. Grandparents usually feel they shouldn't have to end their relationship with grandchildren simply because there has been a divorce. One sister-in-law put it this way: "My brother may have divorced her, but I didn't." When this is the case, the continued contact with the former in-laws can be a source of stress in the new marriage if it isn't handled delicately.

I've found that if contact with former in-laws is to continue, several ground rules are needed.

First, it should be explained at the outset that efforts by in-laws to reunify the divorced couple are not welcome. (If reunification is an appropriate goal, the in-laws still are not the appropriate people to be the driving force.)

Second, both the ex-spouse and the in-laws should avoid discussion of the marriage that could lead to blaming or "What ifs."

Third, contact should be limited and open. Secret meetings cause suspicion and pain even if they are designed to avoid these things.

Finally, in-laws should not be used as go-betweens for ex-spouses. This places them in an awkward situation and prevents the open communication needed for important concerns such as child rearing that are shared by the ex-spouses.

Handling Stepfamily Issues

George and Shana were getting married. George had two boys, ages ten and thirteen. Shana had one girl, age twelve.

Shana's daughter, Shari, was physically mature for her age. Since her mother's divorce, she had been more of a sister than a daughter to her mother. Now, she resented George's assuming a parental role with her, as well as his desire that Shana act more like a mother than a sister to Shari. George felt that if he were going to be living in the same house with this young girl, she should be expected to obey him.

Then another situation arose. George's thirteen-year-old son also was well developed for his age. And since the two weren't really related, he and Shari found themselves attracted to each other. One night when George and the boys had been at Shana's house, George started looking for the boys to tell them it was time to go. He found the younger boy watching television. When he asked where the older boy was, his brother said, "Oh, he and Shari are making out again." George and Shana found the two entwined in Shari's bedroom.

When two families are blended, they rarely relate to one another like the Brady Bunch. Conflicting loyalties, resentments, and differences in habits can surface. Without the God-given and cultural taboos against sex between natural siblings to temper emotions, the rate of incest in stepfamilies is much higher than in blood-related families. I encourage the couple to discuss these and other stepfamily concerns: adoption, name changes, inheritance, rules for relationships between stepsiblings, how relationships with friends and relatives might be changed by the marriage, child discipline (who will fill what roles and how these roles will be phased in), career changes, competition for love and affection, how jealousy will be handled (it can usually be assumed there will be some), and the setting of priorities for the new family.

Discussing a list like this might seem to cast a negative light on the new relationship. After all, it's possible many of these issues won't be a problem for a particular family. Unfortunately, however, we don't know in advance which issues those are. The point of this discussion is to erect warning signs. The family can't afford to be ignorant.

Including the Children

In remarital counseling, our tendency is to work only with the couple. *After all*, we reason, *the children aren't getting married*. The fact is, however, as illustrated by Shana and George's situation, in many ways the children *are* getting married and they will be one of the most important factors in determining whether the new marriage lasts. The number-one cause of divorce in remarriages is conflict over the children. This is true even if the children are old enough to take care of themselves. Children are tied so closely to parents that if the natural parent has to choose between the new spouse and his or her children, the new spouse usually loses.

I normally devote two sessions to discussing the issues *with the children present*. In the first session, I ask them to tell me their understanding of what's happening and what concerns they have. If the children are hesitant to talk (as they often are), I'll ask everyone to write down the topics they think we should talk about; they don't have to sign their lists. If there are children too young to write, I ask them to draw pictures of what they think the new family might be like.

Once I've received the children's topics, I bring up the issues one by one. I find it's usually best to give the people with the least power the chance to talk first. That way, they don't feel they have to conform to what their parents or older siblings have said. I encourage the parents to truly give the children the freedom to talk without fear of penalty, reminding Mom and Dad of the penalty *they* will pay if they don't allow the children to talk early on.

Monitoring the Grief Process

After suffering a great loss, the grieving person experiences shock, denial, anger, a desire to bargain, and eventually an acceptance of what has happened. Only after this acceptance stage is reached can the grieving person began to build a new life on solid ground. In divorce situations, there's the added element of dealing with guilt. If the wounds have not healed by the time the person remarries, chances are high there will be carryover problems in the new relationship, as Joan found out.

Joan's first husband had been unfaithful to her. She was deeply hurt, but she decided to stay with the marriage and try to make it work. Unfortunately, her husband continued in his unfaithfulness, and a divorce followed. A year later, Joan met Paul at a church activity. After a brief courtship, the two became engaged and got married.

Paul's job put him in situations where he met many women, some of them quite attractive. At first this didn't seem to bother Joan. But after a few months, she became distrustful of Paul, eventually accusing him of unfaithfulness. Paul had never been unfaithful to Joan, but her distrust grew until it became too much for Paul. He finally insisted they see a counselor or he would move out. When they came for counseling, Joan's old hurt and bitterness emerged. She had been reacting to her first husband all along, though she didn't seem aware of it.

Active grief can be a problem for widows and widowers as well. One newlywed of six months confided that he was having difficulty accepting his new wife for who she was. He kept wanting her to be like his first wife. As long as the wounds of his grief remained unhealed, he wasn't capable of accepting his new wife.

These wounds can be healed with time and work, but it's difficult to maintain a marriage in the meantime. For this reason, if one or both of the engaged people are still working through the grief process, I suggest they delay the wedding. Normally, I don't encourage remarriage within a year of the divorce or the death of a spouse.

Emphasizing Premarital Purity

Connie was shaking when I first met her. After sitting in silence for a few minutes, she explained that she had been married for twenty years and now divorced for one. She was extremely lonely, so she had been seeing a number of men. When I asked her whether the relationships were providing the companionship she needed, she started crying again. She said they had all provided some companionship and had all led to sexual involvement. As soon as she slept with the men, however, the companionship and the relationship in general deteriorated rapidly. Before long, the men were gone.

Finally Connie looked up at me and asked if I was married. When I said yes, she said, "How long could you go without sex after having it regularly for years? I'm normal, and I have normal needs."

Her question highlights the problem faced by millions of divorced people. Connie was a Christian. She didn't believe in sex outside of marriage. On the other hand, she had grown accustomed to sexual relations during her twenty years as a wife. Like many couples, even during the stormy ending of their union, she and her husband often enjoyed sex. Now she was alone, and she wasn't resisting temptation.

Surveys show that the majority of engaged couples whose partners have already been married are or have been sexually active. Often, even the Christians among them see this as acceptable. One such woman challenged me to give her scriptural documentation that her sexual activity was wrong. When I presented her with a simple word study on the word *porneia*, she reluctantly agreed that she was wrong. But she still wouldn't believe God disapproved of her behavior.

I have learned to meet this problem head on. As with any premarital counseling I do, I routinely inquire about the extent of sexual activity the couple has experienced with each other. The couple is expecting this, because I explain what the counseling will involve when they first approach me. Interestingly, while I encounter a great deal of awkwardness, I have always found couples to be honest.

When I find they have been sexually active, I explain my understanding of Scripture on the subject, and I encourage them to seek forgiveness from God and each other. I then tell them that I hope they will remain chaste until they're married, and that at least during our weeks of counseling, I will be asking them about their progress in this area. I know—and tell them so—that refraining from a sexual relationship won't be easy. And even when couples are willing, relapses are common. But I make no apologies about calling them to the high standards of Scripture.

I'm careful to explain why I ask something so personal. *First*, they have come to me, a representative of the church. While our society tends to value individual freedom over accountability, the church exists to provide guidance to its members.

Second, I ask no more than what God has already commanded.

This law is what's best for us, since God's commands are based in his love for us.

Finally, apart from all moral and spiritual arguments, it's important for a couple to determine how much their relationship is based solely on sex. One young lady challenged my teaching on sex outside marriage, but it turned out she and her fiancé had little else they did together. When they finally agreed to abstain until their wedding, they were forced to look at the weakness of their relationship and consider ways to strengthen it. When they did get married, sex didn't have to carry the burden of their entire relationship.

When couples object to my asking such personal questions, I explain these reasons and tell them I am not willing to do less than my best with them, so I don't make exceptions. I have had many couples, particularly those coming to me from outside my church, elect to go elsewhere. I accept this possibility because I know that if I ignore these important questions, they will suffer for it at some point.

Navigating the Legal Issues

Legal issues are particularly important for remarital preparation because the previous marriage often leaves lingering entanglements. When there are children from a previous marriage, for example, who will have custody? Where will the children live? What will the visitation arrangements be? Will anyone besides the ex-spouse have visitation rights? (It's becoming increasingly common for courts to recognize the rights of grandparents to visit their grandchildren.) Is the stepparent planning on adopting the children? If so, is this likely to be opposed in court? Finally, what is the likely impact of these decisions on the children?

Financial questions also arise out of the legal aspects. Is either partner receiving—or paying—alimony or child support? How will this affect the overall financial picture? Will court action be necessary to make a modification?

I also alert the couple to inheritance issues. How should current wills be modified? Who will be designated guardians of the children should the natural parent die? Will the new marriage change the inheritance of the children? Is a trust fund needed?

Many of these legal questions are outside my expertise as a minister, and the best help I can offer then is to refer the couple to a competent attorney.

Because of the number and complexity of issues in remarital preparation, I try to meet with couples for eight sessions. I realize that's a heavy investment for any minister, but I've found that remarital preparation cannot be adequately carried out in one or two sessions. I also recognize that covering all the possible concerns may seem overwhelming. Nonetheless, I try at least to raise the questions. With careful thought and Christian support, couples who remarry can greatly increase their chances for a stable and lasting union.

Both Brad and Kim were married early in life, and both marriages came to an early end. Their divorces were painful, and the effects of their divorces on their children made it clear to both that divorce was wrong. Unable to undo that wrong, however, they sought support and guidance from the church and the Lord. Eventually, they met each other and grew close. After three years, they decided to get married. The church supported them, and the marriage was an occasion for celebration.

But no one is immune to the problems created by divorce, and Brad and Kim experienced many of the problems I have discussed. After four years of marriage, they are still struggling with problems like child visitation, resentment toward former spouses, and the need to let the new mate be his or her own person. They are struggling through it, however, with the Lord and his church. Their marriage has brought them closer to God, and they serve him eagerly.

We can help many couples like Brad and Kim as we have courage and the love to assist them in working through the unique needs of a remarital union.

25

Grief Aftercare

*The memorial service isn't the place to terminate
ministry; it's the place to begin a different
but no less important one.*

—Kevin E. Ruffcorn

T hings are going pretty well, I thought as I hung my alb and
stole in the closet. I had just completed the funeral for Stan
Conners, the second funeral in the congregation to which I had
recently moved. As I adjusted my collar and slipped into my sport
coat, I ran through a mental check list: *The soloist sang well; I felt
good about my sermon; and the family was pleased with the service.* I had accomplished my goal of providing spiritual comfort.

A comment two days later forced me to question that assumption.

I stopped by the house of a young widow. Three years earlier
this woman's husband had died of a sudden heart attack. She
shared her memories: finding her husband slumped over the
wheel of the car in the garage, telling her school-age children their
father was dead, beginning the struggle as a single parent.

She observed, "The pastor and the church didn't minister to my
greatest needs. Oh, the pastor saw me right after the death, and
he met with me before the service. He said a few words at the
funeral. But I never saw him again in regard to my husband's
death. After the first week, no one from the congregation visited
with us concerning our grief. My real struggles with my husband's
death didn't begin until two weeks after the funeral, and by then,
everyone was out of sight."

We parish pastors usually have a significant pre-death ministry with families. In a majority of situations, death stalks its victim slowly, allowing us to walk with the family through the valley of the shadow of death. Our ministry is important and welcomed.

Other times, death pounces without warning: the sudden, massive heart attack, the middle-of-the-night fatal accident. In these situations we provide emergency spiritual care, visiting with the family several times, sometimes for hours. Then we bow out with the funeral service.

But in either case, the memorial service, I began to understand, wasn't the place to terminate ministry. It was the place to begin a different but no less important one.

In an effort to minister more effectively to the families of Grace Lutheran Church, we created a program of grief aftercare. I've found it has helped people deal with their grief in a fuller and healthier way.

Early Aftercare

Grief aftercare begins before the funeral service, when I tell the family it will take perhaps a year or longer to work through their grief. Occasionally family members say, "As soon as this funeral is over, we can put our lives back in order" or "Just a few more hours, and we can get on with life." I serve as a gentle reminder that death affects us longer than for a few short days.

Most people don't understand grief. They believe things will be back to normal in a month or two. Anything longer indicates they aren't handling the death very well, they aren't "good, strong Christians." Thus, breaking down in tears in the grocery store after hearing a song that reminds them of their loved one confuses and embarrasses them. To let people know such occurrences are normal may not take away the embarrassment, but it does help them realize they aren't going crazy or losing their faith. They are simply human.

The second step is a series of phone calls and visits. A week after the funeral, I usually visit the family. The extended family members usually have returned to their homes and jobs, and friends and neighbors have turned their attention back to their own struggles. The rush of funeral preparations is over, life is quiet, and the family is alone.

Often this is when the reality of their loss hits them. My visit provides the family with an opportunity to express new grief questions or to rehash the old ones.

Many times I hear expressions of loneliness. Mary talked about the unbearable evenings without her husband. Tom lamented the need to make his own supper and how lonely it is at the kitchen table without his wife. Young David mentioned how empty and frightening the house is when he comes home and his mom is not there to meet him. My visits don't take away the loneliness or fear, but they do allow the family to share their grief and to realize someone understands.

Occasionally, I hear soft voices of denial. Donna confessed that she regularly imagined her husband walking through the kitchen door and greeting her with a kiss, just as he always had done. "It seems," she said, "that he's only away on a long trip." Jerry caught himself waiting by the phone for his wife to call from the hospital and ask him to come and take her home. Such struggles are normal to the grieving and not a sign they are going crazy; affirming this comforts the bereaved.

My visit reminds the family that grief does not end at the funeral. Yes, they must get on with life, but they also need to bear the wounds of grief and to allow time for these wounds to heal.

Extended Aftercare

I make a second visit or phone call about three weeks later. One of the main purposes is to assure the family they have not been forgotten. They are still in my thoughts and prayers and also those of the congregation. Another purpose of this visit is to stress that I am available.

Often this is the watershed visit. I'm not sure why. Perhaps after several visits the family members finally believe I'm truly interested in them, rather than in simply doing my "professional pastor thing."

Maybe it takes several weeks and visits for the family members to allow me to walk with them in the depths of their grief. It's one thing to shake hands on Sunday morning or work together on a committee. It's altogether different to trust someone—even a pastor—to come close when one is weak with grief.

Or perhaps three weeks after the loss is simply the point at which people begin to deal with the deeper issues. People hit me with theological questions: "Where is God in the death of my loved one?" "Did God cause this death, did God allow it, or did he have no control over it?" "I'm afraid I'm losing my faith. How do I hang on?" "I'm not sure I believe in life after death. Is there some way I can be sure?"

Anger toward God may boil over: "Why would God allow this to happen?" "What kind of a loving God would do this to us?"

Often people express this God-directed anger in indirect ways. I visited Linda a few weeks after the death of her father. Linda appeared to be handling her grief well, but during our conversation, she mentioned in an offhanded way that she was having difficulty praying. Later she expressed anger that her father had to suffer so much before his death. "How could that be fair?" she pleaded. As Linda spoke, she discovered she blamed God for making her father suffer, and her unvoiced anger toward God affected her prayer life. My pastoral visit defused a potentially harmful situation.

Some families don't seem to need much pastoral care. The family is close and they minister effectively to each other. These families, I've found, still appreciate a pastoral visit. Some use this visit to share memories. Other families express thanks to God for the blessing of their relationship with the deceased. Still others assure me that though struggles remain, they are picking up the pieces of their lives.

I usually try to make a third visit about three or four months after the funeral. By this time any significant difficulties in the grief process are apparent. I encourage the individual to seek additional professional help if symptoms include chronic depression, suicidal tendencies, or eating or sleeping disorders. At other times, the spiritual perspective is all that is needed.

David's fiancée was killed in a freak car accident two months prior to their wedding date. At first David felt intense anger. The anger turned into depression, with which David struggled for months. I suggested that he see a professional counselor, but David opted for a series of pastoral visits.

During one visit, David stated he never would be able to love a person again because of his fear of being hurt by loss. Gradually, he became more and more of a loner. After many hours of conversation, though, he began to see the consequences of his fear. Now he's cautiously stepping toward love again. Grief aftercare helped him deal with his fear before it set into pathology.

One might get the impression I do nothing but visit the grieving. I admit that I consider pastoral visitation important. But I'm able to find time for only ten to fifteen visits a week. So I make my visits to grieving families part of my regular pastoral visitation. Shortly after a funeral, I jot notes on my calendar—one week, three weeks, and three months ahead. When the week arrives, I include the family in that week's visitation.

Following the funeral, the church secretary or I also mark birthday and anniversary dates with a reminder to call the family. Since special occasions compound grief, a call from the pastor then, no matter how short, conveys the comforting message that someone understands. Around Thanksgiving and Christmas also, I call the families of those who died during the year.

Expanded Aftercare   *Community Care*

Ministry to grieving families doesn't fall solely upon my shoulders. A few weeks after the funeral, I contact someone who has gone through similar circumstances and ask that member to visit the family. Having endured a similar situation, the visitor usually understands acutely which words hurt and which heal.

This part of our program is in its infancy. We are, though, beginning to offer a six-week series on grief, active and reflective listening, and a theological understanding of suffering.

Here is what I expect of the visitors:

1. *A one-year commitment.* I suggest visits at least every four to six weeks during the year. (I first ask the grieving family for permission to have a member visit them. I point out that these visits would be opportunities to share their struggles.)

2. *Friendship and concern.* I stress the purpose of their visits

is simply to be available as someone friendly to talk to. Discussion about the struggles of grief need not be the topic of every visit, but it should be legitimate at any time.

3. *Reports of problems or needs.* I ask the visitors to contact me if they have questions about topics raised or concerns about the manner in which the bereaved are handling their grief.

Though just beginning, this program is having an effect. Recently the husband of an eighty-year-old woman died. The couple had been married fifty-five years, during which time the husband had taken care of their financial matters. After her husband's death, the woman was overwhelmed with financial decisions and paper work.

The member I asked to visit this woman was also an elderly widow. Through this woman's intervention, the new widow was given training in budgeting and bookkeeping by members of a retired-citizens organization. Since the visitor had gone through a similar situation, she could assure her charge that God does help and that with God's strength she would be able to carry on.

Ever After Care

Lives being touched by the love and power of the gospel of Jesus Christ—this is what ministry is about.

Just the other day I received a letter from a member who'd lost her husband over a year ago. My day had not gone well. A Bible study had fallen flat, two committees were exhibiting their independence, and some people had telephoned with what I considered nit-picky criticisms of one of my pet projects. I was beginning to wonder if ministry ever gets done right.

Then I tore open the letter and began to read:

> Dear Pastor,
>
> Words cannot express my appreciation for your visits. Your presence helped me go through the most difficult struggle I have ever experienced in my life, the death of my husband. . . .

This letter reminded me that ministry takes place whenever love is expressed and the effort is made to share the power of the gospel. Then God draws alongside with care that lasts forever.

26

Bright, Beautiful, and Deeply Troubled

*Unless a pastor or counselor understands the nature of
borderline personality disorder and takes concrete
steps to establish safeguards, difficulty or
even disaster may follow.*

—Victoria Martin

L inda was the divorced wife of a Presbyterian pastor. She was
bright, articulate, and charming. Inwardly, though, she was
filled with a paralyzing sense of confusion, emptiness, and need.
Having dallied in a number of promiscuous relationships, she had
yet to sate her emotional hunger.

One morning after Sunday school, she approached Jim Smith,
a counselor in our church-related center, about her problem. That
week they met for an initial psychological evaluation, during
which he first suspected the nature of Linda's problem. His sus-
picions were confirmed when a short time later she handed him a
two-page sonnet she composed in his honor entitled *Gantos for
Counsel*.

Here, with her permission, is a portion of her poetic idealization of Jim, whom she had known for less than two weeks:

OBSESSION

I discover my addiction to the hypnotic drug you've
infused my needy spirit. No plant, no flower, no chemist
could proffer an opiate more pure. You care. You accept.
I need not do anything to earn or curry favor. With you I
am that child of God; I am somebody; I am all of myself—

past, present, yet-to-be—the little girl-self in one chair, the
nurturing mother/woman-self in the other, joined/bonded
by my trust in you.
   I am reverent before this Grace.

TEMPTATION

   Without warning a veiled curtain drops suddenly on
our stage, obscuring the glowing exits, shadowing the
players. This flip-side of newfound forgiveness and freedom rears and paws like the alluring, silvery unicorn—
prancing seductively to an illicit glade—knowingly, ca-
ressingly—nudging amorously, playfully.

Notice the effusive praise and alluring seductiveness—two
traits of one of the most difficult of all emotional illnesses to treat:
borderline personality disorder (BPD). Unless a pastor or counselor understands the nature of this problem and takes concrete
steps to establish safeguards, difficulty or even disaster may follow.

Dangerous Liaison

   For some unknown reason, BPD occurs most commonly in
women in their twenties and thirties. Unlike with other psychological problems, someone with BPD does not usually grow worse
over time—at least, younger women often improve and begin to
outgrow the disorder in their late thirties. Women over forty with
this disorder, however, rarely improve.
   People with this illness can drive well-meaning pastors to the
edge of emotional exhaustion. Those with BPD can make unreasonable demands for attention, leading pastors to believe they are
the only ones on earth who understand them. Borderlines will
soak up as much time as a pastor will give them and then want
more.
   Another peril is the borderline's desire for a *special* relationship
with the pastor. In women working with male pastors, this often
manifests itself in a desire for sexual bonding, as Linda's *Temptation* passage reveals. A male pastor struggling with personal in-

securities or a poor marriage is vulnerable to a female borderline in search of intimacy.

Linda was even more explicit in her desires in this brief poem she handed to Jim during the course of her therapy:

> Unconditional acceptance.
> God's gift to me via a human courier.
> Rising, blushing warmth,
> firmly budding breast flowers—
> softly stirring internal petals
> beckoning, musky lubricity
> gently throbbing, sweetly aching contractions
> begging death-union and exquisite release.
> Completeness.

On another occasion Jim was counseling a woman in a professional setting who hugged him on her way out the door. Without warning, she took his hand and put it on her breast. Jim, a professional therapist, immediately reported the incident to co-workers in the office and took steps to make certain such an incident was not repeated.

Drawing the Line

When I was a young intern, I began counseling a woman with BPD. The counselee hooked me into believing I was the only counselor on earth who could help her. Soon the counselee was calling me at home and on weekends. She began bringing me gifts. When I began to restrict how much the woman could contact me, she attempted suicide. She timed her arrival at the emergency room to coincide precisely with her scheduled appointment with me. In fact, I was waiting for her in my office when I was paged by the hospital. This was the counselee's way of forcing me to show care.

The best advice in preventing the above scenario is to construct limits at the outset of the counseling relationship. Doing so is no guarantee that the individual will accept or obey them, but it's much easier at the front end of a counseling relationship than in the middle.

Boundaries are important not only to protect the pastor's time and reputation but as a therapeutic tool. Part of this pathology stems from the borderline's childhood: her boundaries were consistently violated, especially if sexual abuse was involved. As an adult, she is unaware of what constitutes normal demands on others.

Some pastors wrestle with setting limits, believing that it is somehow selfish. They believe they should be fully available. It's helpful to remember the example of Christ, who at times let the multitude press in on him but on other occasions went off away from the people. Jesus set boundaries.

Following are several ways pastors can from the outset protect themselves and still help the member suffering from BPD.

Limit availability. Pastors should counsel the borderline only in a professional setting. Never hold impromptu sessions in a parked car or at home. A secretary or other staff member should be in close proximity, and if at all possible, the door should be left open.

Meet once or no more than twice a week. The beginning and ending time of each session needs to be clearly stated. Unless you guard your schedule, a borderline may spend an entire day with you. Make it clear the session will last no more than an hour. Have your wife or secretary interrupt you when the time is up.

One reason borderlines try to violate established parameters is that it makes them feel as if they're special to the pastor, different from others who have to play by the rules.

Never divulge personal information. Borderline counselees will often try to gain personal knowledge about the pastor. This is an attempt to establish a *personal* relationship with him. They'll ask about the pastor's children or grandchildren. They'll be curious about how his mind works, wanting to know his likes, dislikes, and fears. When this happens, pastors should say, "This session is about you, not me." The personal information a pastor shares with a borderline could be used against him later when the *devaluation* process gets underway (more on that later).

Beware of physical touch. Don't give in to a borderline's request for touching, hugging, or other displays of affection. The worst possible damage a pastor can inflict on those with BPD is to engage in some form of inappropriate sexual contact with them.

Why? Besides the obvious—it's immoral and unethical—borderlines interpret sexual contact as incest, even though they may have initiated it. As in the case of a small child, the authority figure in their life, whom they trusted and adored, violated them.

A wise prayer for the pastor counseling a borderline personality is, "Lord, protect me, even when I don't want to be protected."

Get support. Several years ago, Jim traded a pheasant-hunting weekend for a speaking engagement at a small church in South Dakota. The pastor had a borderline individual in the church and was distraught. The nearest mental health professional was sixty miles away, so the burden for this person fell entirely on this small-town pastor. Jim encouraged him to drive the sixty miles for encouragement and guidance.

If possible, meet regularly with a mental health professional or another pastor, simply for insight or accountability. Doing so is an important defense. Someone outside the church needs to be aware that you're involved in this emotionally draining counseling relationship.

The Stage of Rage

One of the most bizarre aspects of this disorder is the intense rage borderlines can display when they sense someone is backing away from them. Depending on their level of functioning, they may go from simply leaving the church sputtering, "The pastor is unloving," to spreading malicious rumors: "The pastor tried to seduce me."

In either case, when the pastor attempts to backpedal from the relationship, the borderline may try to punish him, having perceived abandonment (similar to the reaction of the woman in the movie *Fatal Attraction*). To maintain the relationship, she may threaten violence, suicide, even blackmail or some form of self-mutilation. Her self-destructive behavior seems to be an attempt to feel something. Even pain is to be preferred to feeling nothing.

Professionals disagree about why borderlines suffer from such an intense fear of abandonment. Some point to genetics: adoption studies that compare the behavior of children separated at early ages from their family of origin suggest some borderline tendencies may be inherited.

Conventional wisdom, though, says their fear, coupled with family instability, abuse, or traumatic disruptions, results from an emotionally unavailable mother. A borderline grows up with radar highly sensitive to rejection or abandonment. The slightest offense is interpreted as exclusion. Anger erupts. In extreme cases, a borderline will even take revenge.

The aforementioned Linda was molested by a relative when she was four years old. When she reported the incident to her mother, her mother threatened to sew her vagina shut. By the time she was thirteen, she was involved in regular intercourse with a young man from church who was planning to enter the mission field. Linda struggles with the origin of her problem:

> I don't know where you came from.
> I wish I could go far enough back in my memory to find your inception.
> Such a gift!
> Who gave you to me?
> My mother?
> My dead abuser brother?
> My long-dead soldier brother?
> My sibling orientation?
> Benign, inadvertent neglect?

Someone has described the borderline's problem this way: Imagine a young child who because of an accident has an arm cut off. As he or she grows older, he or she starts thinking, *Somebody has my arm. If I could only find out who has my arm, I could get them to put it back where it belongs.* They go from one person to another trying to find someone who can fill the void. Of course, no one can do that. Listen to Linda describe her void:

> Pernicious cup bearer!
> My cup from you is always half-empty—never half-full.
> Your dregs are my insatiable craving and neediness for affection and affirmation.

To say it another way, borderlines have a gaping hole in their psyche. Their lives are often an endless search for the person who can fill it.

Sacramental Oxygen

Pastors, because they are caring people, often become one more person in the borderline's search. Borderlines love to extol the help they're receiving. Linda's praise for Jim, peppered with scriptural phrases, is almost idolatrous:

> When I think how in these few weeks you've filled
> the void of my understanding,
> it is oxygen to my faint heart,
> courage to my fear,
> my balm in Gilead.
> I want to shout my joy of freedom
> from childhood's guilt;
> sing hosannas for the validation of my being;
> praise for the return of my prodigal self;
> offer thanks for your sacramental mandate
> to one of the least of these.

Such overstated admiration indicates the person is *idealizing* the pastor, a symptom of those suffering from BPD. Enthralled with the insights they're getting about themselves, they respond with a gratitude that borders on worship. Before long, their unwitting helper can believe he is the Great Healer.

For a discouraged preacher who in a month of Sundays hasn't heard a kind word, such lavish praise can be intoxicating. If the pastor has any narcissistic tendencies, two needy people have just found each other, and the probability for disaster has just increased exponentially. While the pastor needs to be told how wonderful he is, she needs to idealize him, making him out to be morally, intellectually, and spiritually superior to the apostle Paul.

Such unrealism, however, cannot be maintained forever.

When the pastor grows weary of the gifts, presents, and phone calls at home (or perhaps when his wife does), and attempts to distance himself, the borderline fragments—lashing out with unreasonable anger, much like a little child. Listen how Linda describes her volatile state of mind:

> Borderline love
> is the terrible twos
> not quite grown up.
> I stamp my feet, kick at the door,
> and scream: "No! No! No!"
> (Such hot, willful fury only trashes these
> $100 Amalfi's.)
> I sulk and bawl. Cower in the corner.
> Hide my face.
> (Fearful, frustrated tears run, ruin,
> unmask this perfect NM makeover.)

A pastor is often left bewildered how he went from divine status to a scoundrel worthy of Dante's *Inferno*. This process, known as *devaluation*, is the flip-side of idealization. Her hate is equal to the infatuation she once felt. Yet all the pastor may have done is to suggest that the woman quit calling him at home or stopping by without an appointment.

The trigger in each case is the real or perceived threat of abandonment. The borderline uses her anger to cope with the real or perceived loss of the relationship.

Once the pastor begins establishing limits, a borderline might begin making threatening statements about what she will do to herself or, in an extreme case, to the pastor or his family. In less severe cases, she will simply disappear and begin her search again for the perfect caregiver.

What the pastor first perceived as a needy person he now sees as a bottomless pit of unrealistic demands: there is not enough nurture in the world to satisfy her emotional craving. How can a pastor tiptoe out of this minefield?

Warm Care, High Fences

When a pastor or counselor starts feeling smothered by someone with BPD, the impulse is to cut and run, shutting down the relationship entirely. That's a mistake; it will only ignite the borderline's ire.

The better response is to extricate yourself a little at a time, all the while affirming the person. Let the person know he or she can't call you at home anymore, for example, but can call during the day at the office. You might say, "I care enough about you to want you to become whole. I'm not helping that process by allowing you to cross my boundaries."

The borderline who can be helped will eventually come to grips with this. The goal, of course, is for her to begin setting boundaries.

If she reacts by fragmenting (and threatens suicide, for example), the best course of action is to recommend she go to the nearest emergency room. Remember: the strong pastor who does not cave in to her manipulative demands offers the borderline the chance for improvement.

Once a borderline encounters a staff member who puts limits on her behavior, she'll often switch to another. In larger churches, it's crucial that the staff communicate with one another in order to prevent this.

Many therapists refer clients with BPD to other therapists who specialize in treating people with the disorder. Most pastors, when they suspect a person has BPD, would be wise to refer. But this is a ticklish process: borderlines are acutely aware of any step a pastor may take away from her. The key is to frame it in such a way that the borderline sees your special concern for her. Her desire for a special relationship with the pastor can work in his favor.

If he says, "I don't want you to suffer the pain you do. I'm going out of my way to take a day off and find someone who can give you more help than I can," she is more likely to respond positively. A pastor can remain supportive while the borderline receives outside therapy, but he must throw up high fences so the borderline can begin to heal.

Such boundary setting, however, will not be welcomed, and, in fact, resisted at every turn. Linda voices her natural aversion to boundary setting:

> I stick out my tongue and defy:
> "You can't make me!"
> (Selfishness corrupts any vestigial womanly graces.
> I can't even blame PMS.)

Instrument of Peace and Healing

Spiritual growth can play a large part in the healing process for those with BPD. As they come to depend less upon the pastor or counselor, they discover that some of their deepest needs can be met by the Lord. They can begin turning their destructive impulses over to him. A spiritual relationship may not cure their disorder, but it may curb it.

A growing relationship with God may also introduce to them the concept of guilt. Guilt can help them turn away from their seductive behavior to more appropriate ways of seeking intimacy. From my experience, where improvement has occurred in the life of borderlines, the credit is due to a deepened relationship with Christ.

A life of prayer can certainly help them begin to control their behavior. In some instances, Jim and I saw that special prayer for release from spiritual oppression had marked results. One Presbyterian elder who holds a Ph.D. in psychology has seen the release of spiritual oppression help some borderlines live more functional lives. It would be misguided, however, to attribute all BPD to spiritual causes.

In Linda's case, there was marked improvement. Her writings reveal this. At her own suggestion, she began seeing Jim only once a month. Any type of separation is painful for those suffering from BPD, but as they become more functional, they learn to accept that the end of a relationship is not the end of the world. They are not being abandoned, they are being released.

Linda seemed to have such an insight in mind when she sent this final note to Jim.

GRIEF NOTE

Dear and wise friend,
I am thankful upon all our remembrances—
that you have been God's instrument
of peace and healing in my life.
God keep you safe and healthy.
His love and light be with you
In all that you are and

In all that you do.
Remember me in your prayers—
As I shall you in mine—
Amen.

27

Healing Scars of Childhood Abuse

*Sexual abuse of children by adults has a history that can
be traced back to Bible times. No age, race, sex, socio-
economic group, or religion is spared this tragic history.*

—Al Miles

A s a little girl, Andrea was the picture of beauty and innocence.
Secure with her parents and eight brothers on a small farm that
was her world, Andrea loved the country.

"My dad was poor, but I loved him and thought he was wonderful," Andrea says.

"I would run to him, and he'd lift me up to the ceiling. I felt so
proud to be his only daughter. He called me his 'angel,' his 'sweetheart,' his 'princess.' "

But when she was thirteen, Andrea's father added one more
term of affection—"lover."

"It was around 6:00 A.M., already light outside. I woke to find
my dad lying on top of me, sucking my breasts. Scared to death,
I hated him for what he was doing to me. Most thirteen-year-olds
were talking about boys, but I had this man—my father—dam-
aging me forever.

"I looked at the ceiling and prayed he would finish without
going into my underpants. When he didn't, I felt lucky. The only
words spoken were when he said, 'Nothing's wrong with what I
did' and 'You don't have to say anything to your mother about this.'

"When he walked out of my bedroom, I thought I would hate
him forever. I knew my life would never be the same. My mom
continued working nights, so I spent many sleepless nights after

that, scared that Dad would come in my room again. He never did, but I wanted someone to protect me."

For nearly twenty years, Andrea told no one her terrible secret.

"I coped," she recalls, "by pretending it didn't happen or by minimizing its effects. I never forgot, but I told myself it wasn't that bad. It only happened once.

"And, yet," she continues, "I really hated my dad. When Mom asked me why, I was too ashamed to tell her. Somehow I thought what he did was my fault. I thought Mom wouldn't believe me, or if she did, she'd hate him. And I didn't want to break up the family."

Church had always been important to Andrea. As a young adult, it became her refuge from the past. She focused her energy into her spirituality. In her mind, she recreated her father into the man she wanted him to be. Her faith in God and involvement in the church provided her with a deep sense of peace. But the abuse she thought she'd left behind had never really been dealt with.

Nearly ten years later, married with two young children, Andrea and her husband moved into a new home in a large metropolitan suburb. They became successful in their professions and faithful members of a church. The secret of Andrea's childhood sexual abuse was twenty years and a hundred miles removed. Her life was at peace.

Or so she thought.

One day while having brunch with a friend, Andrea unexpectedly found herself talking, for the first time, about her abuse.

It is not unusual for victims of childhood sexual abuse or other traumas to minimize or repress these events for years. Then suddenly, in adulthood, they may encounter confusing, often painful memories from the past.

The memories can surface during an unrelated trauma—being in an automobile accident, for instance, watching a violent movie, or hearing about someone else's abuse. Even happy events can trigger difficult memories—getting married, having a child, or moving into a new home.

Other triggers might be a partner's request to engage in a new act or position during lovemaking or being touched—even in a gentle way.

Andrea told her friend about her abuse. "I hadn't planned to tell anyone, but I felt safe enough to talk about it without feeling ashamed. I felt like I was the only one who had a sick dad."

After her secret spilled out, Andrea realized she had to deal with it so she could be healed and be free from her past, knowing she was not at fault.

Its Prevalence

If Andrea were the only girl to be sexually abused by an adult—even one time—she would still be one too many. But one out of every three females will suffer some form of sexual abuse during their lives.

Sexual abuse of children by adults has a history that can be traced back to Bible times. No age, race, sex, socio-economic group, or religion is spared this tragic history.

The stories told by survivors of sexual abuse have often been discounted, minimized, or ignored. Such responses make victims feel more alone than ever.

When we understand the dynamics of childhood sexual abuse and its ongoing effects on the victims, then we'll be able to begin providing support and healing.

Lynn Powers, a clinical psychologist who for more than fifteen years has worked with women abused as children, says that perpetrators of childhood sexual abuse are "people who have power over children. It could be any adult, but it tends to be adults closest to them—the people in their own homes. It's fathers, grandfathers, uncles, brothers, stepfathers, mother's boyfriends, teachers, baby-sitters, the next-door neighbor."

In their book *I Never Told Anyone*, Ellen Bass and Louise Thornton write that 97 percent of the perpetrators are males. The Minnesota Department of Human Services Child Protective Services reports that approximately 85 percent of the reported cases are committed by persons known to the child and/or her family.

So the places where a girl feels most secure—in her home, church, school, or among the people she trusts—are the places where she faces greater risks of sexual exploitation.

Though one out of every five boys is also sexually abused, we'll focus here on ministering to adult women survivors.

Susan's Story

Susan was the second of six children, the older of two daughters.

"We looked like the perfect family," she says. "Mom was Sunday school superintendent and the president of a church women's group—a caring, giving person who always said yes. Dad was on the church council and taught Sunday school. He knew all the influential people in town. All of us children were respectful and responsible. We were always being patted on the head and told how good we were.

"We moved a lot when I was growing up," Susan recalls, "so I never had any long-term friendships. I went to five grade schools and three high schools. My father had a job in sales. Now I see he was insecure. Any time anyone challenged him, he quit because he could get another job."

She continues: "Our family was the only nucleus of people I was close to as a child. Dad isolated us from Mom's family, and he had no family of his own. Family became central—even sacred—and he became the center of our family. He was both intelligent and manipulative."

He was also a child abuser. When Susan was in the fifth grade, he began a sexual relationship with her.

"Dad took us children with him, by turn, on his sales trips—it was supposed to be a special time to be alone with Dad. But during those times, he started touching my private parts and asking probing questions such as 'Does this feel good?' and 'What turns you on?' This made me feel nervous, nauseous, and confused. He also started showing me pornography.

"By the time I was in seventh or eighth grade, I was almost fully developed. Dad began abusing me even more. I became torn with confusion: part of me wanted to be his little girl, denying the abuse, and part of me didn't trust him.

"I also felt an immense guilt. When my mother was angry with me, I thought it was because she knew. Or I thought she was jealous because he paid so much attention to me. He would buy more for me than the other kids, which also made me feel guilty. I didn't understand that I wasn't responsible for the abuse.

"Sunday morning became a dangerous time. With no senior high group to attend at church, I would be left home with Dad while everyone else went to Sunday school. I would sleep until the last minute. Dad would often pull the covers off me and try to wake me. I felt terrified and pretended to still be sleeping. I think that's when I developed a habit of always being five minutes late for everything. Then I had to rush around to get ready, and he would leave me alone. Dad would be angry, but his anger was easier to deal with than his 'affection.'

"The sexual abuse stopped when I was a junior in high school, but the emotional incest never stopped. Dad never developed his own boundaries. Two years ago he sent me a negligee for Christmas, and he still asks me if I'm alone when he calls at night. To him this is not being inappropriate. His actions make me both angry and sad."

For twelve years, Susan told no one about the sexual abuse.

"My way of dealing with the secret was to forget it—to be part of the façade of the perfect family. I honestly did not remember the abuse."

At age twenty-two, Susan began seminary and took a human sexuality course. On the first day, the group leader asked the students about their first experience with masturbation.

"I cried the rest of the day. Every time he'd come to me in the discussion group, I'd start to cry. So he'd skip over me. About two days later, I told one of the leaders about my abuse. Crying all the time, I had no control over my emotions and became depressed. Not understanding what was going on, I planted myself on my professor's doorstep. Finally I went into counseling."

The following summer, Susan confronted her father about what he'd done to her.

"I told Dad I remembered. He apologized—and to him that simple apology made everything right. 'I said I'm sorry,' he protested. 'No big deal.'

"After that, anytime I brought the topic up he would say,

'You're not remembering right' or 'You're blowing it out of pro-portion.' It became obvious to me that, in his mind, I had started the incest.

"Dad justified his actions," Susan continues, "by talking about the incest of African pygmies or animals. Or he'd say it's society that doesn't accept incest. He even said the church was making me feel guilty.

"He offered to pay for my counseling, but now when I ask him about it, he denies his promise. He lives in his own reality, but it's different than everyone else's."

Perpetrators rarely take responsibility for the abuse they inflict. They are seldom remorseful for their actions. Many feel it is their right to do what they want to any member of the family. Often they justify their actions or construct an elaborate system of blame to trap or threaten their victims.

Susan's father had told her, "People wouldn't understand if they knew about our relationship. People look at this differently, but I'm not doing anything wrong—I'm teaching you. Your mother is a cold person. Nobody ever taught her. I'm trying to teach you to become more comfortable with your body so you'll have more to offer and can be a happier person."

"Everything was for my sake," says Susan. "He diverted any guilt away from himself. He still believes he didn't do anything wrong."

Lynn Powers says, "Some children are told they dreamed everything that happened. We hear stories of sophisticated brain-washing techniques. For example, an abuser might say, 'Do you know what happens to bad little girls who tell on their daddies? I once knew one who was put in a closet' or 'Her mother decided she was a bad little girl and disowned her.' They use language the child can understand so the child accepts the adult version of events. The messages are extremely powerful, so in many cases, they take a long time to get turned around."

Ongoing Effects

Childhood sexual abuse can plague a victim for the rest of her life. It influences the way she feels about and reacts to situations, the way she selects friends or partners, the way she raises her children, and the way she views her relationship with God.

Andrea realizes the long-term effect of her abuse.

"The abuse I endured still affects my self-esteem," she says. "I think I'm ugly. If I do anything wrong, I immediately feel dirty or bad. I want to be perfect at everything. But since I'm not, I become angry and mean to myself and others."

"The abuse," she continues, "affects my relationships, my family dynamics, my choice of a husband, and the way I parent. I have a lot of hatred for men. This is painful because it affects men in my life whom I love—my son, my brothers, my friends, and my husband. I have a lot of rage—sometimes it comes out jokingly, sometimes pointedly. For a long time, I never understood why some women hated men. Now I could be the leader of the pack. I'm much more sensitive to others' abuse or rape."

Help to Escape

Pastors have a unique opportunity to help victims of childhood sexual abuse in their lifelong process of healing. Here are some things we can do:

Listen to her story. A survivor must be believed if she is to be healed.

"When people reveal these tragic events in their lives, the most important thing they need is to be believed," says Powers. "They need someone who can imagine what it was like without reacting strongly. Being too sympathetic or too repulsed probably will not help. Strong emotional reactions generally don't help."

If I, as a minister, think the perpetrator might be innocent, I still will not invalidate the genuine feelings of the woman. If I think she might be exaggerating, I never imply that she is. Raising questions about excessive grief and pain undermines the healing process. If she picks up signals from me that suggest she is out of control or making unfair accusations, she will retreat and suppress her feelings even deeper. Treating the symptoms will not take care of the deeper problem.

Reassure the survivor. Let her know she is not to blame for her abuse. Remind her that she was the victim of someone older and more powerful than she.

Watch your words. Some phrases meant to help the victim gain perspective may actually be harmful to her recovery. I try to avoid the following:

"It only happened once."

"That was a long time ago."

"It's time for you to move beyond this."

"He said he was sorry. Forgive him and get on with your life."

"God wouldn't want you to harbor any resentment toward your perpetrator."

"If you were a mature Christian, you'd forgive him."

"He just made a mistake; we all do."

Such phrases discount or minimize the victim's story and make her a victim again.

"When you've been abused, you don't have a lot of self-esteem or trust," says Andrea. "To hear these kind of responses knocks you one step lower into the ground."

Keep the process open-ended. It's my nature when solving problems to want closure. However, imposing my own timeline or expectations on the survivor can be counter-productive.

Make referrals. Help the victim get to a therapist who specializes in sexual abuse. When we're in over our heads, we can hinder the healing process. However, even after making this referral, we still have a responsibility as ministers to continue our love and support.

The Forgiveness Question

Forgiveness is a complex issue, both psychologically and spiritually, for survivors of childhood sexual abuse.

"Some find themselves differing on the issue of the need for forgiveness," says Powers. "While many have found that forgiving perpetrators is essential for spiritual growth and union with God, psychologists often tell victims that forgiveness is on one end of a healing continuum. Many of them feel it is not necessary for recovery and consequently do not push for it."

Since, however, many survivors have been raised in a religious environment, they will often struggle with the issue of forgiving their abusers. They've been taught that forgiveness is a Christian virtue—necessary to bring them into harmony with God and others.

As director of a transitional housing program for women, Nelda Rhoades Clarke has ministered to hundreds of women recovering from alcohol, chemical, and sexual abuse.

"Women who have been sexually abused struggle with what they have endured," she says. "Being unable to forgive will keep eating away at them, especially if—as is so often the case—they are women of faith. When someone tells them they need to forgive their abuser, they often think that means they have to pretend it wasn't so bad, that they should get on with their lives and forget the abuse ever happened.

"What happened to them is not okay," Clarke insists. "Forgiveness does not necessarily mean they have to return to a trusting relationship with the perpetrator. He may not be trustworthy."

Forgiveness may take different forms. For some it means finding personal peace. Others discover that the perpetrator, though disturbed, is a human being as well. Some survivors experience forgiveness only when they can forgive themselves and complete the healing. According to Powers, "Sometimes a victim must accept the fact that as a child, she was powerless to prevent the abuse that occurred."

Anger is a natural part of this often lifelong process. "Women say," concludes Clarke, " 'I'm still angry because he continues to victimize me.'

"I tell these women, 'Your anger is legitimate,' and they find this helpful. They're often told, 'If you've forgiven, you shouldn't keep thinking about it,' but they will continue to think about it and to have feelings. As a minister my concern is that their anger does not rule their lives."

Survivors of sexual abuse need the freedom to set the agenda, the tone, and the pacing for forgiveness to take place. Andrea eventually confronted her father, but she still struggles with the question of forgiveness.

"He acknowledged he did it. He cried and said he was sorry," Andrea recounts. "Then he asked if there was anything he could do to help me. I said, 'You can't help me because you hurt me.' There was a lot of pain in that."

Andrea remains confused about her relationship with him, unsure of what she wants.

"I still love him," she says. "I still want to take care of him. I'd like to go to his deathbed and say, 'Dad, I forgive you,' and have him die in peace and go to heaven. And yet, I think he was so terrible to do that and everything else he did to me. I know he's sorry, but we will never really have a relationship. Still, I try to be kind to him and include him in family activities, even if only so that my mom can find peace. He looks so sad and lonely in the corner when no one talks to him. But if it were only me and my dad and no one else, I don't know if I'd ever talk to him or see him."

My role as a minister is to remain with Andrea as she continues to struggle.

Susan also struggles with the question of forgiveness: "I can understand my father—his insecurities, pain, and his own abuse. I love him, and in a sense I forgive him for what happened because the memories are mine to deal with. But he continues to be a problem.

"I don't excuse his actions; I hold him accountable. He hasn't corrected what he did. Our relationship is still strained because he can't be trusted. I end up getting sabotaged and hurt every time I go into it naïvely. I keep doing that.

"There is a sense of a child's love being unconditional; that's gospel to me. I still love this man and probably always will. He did good things for me, and I needed to love him. But I wish the love was two-sided. Until he recognizes the pain he caused, the love can't be completely restored."

Adult women survivors of childhood sexual abuse are all around us. They sit in the pews of our churches; teach catechism, Sunday school, and confirmation classes; serve on our boards;

sing in our choirs; and speak from our pulpits. So do their perpetrators. As pastors, the most effective support we can offer survivors is to open our eyes, ears, and hearts to the pain they endure daily.

28

Freeing the Sexually Addicted

Sexual addicts aren't always the dregs of society. Often they're men and women highly successful in their fields.

—Hal B. Schell and Gary Sweeten with Betty Reid

We'd like you to meet some of our friends:

Don is a rising young attorney whose future holds great potential. He has a beautiful wife, Toni, three lovely children, a large home, and important social standing in the church and community. Yet despite these outward signs of success and a solid emotional and sexual relationship with Toni, two or three times a week Don compulsively visits porno shops and prostitutes.

Claire is a high-priced call girl. Like most prostitutes, Claire hates sex. But desperate for male affection, she attempts to prove her self-worth time after time by selling "love" to any man who will pay the price.

Jan is a thirty-five-year-old church musician who grew up in a devout home. He attended a small Christian college and went on to seminary. Married with two children, Jan has been involved in homosexual activities since a professor seduced him in college. He came to us after being picked up for sexual imposition in the rest room of a department store.

These three are composites of people who have come to Spring Forth, College Hill Presbyterian Church's ministry for sexual addicts. As you can see, sexual addicts aren't always the dregs of society. Often they're men and women highly successful in their fields, yet they involve themselves compulsively in sexual activities through which they are bound to be caught and humiliated.

To show some of the dynamics of counseling the sexual addict, we've developed a scenario that outlines our ministry to Jan.

Establish trust

Jan called because he'd been arrested. The initial phone call came to Hal, director of our Spring Forth ministry. Hal listened carefully and compassionately to Jan's crisis and agreed to meet with him for more discussion the next night at 7:30. Hal told Jan the session would include another counselor because we always minister in teams of two persons who are usually the same sex as the counselee.

Before the appointment, Hal and Gary spent time in prayer. We wanted to be sure not to show repugnance toward Jan, even though we viewed his behavior as wrong. We asked God to enable us to model his grace, love, and acceptance. Friends of the same sex who relate in caring but nonerotic ways are crucial in the healing of sexual addicts.

Jan, at the first session, blasted the police for their lack of concern about "real criminals." We listened to his strong feelings and irrational thoughts, knowing they covered deeper feelings of guilt and shame.

Our initial goal is to establish trust and openness. We want to model the love Jesus showed to the woman caught in adultery. So, although we didn't agree with Jan's condemnation of the police, neither did we confront his blame-shifting behavior. After about forty-five minutes, we attempted to get Jan to look more carefully at himself: "Jan, how does this make you feel about yourself?" When Jan saw he was not being condemned, he began to show his true feelings of guilt and condemnation. We listened respectfully, again, as Jan turned his full wrath onto himself.

The volcano of emotions that had been directed at others only minutes before now came full force back to himself. Although the battle was far from over, we at least had gotten to the place of focusing on a real enemy.

Jan knew he was the problem but didn't know how to change. As Jeremiah 17:9 states, "The heart is deceitful above all things. . . . Who can understand it?" Jan was confused about the causes of his behavior. Like Paul, he knew in his mind what was right but found another law in his flesh that kept him from doing what was right.

Our closing prayer in that session emphasized two points: First, that God would speak love and grace to his son Jan. Second, that the Holy Spirit would reveal the broken pieces of Jan's heart to him in preparation for our next meeting. In addition, we made a covenant to pray for Jan daily for protection and strength.

After Jan left, we decided to spend the next few sessions getting a personal and family history, looking for patterns of rejection, emotional trauma, and family dysfunction. We also wanted to see what role Jan was assigned in his family as he grew up.

Look for Patterns

Early in the second interview, we uncovered a powerful pattern in Jan's family. There was a long history of fathers who were absent because of alcohol, divorce, or work, and the predictable pattern of overly concerned mothers whose presence smothered the children.

Jan was the fourth of six children, with three older brothers. By the time of Jan's conception, the entire family desperately wanted a girl. Jan's grandmother chose the unborn baby's name—Janet (after her mother, the saintly matriarch of the family). The closets were filled with frilly, pink dresses, and everyone excitedly waited for little Janet to be born.

When Jan was born, though they did change the name to make it appropriate for a boy, Mother reinforced the rejection by dressing him like a little girl and introducing him as her little boy-girl. Jan actually learned to live as a female and played the role of a girl in the home.

The more Mother babied Jan and enmeshed him into her own emotional system, the more Father withdrew. He was proud only of sons who were good at hard labor and athletics. He disliked Jan and his "sissy music." Although Jan excelled as a singer, arranger, and pianist, he developed a negative self-image, even to the point of saying he hated himself for being trapped in a man's body.

We also discovered the relationship with his older brothers and younger sister was no better than his relationship with his father. The older brothers continually put Jan down. For example, the oldest brother had a favorite TV chair he guarded jealously. If Jan sat in the chair, Steve would lift him out of it and throw him down on the floor, a gesture that literally, as well as symbolically, put Jan in his place.

By age six, Jan "knew" he was different from other boys; they were more masculine than he. These beliefs led to feelings of discomfort in the presence of males, and as a result, he ate in order to gain a lot of weight to give himself protection from other boys. However, that led to classmates' jokes and the nickname "Butterball," all of which reinforced the rejection and shame he already perceived and kept Jan from developing friendships with other males.

A particularly devastating experience occurred when Jan was about thirteen. Being in the nude together in the swimming hole was not unusual for the entire family. On one occasion, his younger sister pointed at Jan's genitals and giggled, "Your thing is so small you'll never be a man."

Sexual addiction is usually the result of perceived trauma, neglect, or rejection at an early age. Such trauma often results in symbolic confusion between sexuality and sexual identity. Although the sexuality (biological gender) of a child is known at birth, sexual identity (masculinity or femininity) is learned from parents—especially the father. In fact, we consider this one of the father's principal roles, because when he doesn't affirm his children's sexual identity, great spiritual, emotional, and sexual damage can result.

Jan's lack of fatherly affirmation caused him to believe he was not good; anybody who really knew him wouldn't love or accept him. Jan was convinced he could trust nobody to meet his true needs, not even God.

Because a homosexual's belief system often causes friendship and warmth to be perceived in erotic ways, we were prepared when Jan made his pass toward Gary just prior to our third meeting. Arriving early, he not-so-subtly asked Gary for a date.

Years before, the first time a counselee had done this, Gary was totally unprepared and told the counselee to "get out of my office and never come back!" Later, through books and talks with fellow counselors, Gary learned the anxiety actually had come from inside, not from what the counselee had said. He'd blown up because he wasn't comfortable talking about homosexuality openly with another man. Gary eventually called the man and asked for forgiveness. Only then was Gary able to deal with the sexual problems of others.

From this background, Gary was prepared emotionally when Jan made his pass, and explained to him he was confusing *philia* (friendship) and *eros* (sexual) love. Gary also could see that such a proposition probably indicated Jan's trust, or that he was testing Gary's ability to deal with the subject.

Take a Sexual History

In the third session we sought the nature of Jan's sexual relationships through taking a sexual history. In this, we want to discover how the client found out about sex and what his childhood experiences with it were. How did he learn about boy and girl anatomy? What did he know about his parents' marital relationship? What have been his experiences with sex? How satisfying have they been? How many partners has he had? Questions such as these are hard to ask for most people—and difficult to answer for the counselee—but they supply vital information.

Many times, the person has never talked about sex with anyone else and finds such conversations embarrassing. Such was the case with Jan. Although he'd been married and had been actively homosexual for years, his knowledge of sex was limited, and he could hardly look at us when we got specific in our discussions. He was shocked that Christians would actually speak openly about such things as masturbation and oral sex. In fact, Jan, like most sexual addicts, saw sex as being dirty and unchristian.

Because Jan had been a practicing homosexual for more than twenty years, his was a long, detailed history. Although sexually involved with men in fantasy since a young child, his first actual physical encounter occurred at a Christian college when a trusted, older male teacher, Walt, led him into a caring, emotional relationship that included sex. This was a powerful experience for two reasons: Jan enjoyed the act itself, and he felt acceptance from this father-like figure. He had, he felt, at long last been accepted just as he was.

Although at the time Jan was "happily" married to a strongly committed Christian woman and had a reasonable sexual relationship with her, he had never before felt the love, care, and affirmation that he now received from Walt. This further reinforced and strengthened the symbolic confusion within Jan's mind and convinced him that he was a "true homosexual."

Jan didn't want to lose Walt's support in the music department, so in many ways, Jan was in bondage to the relationship. However, he soon found he wasn't Walt's only partner; several others from the music department found Walt a loving partner. Hurt and angry, Jan began to look for additional sexual relationships at school. Over a two-year period, he set up numerous one-night stands.

This filled him with conflict. He was married, yet found male sex more appealing. He was studying to be a minister of music, yet afraid of God and panic-stricken at the thought of leading worship. He professed to believe in a strict code of morality, yet he was involved continually in acts that caused him enormous guilt and shame.

Jan tried to stop many times. In fact, he had discussed his dilemma with Walt and the other gay students. In general, they hated their lifestyle but felt helpless to do anything about it. They, like Jan, believed they had been born that way and were sentenced to a life of misery.

Jan had asked for help from visiting evangelists on several occasions because he knew what he shared would leave town with them. One evangelist told Jan sodomites would burn in hell and that if he had his way, all such perverts would be stoned. Another man told Jan that he, too, was gay, and they commiserated by having sex. A third cast out demons and told Jan, "To keep your healing, you have to have faith." Jan evidently didn't.

Finding no help, Jan stopped asking. Finding no understanding and compassion (except from other gays), he stayed within the gay community, which reinforced his beliefs and behaviors. Finding no power to change, he developed cynicism toward God, the church, and the Bible that promised a new life. Finding no faith, no hope, no love, he developed a settled hopelessness that turned into a callous disregard for Christian morals and bitterness toward conservative Christians and their "idealistic, naïve faith."

However, because the wages of sin have not changed over the

centuries, in time things caught up with Jan. He cruised a department store john once too often and got arrested on a police sweep. Wanda, Jan's wife, posted bail, so his secret life came into the light. She had feared for Jan for a long time but was trying to protect him from the pain of being confronted. Fortunately, the police weren't as interested in protection, and Jan began to get help.

All this came out over several sessions dealing with sexual history. It wasn't a pretty picture, but it needed to be uncovered.

Make Connections

In order to heal a sexual addict, we try to hold in tension two paradoxical beliefs: addictive behavior is both a disease and a choice—bondage and rebellion. Therefore, we want to get to the root of the disease—the trauma, pain, rejection, and poor parenting that the child received. In this, the child had no choice; he is in bondage to the sins of others. But we must face concurrently the choices the addict has made along the road—choices toward sin. If both sides of the problem aren't confronted, change is impossible.

While taking Jan's family history, we began to connect what happened in his family and what he was acting out unconsciously in promiscuous behavior. At the same time, we knew Jan did have a choice in determining the exact results of the trauma he received. His choices had resulted in anger toward parents and God.

The book of Hebrews says, "Be careful lest any of you fail to obtain the grace of God whereby a root of bitterness will spring up and defile many people." Jan had failed to apply God's grace to himself, his siblings, and his parents. As a result, he had developed numerous roots of bitterness.

Jan didn't want to accept responsibility for his sexual behavior. "My father neglected me, and Mom was overprotective," he protested. "It's not my fault." Although it's true he was reared in an imperfect world, we taught Jan that his only hope for healing lay in forgiving his family and in seeking forgiveness himself.

When Jan learned the distance of his father mattered less than his childhood judgments of that father, he was able to confess his sin of judgmentalism, receive cleansing from the Lord, and then forgive his dad. Jan's feelings changed toward his family after his confession and forgiveness.

With the pattern of mutual rejection with his eighty-year-old father broken, Jan's relationship with other men improved. Whereas being out of fellowship with his father had resulted in sexualizing the friendship of other men, being in relationship with Dad now allowed Jan to be a friend to men in a healthy way. He was deeply struck by the change: "It's amazing! I can have friends without getting sexual."

As we continued to work with Jan, he began to see places where he went wrong. He gradually understood that he was not hopelessly homosexual, but that deficiencies in personality and lack of affirmation had caused his behavior. He began to see the roots of his symbolic confusion and how these drove him to act out sexually. Best, he started to understand that it was only through a personal relationship with Jesus Christ and fellowship within the body of believers that he could know true love.

Break Behavior Patterns

Though Jan had been arrested, was confronted by the church and his family, and was in counseling, he still was tempted by homosexual activity. He tried to stop, but seemed unable to do so completely. A breakthrough occurred, however, when Jan came to see us right after a sexual experience, and we examined the events that led up to it.

Jan related that on Sunday he'd been criticized for the worship music. On Tuesday, he and Wanda had been defeated badly in tennis. On Wednesday, Wanda had criticized his discipline of the children.

In rapid succession, Jan had faced crises in his professional, social, and family life. On Thursday, he went looking for a sex partner. Perceived rejection led Jan to feel depressed, and his drug of choice for depression was sex with a man. The habits of many years were hard to break.

Early in the session, Jan said, "I went into the department store rest room and was tempted." For the next hour and a half, we helped Jan diagnose the disappointing experiences earlier in the week that led him to the department store. We look for patterns in the events preceding a sexual temptation, since real conversion depends upon changing a person's response to perceived rejection. Resisting temptation really means resisting the feelings of condemnation that cause a person to seek sexual relief. Had we not helped Jan renew his mind and emotions around the issue of rejection, in his heart he could not have repented of sexual sin. He may have been able to stop sex physically, but not mentally.

Once he began to see this pattern, progress followed. Weeks and months would go by without a sexual fall. Occasionally, Jan would fail to deal with stress and revert back to the old patterns of using sex as a drug.

When those falls occurred, we found it was his old, unrenewed belief system causing the failure. A sexual addict's belief system is filled with negative, self-rejecting thoughts. In addition, many addicts are performance-oriented and live lives full of shoulds and oughts. Their constant failure to achieve irrationally high performance goals reinforces the negative self-talk and low self-esteem. Because of this, we worked to build the new Jan.

Correct False Beliefs

One continuing struggle we faced was Jan's negative view of God the Father. He couldn't trust God to meet his needs, because he projected the failures of his earthly father on the heavenly Father. Over and over we washed Jan's mind with the truth of Scripture in order to overcome the lies of his irrational belief system.

We gave Jan, as we do all our counselees, tools to assist him in analyzing his behavior through understanding his belief system. We showed him the ABCDs of his emotions: that Activating Events (A) are interpreted by his Belief System (B), causing Consequential Feelings (C) in him, which result in Decisive Behavior (D). We have no control over Activating Events, and Consequential Feelings are caused by what we believe about the events. The Decisive Behavior results directly from feelings. Therefore, the place to work is the Belief System.

By hitting repeatedly on his misconceptions, over time we were able to help Jan see just how irrational his belief system was, so his mind could be renewed according to Scripture. Unfortunately, much of his irrational self-talk came from the rigid theology of his youth, and this made our task more difficult.

Another young man's experience demonstrates how the belief system affects us. For six months we hadn't been able to identify any causes of his homosexual tendencies. Then in a routine counseling session, he began to tell us about something that had happened when he was sixteen. He began, "As usual, my father said, 'Why are you so dumb?'" The "as usual" caught our attention. When we probed, the man told how he often had sought his father's advice and his father had given it to him, but always beginning with, "What makes you so dumb? Can't you remember anything I told you before?"

Because of these words, the young man believed he was inadequate. He'd decided, *I'm never going to be capable, to measure up.* This became a powerful belief system. Change began when he saw what the Bible had to say about him. In fact, he memorized many Scriptures that affirmed his position in Christ.

With Jan, we worked weekly for about eight months until he was able to handle stress by himself without yielding to the old temptations. After that we saw him periodically for a year. Recently Jan said not only are his temptations becoming weaker and less frequent, but he no longer yields to them. Now he can even worship God in church.

Work With Family

At the same time we were counseling Jan, we also worked with Wanda. Like many mates, she was a co-dependent who actually facilitated his addiction. When Jan felt temptation coming, he'd withdraw from the family. Wanda saw that as a signal for her to take over. This reinforced the "I'm not a real man" syndrome and encouraged Jan to act out his frustration in homosexual contact.

Early in their marriage, Wanda was ignorant of the depth of Jan's addiction, but she became addicted to taking care of him. After the arrest, she was at a loss. She tended to be angry yet continue as the super caregiver.

We taught Wanda how to communicate with Jan about her own needs and wants so she would treat Jan as an adult. Strangely, we found it harder to get Wanda to change than to help Jan. He knew his behavior was wrong, while Wanda's actions seemed good and caring.

Just as a teeter-totter operates on the principle of balance, so does a family. When Wanda was over-responsible, Jan would edge toward the end of the teeter-totter labeled "irresponsibility."

Making this particular match even more difficult to untangle was the support Wanda received for her martyr compulsions, especially after Jan's perversion became known. Wanda's friends acted like Job's "counselors," encouraging her to be "a strong Christian wife and mother now that her husband had revealed how weak-willed he really was."

Convincing her she was addicted to strength was difficult, but the notion of mutual submission slowly took root and flourished. We learned eventually that her addiction developed when she was the eldest child in an alcoholic family. She had become an expert at being a co-dependent. Although growing, Wanda has much more work yet to do than Jan.

The Rest of the Stories

We've used Jan's case to illustrate our work, but perhaps you've wondered what happened to Claire and Don.

Many women who become addicted to prostitution come from families in which they were molested as children. However, Claire revealed instead a childhood filled with rejection from both parents. Claire perceived she constantly was rejected by her father, and her mother sided with him. She was the family scapegoat, making her self-esteem negligible.

Through prayer and Scripture, we helped Claire forgive her parents and accept God's forgiveness. This step posed few difficulties. However, helping Claire forgive herself was much more difficult. It took more than eighteen months to help Claire find her way to substantial wholeness.

Don's story is not unlike Claire's. Being the third of four sons, he also got lost in his family of origin. Because Don was not athletically inclined, his father was displeased. As a result, Don had serious difficulty believing he was a real man. Despite numerous visits to prostitutes—each time with the unconscious assumption that this time he would feel like a real man—it never worked. The counseling process with Don resembled that with Jan and Claire.

The particulars may differ, but the principles remain constant. We always listen carefully for the hurts and beliefs of the deep heart, for Jesus said, "For out of the overflow of [the] heart, [the] mouth speaks" (Luke 6:45). Once we discover trauma, roots of bitterness, or lack of forgiveness, we move in with prayer, confession, and forgiveness to bring healing and growth. Whenever we discover irrational belief systems, we work to renew the mind.

Don, Claire, and Jan were all particularly responsive clients who worked hard, did their homework, and exposed to us the deepest parts of their hearts. Many resist healing and won't work like that to change. They adopt a victim attitude that says, "*You're* supposed to heal/counsel/cure me." Such an attitude breeds certain failure, because trying to rescue the victim causes the rescuer to become the victim.

Because these clients worked hard, they were able to achieve substantial freedom from their lifelong addictive thoughts and acts. Free from their addictions, they were ready to contribute to life and ministry as whole people. Seeing such results makes the admittedly difficult counseling process worth every minute.

29

Counseling the Rape Victim

*The rape victim's loss is profound. She has not lost
another loved one, she has lost her
own loved one, herself.*

—Danny Armstrong

She will come to your office like most others do, by appointment. The rape took place quite some time ago, perhaps months, perhaps years. Only now has she worked up enough courage to talk about it. At first she will probably not mention the rape itself, but some of her resultant problems: a feeling of despair, inability to trust people, fear, and others. If you really listen and feed back her feelings accurately, chances are she will proceed past these presenting problems to the one she really came to talk about—her rape. Your first obligation, then, is to listen. Without this crucial step, she may never reveal her true problem.

If she accepts the risk and reveals that she has been raped, you should know seven feelings common to rape victims. There are others, but these seem to be recurrent.

What They Feel

Number one is *anger*. Rape victims are some of the most intensely angry people I have ever met. They are "mad as hell," and would kill their rapist if they knew who he was and if they could get away with it. But they are not only angry with their rapist. They are angry about people's attitudes who look upon rape as a sexual crime instead of a crime of violence. They are outraged at injustice, as rapists are set free on bonds, given light or suspended sentences, or early paroles. They are furious at having been personally violated.

Number two is *dirty*. Despite numerous bathings, the rape victim cannot feel clean, at least not for a long time. She feels contaminated and degraded. Even her right to cleanliness and hygiene has been taken away from her.

Number three is *hopeless*. One day she was happy, optimistic, productive, and future-oriented. The next day she was raped. And the day after that she lost life. She was robbed of the intangibles that make life worth living. Now she can barely see or think ahead until the next day. Next week is beyond her vision, next month is unthinkable, and next year unimaginable.

Number four is *guilty*. Few people have given her any sympathy. The unspoken prejudice is that only loose women are raped. Those with whom she has been able to talk about her rape have had a morbid curiosity about the sexual aspects. It doesn't take long for the message, whether verbal or facial, to come through—the rape victim is really not a victim but a conspirator. She quickly learns to play the "If only" game:

"If I had only installed door and window locks."

"If I had only used them."

"If I hadn't gone out that night."

"If I had left a little earlier."

Number five is *alone*. Being raped is not dinner-table conversation. You just don't talk about it. But eventually she must, so she risks it with a few friends she thought would understand. They don't, and she learns to withdraw. She feels estranged, alienated, and alone. Her whole worldview has been turned upside down so that she is no longer the carefree, trusting person she was. She finds it extremely difficult, if not impossible, to make new friends, and the ones she had from before are drifting away because "you've changed so much."

Number six is *fear*. When a woman is being raped, she is sure she is going to die. Never before has the victim experienced or even imagined such violence. To say that the rape victim is afraid during the rape is a gross understatement. Terrified is more like it, but words cannot suffice. And the fear doesn't leave with the rapist. The victim is now a nearly classic paranoid, fearing everyone and everything. Sleep comes reluctantly. Life is now lived on edge.

Number seven is *grief.* We grieve when we lose something important to us. The rape victim's loss is profound. She has not lost another loved one, she has lost her own loved one—herself. She feels less than whole. She has lost control of her life. She has lost hope. She has lost dignity and self-worth.

Ways to Begin

Remember that up to this point you have still not spoken. You have taken a moment to sense the rape victim's state of mind and emotions. Now it's time to respond. What should you say first?

Whatever it is, *make sure it is clear to her that you're siding with her.* Probing and asking questions demonstrates conditional acceptance, a form of rejection. For many rape victims, the pastor or priest is their last hope of understanding or sympathy. Rejection here is devastating. She needs to know immediately that you are an advocate, one who will take her side, one who understands. The circumstances surrounding the rape don't make any difference. She has not come for counseling as a chief witness in the midst of a trial, but as a victim in the midst of a tragedy. The pastor or priest is God's representative, and God accepts people unconditionally.

Having sided with her, you must now try to meet her needs in terms of the feelings she is having. This can't be done in a single session, nor should it be rushed. But as time and circumstances allow, several steps may be taken. Keep in mind that she has chosen to come to the minister as a "holy person," a man or woman of God, and therefore expects insight and comfort from a spiritual perspective.

Initially, let her ventilate her angry feelings. Point out that anger is sometimes not only appropriate, but right. Jesus became so angry that he made a whip and physically drove the money-changers out of the temple (John 2:15–16). The Bible differentiates between anger and sin. The two do not always equate. "In your anger do not sin," wrote Paul (Ephesians 4:26).

Hatred and anger go hand in hand, and the rape victim feels

both. Anger, however, is more general in nature. Hatred is reserved specifically for the rapist. It is more enduring, too, outlasting the multidirected anger by far. At some point, after rapport and spiritual maturity are present, you have an obligation to assist the victim in letting go of this hate. As long as she hates, she is still subject to the rapist's control. Her emotional and psychological energy is consumed by her hatred. Only when she can let go and volitionally forgive will she regain complete control of her life. As Jesus explained it, "I tell you the truth, everyone who sins is a slave to sin" (John. 8:34).

Your chief instruments of cleansing are prayer, the Scriptures, and, for many, addition of the sacraments. Like the ten lepers who felt dirty, not because of something they had done, but because of something that happened to them, the rape victim needs to know that she can be completely cleansed and restored (Luke 17:11–19). Ephesians 5:25–27 fits beautifully, as Paul describes the cleansing power of Christ upon his church: ". . . cleansing her by the washing with water through the word, and to present her to himself as a radiant church, without stain or wrinkle or any other blemish, but holy and blameless."

Baptism and/or communion might be meaningful experiences of cleansing for the rape victim. Baptism, of course, is an initiatory rite into the Christian community and should be so regarded. But in format, it is a ceremony of cleansing, and if appropriate, might be so used. Communion, with its elements of bread and wine representing the body and blood of Christ, is also a ceremony of cleansing. Reflect for a moment on Revelation 7:14: "These are they who have come out of the great tribulation; they have washed their robes and made them white in the blood of the Lamb."

Affirm the future by holding out the hope that a return to normal living is possible. If the victim appears open to such a message, the pastor may want to affirm that our God is a God who can make evil turn against itself, that he can make good come out of evil. "We know that in all things God works for the good of those who love him" (Romans 8:28).

In addressing feelings of guilt, take a two-pronged approach. We all feel both real guilt and false guilt. False guilt is placed on rape victims by the attitudes and comments of others. She needs to hear again of her goodness, of her worth and value. She needs to be certain that she is the victim and not the criminal.

Real guilt lurks behind the scenes of every human event, and in a cause-effect world, it is difficult not to see God involved somehow. Every rape victim can look back into her own life, as each of us can, and recall the "sins" for which we may believe God is punishing us. Two things need to be done here. One is to relieve anxieties about that real guilt. This can be done fairly straightforwardly. "If we confess our sins, he is faithful and just and will forgive us our sins and purify us from all unrighteousness" (1 John 1:9). The more difficult problem has to do with her view of God. Is he aloof, withdrawn, and unconcerned about the individual tragedies of our lives? Is he a stern taskmaster, a "you made your own bed, now lie in it" God? Is he a harsh disciplinarian, punishing us for our sins? Or is he a loving Father who hurts when we hurt and who wants to meet our needs?

To help her work through her sense of loneliness, be not only an advocate, but a friend—someone to talk to, who will listen without an agenda, except when advice is asked for. A referral to another rape victim or a support group may be appropriate, but it should not be a way of copping out. She came to the minister to find a religious perspective. Encourage her to attend and participate at church, particularly in those activities centered on fellowship.

Encourage her to call whenever she wishes. She may need assistance in getting locks and security devices installed in her home. Pray with and for her. Encourage her to read the twenty-third and twenty-seventh Psalms. "Even though I walk through the valley of the shadow of death, I will fear no evil" and "The Lord is my light and my salvation—whom shall I fear?" are comforting words.

Finally, her grief should be ministered to as any other grief. The ministry of presence is of value. Learn what a normal grief process is like and assist her through its phases. Granger Westberg's *Good Grief* was written with a view to those whose loved ones have died, but its table of contents reads like the rape victim's diary: "We are in a state of shock. We express emotion. We feel depressed and very lonely. We may experience physical symptoms of distress. We may become panicky. We feel a sense of guilt about the loss. We are filled with hostility and resentment. We are unable to return to usual activities. Gradually hope comes through. We struggle to affirm reality."

30

A Powerful Presence

*What hurting patients need is someone who will honestly
listen to them, understand their feelings,
and not hasten to change the subject.*

—Richard Exley

M y introduction to local church ministry, nearly twenty-five
years ago, was a baptism by fire, or perhaps I should say, by
sickness. A number of people in the church were hospitalized, and
I went to visit, to encourage, to pray. But I felt horribly out of
place.

This was a world of science and medicine. What good could I
possibly do? Of what value were Scripture and prayer compared
to surgery, therapies, and miracle drugs? I was intimidated. Still, I
faithfully visited the sick and sat with their families during those
critical hours in surgery when things could go either way.

I did what I thought was expected of me—administered Scripture and prayer. Not knowing what else to do, I simply tried to be
there. I listened without saying much, mostly because I didn't feel
I had a lot worth saying.

Then I began receiving thank-you notes. "It meant so much to
have you there when I was facing surgery." "I can't tell you how
much strength I gained from your visit."

I couldn't believe it. The little I did had helped?

About two years later, I learned firsthand the dynamics of pastoral care.

Nine days after our daughter was born, my wife, Brenda, hem-
orrhaged. I rushed her to the hospital. By the time we arrived, she

was nearly unconscious from loss of blood.

Immediately she was whisked away to surgery, and after I signed the consent forms, I was left alone with my fears. A host of terrifying possibilities set upon me. I paced the floor in agitation.

Then my mother arrived. She didn't say anything, at least nothing I can remember, but I felt better just knowing she was there. Somehow I was strengthened, comforted, and encouraged by her presence.

The surgery was successful, and my wife recovered. But I have never forgotten the ministry I received from my mother's presence that day.

Since then I've become highly sensitive to what makes for a welcome presence and what types of pastoral presence are definitely unwelcome.

World of the Sick

I find it helpful to remind myself what seriously sick people are experiencing.

First, there's the pain, constant and unrelenting, as persistent as gravity, blotting out all else, until their world is reduced to the size of their sterile room.

Then there's the weakness, the inability to control their body, which no longer functions on command. It, too, becomes an enemy, undermining their morale, even their faith.

On a psychological level, the sick experience a loss of power. Their familiar environment is gone. Now they live in a hospital, where they have little or no control over their lives. Before, they set much of their schedule. They decided when to get up and when to go to bed; what to eat, how to prepare it, and when to eat it.

Suddenly all of that's changed. They may receive the finest medical care possible, but they're no longer free to come and go. They're told when to sleep, when to wake up, when to shower, and on occasion, they must even relieve themselves on command. They're subjected to humiliating procedures, stripped of all modesty, poked and prodded and experimented with, all in the name of medicine. Eventually the medical vandalism may produce healing, but initially it can be demoralizing.

Finally, there's the fear. Fear of the unknown. *What's going to happen to me? Will I get well? Will I be able to provide for my family, care for my children? Will I still have a job when I get well? Will insurance cover the hospital bills? Do I have enough sick leave?*

Interlaced with these concerns is the ever-present possibility that they may not recover, which only creates more questions. *Am I going to die? What will become of my family if something happens to me? Who will look after the children?*

Faced with such naked need, I, as a minister, may fall prey to my unrealistic expectations. Although I know that I cannot work miracles, I still feel somehow diminished when there seems to be so little that I can do. Not infrequently, I am tempted to revert to platitudes, false assurances, or a premature prayer in a misguided attempt to provide comfort.

Premature Prayer

One lady, a victim of cancer, told me that when her pastor came to the hospital to see her, he would breeze in and out of her room, chatting all the time, hardly giving her a chance to get a word in edgewise. He did ask how she was doing. But she didn't feel encouraged to respond honestly. After a few short minutes, he would pray and then leave.

She quickly tired of his insensitivity, and being an assertive person, she determined he was going to hear her out. When he arrived for his next visit, she was ready. He breezed in with his usual chatter and hurried questions: "How are you feeling today? Did you sleep well? Are you having much pain?"

When he paused, she unloaded, not angrily, just honestly.

"My pain is absolutely intolerable," she said, looking him straight in the eye. "I'm afraid I'm dying. I pray day and night, but it seems that God has forsaken me. He never answers me, never makes his presence known."

By now her pastor was visibly uncomfortable, and when she paused for a breath, he said, "Let's pray."

Before she had meekly followed his lead, but not today.

"Don't do that to me," she said. "You're always using prayer like some kind of escape hatch. Every time I start to tell you what it's like being barely thirty, the mother of two, and dying with cancer, you want to pray.

"But your prayer isn't real. It's just religious words, a smoke screen, so you can make a quick exit. Today you're going to hear me out; you're going to walk with me through my valley of the shadow of death. That's what you're supposed to do, you know. That's why you're here—so I don't have to face death alone!"

He stayed until she finished, but it was a long time before he visited again.

Premature prayer can effectively isolate a sick person. The seriously ill have taught me the importance of timing and sensitivity.

One grieving father, following his son's untimely death, said, "I know all the 'right biblical passages.' While the words of the Bible are true, grief renders them unreal."

The same can be said about prayer. Nothing is more powerful than prayer; yet prayer can come across as unreal, too, if it doesn't reflect the seriousness of the suffering. Prayer is appropriate in the sickroom, of course. But prayer should usually follow a time of listening deeply, and with compassion, to the sick and their families.

This is hard for those of us who are used to getting things done. It's hard to sit and wait, to watch—powerless—as disease does its dirty work. We want to do something, anything. We are often gripped with an almost irresistible urge to exert our authority, to regain control of our world.

When we can't bring a quick solution to the situation, our discomfort tempts us to flee the situation, at least emotionally. Or else we respond the wrong way. Patients frequently say things like "I don't have much to look forward to anymore" or perhaps even "I think I'm going to die soon."

We may respond by changing the subject, or with false assurances: "Don't talk like that. You're going to live for years. Why, you'll probably outlive me!"

While our intent may be to bring cheer, it seldom works. Instead, such a response effectively isolates the patient. It invalidates the fear, leaving him or her to face sickness and suffering alone. What patients need in that moment is someone who will honestly listen to them, understand their feelings, and not hasten to change the subject.

This Present Comfort

Not long ago, I received a telephone call from a young woman named Diane, telling me that her three-year-old daughter was in intensive care. For eleven days she had maintained her bedside vigil, and when she finally called, she was nearly frantic. I comforted her as best I could and promised to come to the hospital as soon as I finished my appointments.

By the time I arrived, her daughter, Carrie, had been moved from intensive care. Her condition was still serious, but the prognosis was positive.

Now that her daughter was out of immediate danger, Diane tentatively voiced another concern. It involved her husband, Dave. He hadn't been to the hospital for three days and was barely civil when he called.

The trouble had begun four nights earlier. He had insisted that she leave Carrie alone at the hospital and spend the night at home with him. "You're going to get sick if you don't get some rest," he repeated.

Reluctantly she had agreed. Once they were in bed, his "real" motive became obvious. When she resisted his advances, a terrible argument ensued, and she returned to the hospital in tears.

"What kind of a man would do something like that?" Diane demanded.

I breathed a prayer for wisdom before I ventured an answer. "Although Dave's behavior seems extreme, it's not that unusual. In times of stress, men often seek intimacy with their wives, especially if they have a healthy marriage."

"But how can he even think of sex at a time like this? I mean, Carrie is in the hospital—practically at death's door—and I'm totally exhausted. Making love is the farthest thing from my mind."

"His behavior was insensitive, I'll grant you, but he's probably not as unfeeling as you think. He's hurting, too, and undoubtedly afraid to face the possibility of Carrie's death. Making love with you may have been his way of coping."

Before she could respond, Dave walked in. Ignoring me, he said, "I'm sorry, Diane. I've been acting like a fool."

Illness of any kind produces stress, especially a critical illness. No member of a family is immune, and research indicates that many marriages fail under the pressure. In addition to the obvious difficulties of maintaining a normal homelife, there are also enormous psychological pressures, which men and women often react to in decidedly different ways, creating additional tension and misunderstanding.

The overriding feeling is often a sense of helplessness. A beloved spouse or child is suffering, perhaps even facing death, and no one can do anything about it. Men often respond in one or two ways: anger or escape.

An assertive man, who is used to taking charge and getting things done, will grow angry because of his inability to rectify the situation. He may take his feelings out on the doctors and other health professionals, accusing them of incompetence or worse. Or he may direct his anger toward his own family.

His rage is really directed toward the disease that threatens his loved one or toward God who has "allowed" this to happen or even toward his own helplessness.

Other men try to escape. They lose themselves in their work or in household chores. Frequently they deny the seriousness of the situation, refusing to face the possibility of impending death. This, in effect, isolates them from both their family and the patient. The resulting loneliness and resentment further strains the already over-stressed family.

A woman, on the other hand, tends to invest herself totally in the sick person, especially if the patient is her child. For her there is no world outside of that small hospital room, no concern except the welfare of her suffering child. When other concerns press upon her, she thinks, *Others will have to understand. This is an emergency. Nothing else matters.* The resulting jealousies and tensions add to the family trauma.

I understood these things, at least in theory, but could I help Dave and Diane come to grips with them?

I suggested to Dave and Diane that we go to the hospital cafeteria for coffee. Once we had our cups and were seated, I leaned toward Dave and asked, "Been pretty rough, has it?"

For a long time, he didn't say anything, just stared at the steam rising from his coffee. Finally he took a deep breath and said, "I feel so helpless. The two people I love most in all the world are hurting, and I can't do anything. It feels like I'm losing them both."

"Can you tell me about it?"

"When Carrie got sick, I was scared. Real scared. But I put on a brave front for Diane. Then it seemed she shut me out, too."

"What do you mean?" I asked.

"She was, you know, so preoccupied with Carrie. She would hardly leave her bedside, even to eat. It was like no one else existed, not me, not anyone."

I nodded, and he continued, "I care about Carrie, too, but life goes on. I still have to get up, go to work, and make a living. For Diane, none of that matters. When I try to tell her how I feel, she just clams up, or else she accuses me of not caring about Carrie."

Many couples coping with a serious illness face similar tensions. By being there, I try to feel their hurt and anger and help them understand each other.

I suggested to Diane that Dave is not an unfeeling brute in desiring sexual intimacy; it's his way of trying to connect with his wife at this time.

And I told Dave, "Diane does not have an abnormal fixation. She is simply responding as mothers have always responded. Her child is deathly ill, and all her maternal instincts demand that she be near her. The fact that she can do nothing but maintain her bedside vigil does not, in any way, diminish her sense of responsibility. She does not explain her feelings, doesn't even imagine that she should. In her way of thinking, you must surely feel the same way. After all, Carrie is your child, too."

Once a couple accepts the legitimacy of each other's feelings, they can better understand what is happening to them. Such understanding enables them to face the common enemy of illness united, rather than mistakenly attacking each other.

Although, in the case of Dave and Diane, explanation was part of the ministry I provided, the real power was my presence. They were able to hear my explanations because I first was willing to share their pain.

The Presence in My Presence

A few weeks ago, a young wife in our congregation learned she had a malignant tumor. It was, of course, disconcerting news, though the doctor's prognosis was quite positive. On the morning of the scheduled surgery, my wife, Brenda, and I drove to the hospital, arriving just as the woman and her husband were getting out of their car. We accompanied them as she was admitted to the hospital and prepared for surgery.

It was a tense time. Jerry, her husband, was quietly attentive to her, not daring to miss a single moment of this precious time. She was brave, glad the waiting was almost over, eager to get the whole thing behind them.

Brenda and I listened as they made small talk about their boys. Just that morning, the car had rolled out of the garage and was at that moment straddling the mailbox in front of their house, awaiting the tow truck.

After a while the room grew still, each of us silently entertaining our thoughts. Finally, I shared some Scripture, and we all prayed. Soon the attendants came for her, and she was wheeled away to surgery.

Just yesterday we received a note from her. To Brenda she wrote, "Thank you for loving, caring, crying. . . . It meant so much to see you before my surgery. Your presence, prayers, and concern made a difficult time bearable."

To me she wrote, "Jerry and I were touched and loved when you and Brenda came to the hospital the morning of my surgery. I think it was neat of God to send you there early enough to escort us from the parking lot. We drew on your strength just having you there."

Years ago I might have puzzled over her card. Not anymore. I still don't fully understand how my presence helps, but I know it does. Even when it seems we aren't doing much, when it seems that the best we can manage are silent tears, a quick hug, and a shared prayer, God makes it enough.